On Mount Vision

Contemporary North American Poetry Series

Series Editors Alan Golding, Lynn Keller, and Adalaide Morris

On Mount Vision

FORMS OF THE SACRED

IN CONTEMPORARY AMERICAN POETRY

by Norman Finkelstein

UNIVERSITY OF IOWA PRESS, IOWA CITY

University of Iowa Press, Iowa City 52242
Copyright © 2010 by the University of Iowa Press
www.uiowapress.org

Printed in the United States of America

Design by Omega Clay

The University of Iowa Press is a member of Green Press Initiative and is
committed to preserving natural resources.

Printed on acid-free paper

Library of Congress Cataloging-in-Publication Data
Finkelstein, Norman, 1954–
On Mount Vision: forms of the sacred in contemporary American poetry /
by Norman Finkelstein.
p. cm.—(Contemporary North American poetry series)
Includes bibliographical references and index.
ISBN-13: 978-1-58729-857-8 (cloth)
ISBN-10: 1-58729-857-0 (cloth)
     1. American poetry—21st century—History and criticism. 2. American poetry—
20th century—History and criticism. 3. Religious poetry, American—History and
criticism. 4. Postmodernism (Literature) —United States. I. Title.
PS310.R4F56 2010
811'.5409382—dc22   2009028670

for Ronald Schuchard

Contents

Acknowledgments ix

Introduction 1

1 ROBERT DUNCAN
From Poetry to Scripture 27

2 RONALD JOHNSON
The Poetics of Kosmos 65

3 JACK SPICER
A Reason to Be- / Leave 95

4 SUSAN HOWE
History as Séance 114

5 MICHAEL PALMER
The Problem of Spirit 138

6 NATHANIEL MACKEY
Shamanism and the Unity of All Rites 183

7 ARMAND SCHWERNER
The Sacred and the Real 208

Afterword 232

Notes 235

Works Cited 263

Index 275

Acknowledgments

First, and most importantly, I must acknowledge the poets and their po-
ems: their work is a fundamental part of who and what I am. Jack Spicer died
when I was still a child, but by the time I was a young man I was deeply im-
mersed in his poetry, and remain so. I never met Robert Duncan, but I did
have the privilege of hearing him lecture once, at the Modern Language As-
sociation convention in San Francisco in 1979. That event confirmed what
I already knew, partly from reading his poems: that poetry was a *vocation*.
I corresponded with Ronald Johnson and hosted him at Xavier more than
twenty years ago; I even made him dinner, which in retrospect took a lot
of nerve. Susan Howe, Michael Palmer, and Nathaniel Mackey have like-
wise visited Xavier over the years and have given extraordinary readings.
Michael was a great help while I was coming to terms with his Zanzotto
poems, and Nate has honored me on a number of occasions by including my
poems in his journal *Hambone*. Armand Schwerner, gone ten years now, was
a dear friend for all too short a time.

Second, my thanks to the friends and colleagues who provided support,
advice, and guidance while I wrote this book: Michael Heller, Robert Mur-
phy, Donald Revell, Mark Scroggins, Eric Murphy Selinger, Henry Wein-
field, and Tyrone Williams. And especially Peter O'Leary, whose book
Gnostic Contagion proved a model and inspiration for what I have attempted
here. Peter, as it turns out, was also one of the readers of the book for the
University of Iowa Press, so I owe him double thanks. And thanks also to
Brian McHale, the second reader.

Next, the editors and staff at the University of Iowa Press. I am delighted
that this book is part of the Contemporary North American Poetry Series,
edited by Alan Golding, Lynn Keller, and Adelaide Morris. Alan too is a
friend of many years and I was touched when he asked to see the manu-
script as I was completing it last year, and happy to wrestle with it whenever
he challenged me about it. Lynn's and Dee's enthusiasm for the manuscript
has also been tremendously encouraging. Likewise, acquisition editor Joe

Parsons, whose profile pictures on Facebook are a never ending source of amusement.

The Faculty Development Committee of Xavier University awarded me two semester-long research sabbaticals, in 2004 and 2008, that helped me begin this book and bring it to a conclusion. I could not have written *On Mount Vision* or any of my earlier books without the support of my home institution, and I remain grateful.

It gives me great pleasure to dedicate this book to Ronald Schuchard, my dissertation director and mentor at Emory University. His patience and dedication as a researcher, his sense of responsibility to the poets he studies, his contributions toward understanding Yeats and Eliot—in all this, Ron remains my model of the scholar-teacher.

And finally, love and thanks to my wife Alice, who, now that she's completing an M.A. in English, knows even better than ever why her husband is a little *meshugeh*.

:::

A version of chapter 1 appeared in *Twentieth-Century Literature* 51.3 (Fall 2005) under the title "Late Duncan: From Poetry to Scripture." A version of chapter 2 appeared in *Ronald Johnson: Life and Works*, edited by Joel Bettridge and Eric Murphy Selinger (National Poetry Foundation, 2008), as "Exploring the Johnson-Duncan Connection." A version of chapter 4 appeared in *LIT: Literature, Interpretation, Theory* 20.3 (2009) as "'Making the Ghost Walk about Again and Again': History as Séance in the Work of Susan Howe." A version of chapter 6 appeared in *Contemporary Literature* 49.1 (Spring 2008) as "Nathaniel Mackey and the Unity of All Rites." Parts of chapter 7 appeared in the *Wallace Stevens Journal* 24.2 (Fall 2000) as "Wallace Stevens, Armand Schwerner and, 'The The'" and in *American Literary History* 17.2 (Summer 2005) as "The Sacred and the Real in *The Tablets* of Armand Schwerner." My thanks to the editors of these publications.

:::

I gratefully acknowledge the following for having given me permission to quote from published work:

Excerpts from Robert Duncan's "A Seventeenth Century Suite" and "Santa Cruz Propositions," from *Ground Work: Before the War / In the Dark*, copyright © 1968 by Robert Duncan. Reprinted by permission of New Directions Publishing Corp.

Excerpts from Robert Duncan's "Coda" and "Passages 35: Before the Judgment," from *Ground Work: Before the War / In the Dark*, copyright © 1984 by Robert Duncan. Reprinted by permission of New Directions Publishing Corp.

Excerpts from Robert Duncan's "Illustrative Lines," from *Ground Work: Before the War / In the Dark*, copyright © 1985 by Robert Duncan. Reprinted by permission of New Directions Publishing Corp.

Excerpts from Robert Duncan's "After a Long Illness," from *Ground Work: Before the War / In the Dark*, copyright © 1987 by Robert Duncan. Reprinted by permission of New Directions Publishing Corp.

Excerpts from Susan Howe's "A Bibliography of the King's Book or Eikon Basilike" and "The Nonconformist's Memorial," from *The Nonconformist's Memorial*, copyright © 1993 by Susan Howe. Reprinted by permission of New Directions Publishing Corp.

Excerpts from Nathaniel Mackey's "Song of the Andoumboulou: 42," "Song of the Andoumboulou: 52," "Song of the Andoumboulou: 56," and "Sound and Sentience," from *Splay Anthem*, copyright © 2002, 2006 by Nathaniel Mackey. Reprinted by permission of New Directions Publishing Corp.

Excerpts from Michael Palmer's "From the Anthology (W's Dream)," "Letter 1," "Letter 6," "Letter 7," "Letter 8," "Under the Perseids," and "Untitled (September '92)," from *At Passages*, copyright © 1995 by New Directions Publishing Corp. Reprinted by permission of New Directions Publishing Corp.

Excerpts from Michael Palmer's "A hundred years ago I made a book," "A man undergoes pain sitting at a piano," ". . . by the name of Ceran," "Dear Lexicon, I died in you," "Said the Speaker," "She says, Into the dark—," and "Words say, Misspell and misspell your name," from *Codes Appearing: Poems 1979–1988*, copyright © 1981, 1984, 1988 by Michael Palmer. Reprinted by permission of New Directions Publishing Corp.

Excerpts from pages 44, 49, and 50 of Susan Howe's *Singularities* copyright © 1990 by Susan Howe. Reprinted by permission of Wesleyan University Press.

ACKNOWLEDGMENTS

Excerpts from pages 200, 232, 302, 380, 383, 412, 413, and 416 of Jack Spicer's *My Vocabulary Did This To Me*, copyright © 2008 by Peter Gizzi. Reprinted by permission of Wesleyan University Press.

Excerpts from various poems in Ronald Johnson's *ARK*, copyright © 1996 by Ronald Johnson. Reprinted by permission of the Literary Estate of Ronald Johnson.

Excerpts from various poems in Armand Schwerner's *The Tablets*, copyright © 1999 by Armand Schwerner. Reprinted by permission of the Literary Estate of Armand Schwerner.

On Mount Vision

The subject of this book is religious revisionism in contemporary American poetry. It is an attempt to understand how and why the sacred remains a basic concern of poets today, especially of a group of poets who have written ambitious, complex, and often extravagant long poems of an experimental nature.[1] Therefore, this book is also about the shifts in form and genre taking place in recent long poems. The experimental nature of these works, however, is constantly mediated by their authors' highly refined and self-conscious sense of tradition: the tradition of long American poems that precede them (all equally experimental and unconventional), and of course, the much older and endlessly vexed tradition of sacred poetry itself. Perhaps I should say instead "the traditional conflict between poetry and the sacred," since poetry never subordinates itself completely to the sacred, and the sacred always adheres to what may appear to be even the most resolutely secular poems. As Geoffrey Hartman puts it:

> As all poetry and indeed all writing—not only that of prima facie religious eras—is scrutinized by the critical and secularizing spirit, more evidence of archaic or sacred residues come to light. We may not value them, but they are too prevalent and integumented to be undone. The sacred has so inscribed itself in language that while it must be interpreted, it cannot be removed. One might speculate that what we call the sacred is simply what must be interpreted or reinterpreted, "A Presence which is not to be put by." ...
>
> It would be a great relief to break with the idea of the sacred, and especially with institutions that claim to mediate it. Yet the institution of language makes every such break appear inauthentic. (*Criticism in the Wilderness* 248–49)

Hartman's rabbinic speculation regarding the sacred and the interpretable is of fundamental importance to this book, for as I have come to understand the work of the poets I examine here, the presence of the sacred must be interpreted and cannot be removed. Likewise, given Hartman's understanding of language in this passage, we may conclude that the scriptural nature of poetry, its inevitable engagement with the sacred, is always assured. That

1

we are led to this conclusion by what Hartman identifies as "the critical and secularizing spirit" is a fascinating irony in itself, since as Hartman well knows, the hermeneutical impulse in criticism that lays bare the "archaic or sacred residues" in poetry has its own origins in religious textuality too, and is therefore never wholly secularizing.

This leads me to another, closely related assertion by Hartman's colleague Harold Bloom, one that has had a profound influence on the way I read literature:

> The scandal is the stubborn resistance of imaginative literature to the categories of sacred and secular. If you wish, you can insist that all high literature is secular, or, should you desire it so, then all strong poetry is sacred. What I find incoherent is the judgment that some authentic literary art is more sacred or more secular than some other. Poetry and belief wander about, together and apart, in a cosmological emptiness marked by the limits of truth and of meaning. (*Ruin the Sacred Truths* 4)

In Bloom's terms, one of my goals is to chart the wandering, "together and apart," of poetry and belief, as it takes place in a number of major poems of our time. That they are probably not the poems that Bloom would regard as major in any sense is yet another irony with which I must contend, given the importance of his theoretical insights to my commentaries.[2]

In the passage just quoted, Bloom presents imaginative literature as *resistant* to the categories of sacred and secular, but in the debate between the aesthetic and the religious, we know where his sympathies lie: "From our perspective, religion is spilled poetry" (*Kabbalah and Criticism* 52). Contrary to Matthew Arnold, who, according to Bloom, "reads religion as abiding in poetry, as though the poem were a saving remnant," it is more likely that "the saving remnant *of poetry* is the only force of what we call theology. And what can theology be except what Geoffrey Hartman anxiously terms it: 'a vast, intricate domain of psychopoetic events'" (*Agon* 152). But if poetry insists on its precedence over religion, and if we know the sacred only through the mediating power of poetic form, then, conversely, the poem will always and unavoidably remind us of its religious heritage and associations, even if it seeks to deny them. Allen Grossman presents a somewhat less conflicted view of the matter when he observes that "*poetic vocation, always personal (vocation is of persons), requires to make it social (i.e., public) a mediating institution other than poetry. . . . Most commonly in the West the*

mediating institution is the religion of the state, and the requirement of media-
tion arises because of the social necessity of regulating the relation to the sacred"
("On Communicative Difficulty" 144). Grossman mentions other mediat-
ing institutions ("mythological nationalism" in relation to Whitman, Yeats,
and Hölderlin; fascism in relation to Pound), but given his emphasis on "the
social necessity of regulating the relation to the sacred," it seems to me that
even in a predominantly secular society such as ours, poetry and the po-
etic vocation will always, at some level, be at work in the regulation of the
sacred.[3]

"Or maybe this / is the sacred" begins "Untitled (September '92)," a poem
in the series called Untitled, from Michael Palmer's collection *At Passages*
(1995). For me, it is one of the most important moments in Palmer's entire
career. What has been simmering below the surface, partially repressed,
sometimes approached but more often avoided, is finally articulated. It is
uttered quietly, coolly, in the typical Palmer style, with the offhanded "Or
maybe," as if we are overhearing a conversation already in progress. And in
a sense, we are: it is a conversation that Palmer has been conducting with
himself, with his precursors, with his contemporaries, and with the culture
at large, for a long time. It is a conversation about the role, or to be more ex-
act, the *place* of the sacred in modern poetry, the poem itself being one of the
unspecified phenomena to which the "this" in the first line refers.[4] Today,
in the light of postmodern forms of knowledge and of an experimental po-
etry such as Palmer's, apparently dedicated to deconstructive procedures,
to linguistic and epistemological skepticism, and to a radically secular
worldview, we may be reluctant to discuss the relationship of poetry to the
sacred. Indeed, some would say that the matter is beside the point, perhaps
dismissing what I take to be the strong arguments of critics such as Gross-
man, Hartman, and Bloom. Yet the notion that the poem can still become
a holy site, or a space wherein the sacred and the secular may be contested,
haunts contemporary poetry, making poets and readers alike susceptible
to a return of the repressed in regard to poetic subject matter. If I may be
forgiven a pun, spirituality becomes a spirit for these readers; it constitutes
the *unheimlich* as do few other matters. As Freud writes in "The Uncanny,"
quoting Jentsch, a feeling of the uncanny arises when one "doubts whether
an apparently animate being is really alive; or conversely, whether a lifeless
object might not be in fact animate." Is the object we face here animate or

3

inanimate, alive or dead? The question must be asked, because the fate of poetry, whether we wish to admit it or not, is always bound up with the cultural conditions of the sacred at any given time. Indeed, if I can play upon the words of another theorist of grand master-narratives, a specter is haunting modern poetry, and that specter is the notion of spirit, or of the sacred itself.

Palmer's *At Passages* takes its title from lines that appear a little later in "Untitled (September '92)": "At Passages we peer out / over a tracery of bridges // patchwork of sails" (74). Palmer's use of the term Passages invokes the serial poem by that name of his precursor and mentor, Robert Duncan, a poet for whom a postmodern understanding of the sacred is of paramount importance. Like Palmer's text, Duncan's Passages is also a "tracery of bridges": its interlaced, highly ornamented lines, weaving their way over the years and through a number of his books, endlessly bridge or connect the orders of being to form a boundless vision of *kosmos*, "a contrapuntal communion of all things" (*Bending the Bow* 78) or "a poetry of poetries, *grand collage*" (vii). Palmer defines Duncan's *grand collage* as "grounded in the authority of timeless heretical *gnosis*, "a constellation of myriad myths and voices from an eternal counter-tradition, as well as of impulses, accidents and intrusions, disciplined and informed by an attention to the poem's ratios or measures" ("Robert Duncan and Romantic Synthesis"). Although there is a much greater degree of what might be called *negativity* in Palmer's poetic, and a greater insistence on the materiality of language, it is Duncan and the complex traditions he represents (theosophical, gnostic, romantic, symbolist . . .) that leads Palmer to an engagement with what he names, in his precursor's work, "the dimension of Spirit, with that troublesome, rebarbative capital letter" ("Robert Duncan and Romantic Synthesis").

Duncan's understanding of "Spirit" has a profound effect upon his poetic practice and his sense of himself as a derivative poet. His notions of poetic identity, tradition, and form in turn influence every poet under study in this book. But although he is the subject of my first chapter, and the earliest poet I consider, I am not really attempting to define a school of Duncan, which would, in any case, run contrary to Duncan's own conception of poetic receptivity, calling, and investment. Rather, I would read him as a paradigm of the contemporary poet who seeks to work through matters of the sacred, of spirit, of ritual, and of religion, especially in long, open, serial forms. Following Duncan, it is no accident that Palmer's investigation of the sacred as a return of the repressed, the sudden eruption of the sacred in the poem as a category to be defined, a condition to be analyzed, an illness to be cured, occurs within the context of a seemingly heterogeneous *series* of poems that defy categorization and definition—even to the point of being called, paradoxically, Untitled. Duncan's extraordinary conception of form, of the poem as a "place of first permission" (*Opening of the Field* 7) that is simultaneously an unveiling or revelation of what has been previously hidden in the recesses of the world and of language—that is, previously *unnamed*—resonates powerfully for the poets who come after him, whether or not they explicitly acknowledge him as an influence.

Beginning with Duncan's Passages, the poems that I examine here, all of them related to but not defined by conventional genre designations such as lyric and epic, are engaged in cultural work that is derived from or in dialogue with what may be broadly understood as practices of faith and spiritual experience. Sometimes they address (or revise) specific religious doctrines or beliefs, but more often they participate in what Duncan calls "the symposium of the whole." "[O]ur ideal of vital being," Duncan declares, "rises not in our identification in a hierarchy of higher forms but in our identification with the universe." Such being the case, "religion and art may both be fictional and the intensity of their truth and reality the intensity needed to make what is not actual real. The crux for the poet is to make real what is only real in a heightened sense" (*H.D. Book*, 91, 123).

As Duncan indicates, the "fictional" nature of religion and art, these two related spheres of human activity, means that they paradoxically transform and intensify reality. Duncan returns to this idea repeatedly throughout his writings. In the introduction to *Bending the Bow*, the power of what he names *IT*, a "primal Eros" that energizes the cosmos, is acknowledged by the "gnostics and magicians" who "claim to know or would know Its real nature, which they believe to be miswritten or cryptically written in the text of the actual world." Yet despite his sympathy for the traditions such figures represent, Duncan argues to the contrary that "[William Carlos] Williams is right in his *no ideas but in things*; for It has only the actual universe in which to realize Itself. We ourselves in our actuality, as the poem in its actuality, its thingness, are facts, factors, in which It makes Itself real" (vii). Not only is this an instance of Duncan's famous synthesizing of romantic/symbolist

5

and modernist/objectivist poetics, it is also a representative expression of his religious imagination. We find a similar expression, including that same use of the destabilizing term "fiction," in his important essay "The Sweetness and Greatness of Dante's *Divine Comedy*," when he declares that "with Dante, I take the literal, the actual, as the primary ground. . . . It is, finally, I believe, the only ground for us to know; for it is Creation, it is the Divine Presentation, it is the language of experience whose words are immediate to our sense; from which our own creative life takes fire, *within which* our own creative life takes fire. This creative life is a drive toward the reality of Creation, producing an inner world, an emotional and intellectual fiction, in answer to our awareness of the creative reality of the whole" (*Fictive Certainties* 145).

Duncan's "awareness of the creative reality of the whole" calls to mind the modern situation that Steven M. Wasserstrom calls *"religion after religion,"* in which "the most 'traditional' theosophy appears as an expression of a curiously emphatic modernism: antinomian, individualistic, and secular" (65). In his study of Gershom Scholem, Mircea Eliade, and Henry Corbin (all religious thinkers whom Duncan read), Wasserstrom argues that in our era,

> the history of thinking on religion . . . starts from the fact of being religiously numerous—and goes from there to defend against that fact, inescapably doing so through the very forms of that fact. This *dédoublement*, in which the thinker imaginatively projects into a unifying perfection outside pluralistic social conditions, into a singular theophany accessible as symbols, disrupts an unproblematic relation to everyday belief and practice. It thus seeks, out of this originative rupture, a religion resistant to rupture. Such reintegration is found in the "hidden life" that is the real Tradition, in the theosophical history of *religion after religion.* (51)

This book may be understood, therefore, as consisting of chapters in this "theosophical history," as related through the work of some of the most spiritually acute poets of our time.

Because my primary concern is to examine a relatively small number of recent poems, it would not be helpful—even if it were possible—to fully survey the history of modern American poetry's relationship to the sacred and to religious belief. Then again, to proceed inductively, moving directly to considerations of the individual works, would soon prove to be an inadequate approach, even if one were to take into account each poem's literary historical context. Despite a common lineage and, to a certain extent, shared methodological assumptions, these poems vary in style and in their specific orientation to religious experience. Yet the attitude toward the sacred that may be observed in all of them—heterodox, syncretic, and revisionary—needs to be addressed deductively, and that means establishing at least some general historical ground.

:::

Since the poems I read here are all American, it would make sense to start with the figure who establishes the American difference in literature, and that of course is Emerson. And yet one proposes Emerson as a point of historical origin with some risk, at least according to Harold Bloom. For Bloom, Emerson's "Gnosis begins with the reader's Sublime, a Freudian Negation in which thought comes back but we are still in flight from the emotional recognition that there is no author but ourselves. . . . Emerson's Gnosis rejects all history, including literary history, and dismisses all historians, including literary historians who want to tell the reader that what he recognizes in Emerson is Emerson's own thought rather than the reader's own Sublime" (*Agon* 170). I suppose I will have to take this risk, while acknowledging the degree to which one sees one's "own Sublime" in the text of another, especially that of Emerson, who insists that we rely upon ourselves as the sole source of meaning when we engage in any interpretive process: "How much can you know of your own history, when your knowing is itself a crucial moment in that history?" (8). As always, Bloom serves as my provocation. Having spent ten years writing a serial poem that wrestles with religious issues in ways that are similar to the works under consideration here, I can make no claim to the disinterest of the literary historian.[5] One reason I write literary criticism is to explain to myself why I have come to value the work of another poet. I cannot say whether this is a matter of Bloomian anxiety, but I would venture to guess that this takes me at least part way down the path toward self-reliance.

But even if a critic could consider the Emersonian tradition in and of itself, he or she is bound to meet resistance. Richard Poirier informs us that "Emerson is quite disconcertingly mistrustful of the value of human culture as it has so far evolved" (86); it is for this reason that Emerson has had remarkably little impact on the institution of Anglo-American literary criticism. Against Arnoldian "touchstones," which seek to conserve, as Arnold tells us, "the best which has been thought and said in the world," Emersonian "genius" enters into written form only by becoming "repressed and deformed even before it is further adulterated by institutions of reading" (89). Poirier therefore concludes that "For Emerson, the reading of life or of art is not a search for morally stabilizing moments or summary, but for infusions and diffusions of energy, for that constant redistribution of forces called troping, including the troping of the self" (92). As we shall see, this contrast between stabilization and "troping" equally applies when one compares the Arnoldian and the Emersonian perspectives on the relation of poetry to religion.

"All that we call sacred history attests that the birth of a poet is the principal event in chronology," declares Emerson in "The Poet" (1844); "poets are thus liberating gods" (451, 461). Part of the poet's liberating power lies in his heightened awareness that "things admit of being used as symbols, because nature is a symbol, in the whole and every part" (452). Articulating a theory of symbolic correspondences with its religious and philosophical origins in antiquity (and directly influencing Duncan's understanding of the universal "orders" of being), Emerson envisions the poet as shaman, a dæmonically possessed priest of nature. "Therefore," he explains, "all books of the imagination endure, all which ascend to that truth, that the writer sees nature beneath him, and uses it as his exponent. Every verse or sentence, possessing this virtue, will take care of its own immortality. The religions of the world are the ejaculations of a few imaginative men" (463). For Emerson, poetry brings forth religion, and the poet's imaginative awareness of the correspondences between the natural and supernatural worlds is at the root of all religious doctrines and creeds. Poetry is spiritually transformative; it is the melodious medium through which we may know the soul of things: "Like the metamorphosis of things into higher organic forms is their change into melodies. Over everything stands its dæmon, or soul, and, as the form of the thing is reflected by the eye, so the soul of the thing is reflected by a melody" (458). Poetry provides access to "the true nectar, which is the ravishment of the intellect by coming nearer to the fact" (460), and by "fact," Emerson appears to mean *that which is*, both physically and metaphysically. We are close to what is usually understood as a basic religious concept, but here it is poetry, not religion, that serves as the revelation of truth. Earlier, in *Nature* (1836), Emerson observes that "We make fables to hide the baldness of the fact and conform it, as we say, to the higher law of the mind. But when the fact is seen under the light of an idea, the gaudy fable fades and shrivels. We behold the higher law. To the wise, therefore, a fact is true poetry, and the most beautiful of fables" (48). Under what Emerson calls "the higher law," poetry is fact and fact is poetry. Are religions among the fables that we make? If so, then poetry is indeed the essence of religion.

For Emerson, "America is a poem in our eyes," yet "I look in vain for the poet whom I describe," the poet whose intellect, having been ravished by the poetic fact that is America, is commensurate with "its ample geography" that "dazzles the imagination" (465). But Emerson does not have long to wait. Walt Whitman, called forth by Emerson's vision of the poet, maintains his master's understanding of religion's essentially poetic nature, stating it even more directly in both prose and verse. Poirier observes that "the desire which produces works of art is variously associated in Emerson with God or Divinity or the soul *in* each of us. His religious vocabulary is in itself part of the problem he sets for himself, or that is set for him by the historical condition of the language of his time.... words like 'soul' or 'God' or 'Divinity' designate for him the very limitations which human desire must always want to transcend" (15). This applies equally to Whitman and, as we shall see, to Dickinson as well. In Whitman's straining, overreaching lines, the religious vocabulary he inherits always seems at the point of transcending itself, indicating a surplus of spiritual (and psychosexual) energy that can neither be contained by conventional notions of poetic form nor articulated as normative religious concepts. As he proclaims in "Song of Myself," "Divine am I inside and out, and I make holy whatever I touch or am touch'd from, / The scent of these arm-pits finer than prayer, / This head more than churches, bibles, and all the creeds" (211).

According to the preface to the 1855 edition of *Leaves of Grass*, the poet's "thoughts are the hymns of the praise of things. In the talk on the soul and eternity and God off of his equal plane he is silent. He sees eternity less like a play with a prologue and denouement... he sees eternity in men and women" (9). As in Emerson, we see an emphasis on the spirituality of *things* as revealed by the poet, and on the eternal embodied in the immediate and in the person of the American individual, as opposed to the "play," or drama of the Christian alpha and omega, Genesis and Apocalypse. Thus, in "Song of Myself," "I have heard what the talkers were talking, the talk of the beginning and the end, / But I do not talk of the beginning or the end" (190). The silence of the poet regarding "the soul and eternity and God" indicates that an abstract religious discourse on such matters, apart from the lives of men and women, is simply beside the point. "There will soon be no more priests," declares Whitman. "Their work is done. . . . A new order shall arise and they shall be the priests of man, and every man shall be his own priest. The churches built under their umbrage shall be the churches of men and women. Through the divinity of themselves shall the kosmos and the new breed of poets be interpreters of men and women and of all events and things. They shall find their inspiration in real objects today, symptoms of the past and future. . . . They shall not deign to defend immortality or God or the perfection of things or liberty or the exquisite beauty and reality of the soul. They shall arise in America and be responded to from the remainder of the earth" (24–25). The poet as priest of what Bloom calls "the American Religion," founded by Emerson and proclaimed by Whitman, interprets life, not texts. What are traditionally regarded as religious categories—immortality, God, the soul—are simply assumed, and subsumed by poetic inspiration, "inspiration in real objects today."

Whitman's insouciance toward these categories (which is unrivaled by the poets who follow him) is everywhere apparent in "Song of Myself." "I do not despise you priests, all time, the world over," begins section 43. "My faith is the greatest of faiths and the least of faiths, / Enclosing worship ancient and modern and all between ancient and modern" (236). The section then proceeds to a catalogue of practices and rituals from religions of "all time, the world over," as well as an equally inspired evocation of "down-hearted doubters, dull and excluded," lost in "the sea of torment, doubt, despair and unbelief." Religious practices, like religious categories, are subsumed by the poetic self, so that faith as a matter exterior to the self, a matter of self and other, cannot be judged as either "greatest" or "least." For Whitman, as he says in section 48 of "Song of Myself," "nothing, not God, is greater to one than the self" (244); that is, the "Me myself" whom he first presents in section 4. As Duncan asserts in his "Changing Perspectives in Reading Whitman," "In Whitman there is no ambiguity about the source of *meaning*. It flows from a 'Me myself' that exists in the authenticity of the universe. The poet who exists close on the vital universe then exists close on his Self" (*Fictive Certainties* 191). True communion with the self precludes any normative religious inquiry either within or beyond the bounds of any given creed. "Be not curious about God," cautions the poet, "For I who am curious about each am not curious about God . . . I hear and behold God in every object, yet understand God not in the least, / Nor do I understand who there can be more wonderful than myself" (244). The "wonderful" self is miracle and mystery; its sufficiency is an answer to religious doubt.

This sublime confidence, with its Emersonian roots, is also found in Emily Dickinson, but with certain crucial differences. In *My Emily Dickinson*, Susan Howe observes that "Dickinson chose not to celebrate and sing herself with Whitman; nor could she declare confidently with Emerson that '. . . the Poet is the sayer, the namer, and represents beauty. He is a sovereign, and stands on the centre'. She said something subtler. 'Nature is a Haunted House—but Art—a House that tries to be haunted'" (13). Dickinson revises Emerson on the issue of natural symbolism and universal correspondences. "The Universe is the externisation of the soul," Emerson declares in "The Poet" (453), but it takes Dickinson's darker sensibility to recognize the truly uncanny implications of such a statement. Nature is haunted by Divinity, and if Art is in any manner a second Nature, then it must be haunted too, which means being receptive to the ghosts that bring us—or that are themselves—poems, however terrifying they may be. In that respect, the soul in its house is likewise haunted, as in #512:

> The Soul has Bandaged moments—
> When too appalled to stir—
> She feels some ghastly Fright come up
> And stop to look at her—
>
> Salute her—with long fingers—
> Caress her freezing hair—
> Sip, Goblin, from the very lips
> The Lover—hovered—o'er—
> Unworthy, that a thought so mean
> Accost a Theme—so—fair— (250)

If the psychosexual vision of the soul in Whitman is masturbatory, with the soul freely jetting into the cosmos that he himself contains, the vision in Dickinson is necrophiliac, with the soul visited by the "Fright" or "Goblin" who supplants the "Lover" to whom she is properly bound. Though "The soul has moments of Escape" when "She dances like a Bomb," she is invariably "retaken," a "Felon led along, / With shackles on the plumed feet, / And staples, in the Song." For Whitman, the poem is a liberation; for Dickinson, an incarceration, an act of bondage, whether in the home, the prison, or the tomb. Yet in both poets, the transaction between the soul and that which is beyond it takes place in moments alone, apart; as Dickinson says, "These, are not brayed of Tongue."

In those moments when Dickinson communes with herself and feels her power most intensely,[6] however, the result is as sublime (and perhaps even more self-conscious) as any passage in Emerson or Whitman:

The Soul's Superior instants
Occur to Her—alone—
When friend—and Earth's occasion
Have infinite withdrawn—

Or She—Herself—ascended
To too remote a Height
For lower Recognition
Than her Omnipotent—

This Mortal Abolition
Is seldom—but as fair
As Apparition—subject
To Autocratic Air—

Eternity's disclosure
To favorites—a few—
Of the Colossal substance
Of Immortality (144)

This poem, #306, is in the same vein but goes a good deal further than, say, the more well known #303, "The Soul Selects her own Society," and it appears to take place once the soul "shuts the Door." The trope of extreme height that is associated with the sublime is connected here to an awareness of immortality, autocracy, and omnipotence, either of the soul herself or of the divine power, "the Colossal substance," to which she is conjoined. Because she is one of the "favorites" who are privy to "Eternity's disclosure," Dickinson bears the same assurances as Whitman when he declares that "I know that the hand of God is the promise of my own, / And I know that the spirit of God is the brother of my own" (192)—though in Dickinson, it is more a matter of Calvinist election than democratic brotherhood.

This is obviously not the place to rehearse the poet's religious development, which remains the subject of endless debate among Dickinson scholars. But if we regard this and similar poems as expressions of the uppermost limit of Dickinson's psychic power, as assertions of omnipotence that derive their rhetorical conviction from an uncanny sense of self-reliance that Emerson himself only occasionally achieves, then we can begin to appreciate the extremity of her religious revisionism. It ranges from the relatively easygoing undoing of convention in slyly subversive poems like #324 ("Some keep the Sabbath going to Church") to the mysterious hermetic intensities of a late piece like #1620 ("Circumference thou Bride of Awe"). More in the line of Whitman's attitude toward religion, but far more sardonic, is the delicious #1545:

> The Bible is an antique Volume—
> Written by faded Men
> At the suggestion of Holy Spectres—
> Subjects—Bethlehem—
> Eden—the ancient Homestead—
> Satan—the Brigadier—
> Judas—the Great Defaulter—
> David—the Troubadour—
> Sin—a distinguished Precipe
> Others must resist—
> Boys that "believe" are very lonesome—
> Other Boys are "lost"—
> Had but the Tale a warbling Teller—
> All the Boys would come—
> Orpheus' Sermon captivated—
> It did not condemn— (644)

Transforming herself into a new Orpheus, Dickinson captivates but does condemn. She becomes her own proof that poets, as she says in #569, "Comprehend the Whole," which includes "the Heaven of God" (277). Yet as Poirier observes of Emerson, and as we saw in regard to Whitman, the religious language that Dickinson inherits remains part of the psychopoetic problem she sets for herself. Late in her career, Dickinson may feel that she is among those "Others" who need not resist "Sin," but she is still warbling a *sermon*: biblical allusions and the religious frame of reference they imply remain part of the array of powers that the poet must confront and overcome. The range and tone of #1545 is more confident than the wonderful early poem "A little East of Jordan" (#59), in which she identifies with Jacob wrestling the angel (or God, as Dickinson reads the episode). Nevertheless, for Dickinson, from first to last, the Bible, written by "faded Men" but truly authored by "Holy Spectres" *is* the religious imagination as it comes to her. Like Milton (and surely there is something of *Paradise Lost* in "Satan—the Brigadier"), Dickinson produces a countertext that revises and completes Scripture. The difference is that Dickinson does not write an epic but a body of lyrics that come to constitute a single haunted house.

Dickinson's Frights or Goblins, her Holy Spectres that "suggest" scripture to human authors, remind me of her poetic and spiritual descendent, Jack Spicer, whose religious agon is the subject of chapter 3. Spicer's poetic of spooks and Martians, his understanding of the poem as a house in which lights go on and off as one goes from room to room and the ghosts move the furniture about, owes a great deal to Dickinson, though in Dickinson, the experience is altogether more frightening. Her sense of poetry as a series of haunted moments is as important to our concerns as Whitman's accretive and projective conception of *Leaves of Grass*, which, as we know from his essays on Whitman, shapes Duncan's project starting with *The Opening of the Field*. American originals whose formal innovations are inextricable from their religious revisionism, Whitman and Dickinson remain critical, and often surprisingly direct models for poets working over a hundred years after them.[7]

In comparison to Emerson and his followers, Matthew Arnold has already been presented as a more cautious thinker regarding poetry and religion. Nevertheless, his position must be examined, considering the precision with which he frames the issue and his influence on the modern Anglo-American literary academy.[8] Arnold remains one of the first figures who comes to mind when one considers the role of the sacred in modern poetry, and vice versa. "Vice versa" is precisely the issue: as Bloom and Poirier know full well, the Emersonian view that poetry always empowers religion differs significantly from the Arnoldian supposition that in modern times, the core values of religion will be preserved in poetry. In *Culture and Anarchy* (1869),

Arnold, examining the relative strengths of poetry and religion in Victorian society, states that "the idea of beauty and of a human nature perfect on all sides, which is the dominant idea of poetry, is a true and invaluable idea, though it has not yet had the success that the idea of conquering the obvious faults of our animality, and of a human nature perfect on the moral side,—which is the dominant idea of religion,—has been enabled to have; and it is destined, adding to itself the religious idea of a devout energy, to transform and govern the other" (99–100). Arnold goes on to develop this notion of poetry's religious destiny in a famous passage from "The Study of Poetry" (1880), declaring that "more and more mankind will discover that we have to turn to poetry to interpret life for us, to console us, to sustain us. Without poetry, our science will appear incomplete; and most of what now passes with us for religion and philosophy will be replaced by poetry" (161–62).

In this passage, poetry replaces religion and philosophy in its continued capacity to console, to sustain, and to interpret life, functions that, I would argue, have been of the highest priority to British poets since Wordsworth, but are actually of much less concern for American poets, even in times of psychic or historical crisis.[9] For them, poetry is less an interpretation of life than an enactment of life, an instance of power and not a commentary on it, except to the extent that all texts are in some ways commentaries. With Emerson in "Self-Reliance," American poets understand that "life only avails, not the having lived. Power ceases in the instant of repose; it resides in the moment of transition from a past to a new state, in the shooting of the gulf, in the darting to an aim. This one fact the world hates, that the soul *becomes*" (271). Because spiritual power is in a constant state of movement and transition, "the soul *becomes*," and this is why poetry, insofar as it embodies spiritual power, always moves us closer to what Emerson, as we have seen, designates as "the fact." Granted, for Arnold too, "poetry attaches its emotion to the idea; the idea *is* the fact"; this is why "the strongest part of our religion is its unconscious poetry" ("The Study of Poetry" 161). But Arnold (despite, oddly, his devotion to Goethe) lacks the Emersonian sense of becoming, or what Charles Olson, in a not altogether different context, would later call "the *kinetics* of the thing" (240). Rather, it would appear from his remarks that poetry and religion have always abided in each other; for Arnold, this is *fact*. This makes perfect sense, given Arnold's generally conservative bent, including his desire to conserve what is best in organized religion, which poetry as the truest expression of religious values will rescue, whether we are conscious of this or not. Clearly, however, Arnold wishes his readers—those engaged in the pursuit of culture, of sweetness and light—to become conscious of this relationship, and to value poetry all the more because of it.

Arnold's understanding of the role that poetry can play in the modern spiritual crisis comes, of course, as much from his practice as a poet as from his later observations as a cultural critic. Indeed, Arnold's belief that the strongest part of religion is unconscious poetry, comes in part from the traumatic firsthand experience of the withdrawal of religious faith from his own poetry. According to Ronald Schuchard, "Arnold was the first English poet to describe a disturbing new phenomenon in modern letters, a 'mysterious malady' that had affected him in the composition of 'Empedocles on Etna' (1852), in which his persona struggles with 'some root of suffering in himself, / Some secret and unfollowed vein of woe'" (4). By reminding us of Arnold's decision to suppress "Empedocles" when he publishes the first edition of his *Poems* (1853) because of its "destructive subjectivity" and a burdened sense of the self that "led only to paralysis and despair" (4), Schuchard points to the darker spiritual path that extends from Arnold into the early twentieth century. Borrowing the title of Lionel Johnson's poem, Schuchard names Arnold's "mysterious malady" "The Dark Angel," a "sensual-spiritual malaise" (5) that moves on past Arnold himself to manifest itself with disastrous results in the British poets of the 1890s and ultimately to afflict T. S. Eliot, whose struggle with the angel spans his entire career.

Eliot may first witness this modern struggle in Arnold, but he goes much further than Arnold in his understanding of the religious dimension of literary culture. In "Francis Herbert Bradley" (1927), Eliot takes obvious pleasure in presenting Bradley's "Arnold-baiting" (*Selected Prose* 201), and does a bit of his own: "In *Culture and Anarchy*, which is probably his greatest book, we hear something said about 'the will of God'; but the 'will of God' seems to become superseded in importance by 'our best self, or right reason, to which we want to give authority': and this best self looks very much like Matthew Arnold slightly disguised" (201–2). As witty as this remark may be, it also reveals Eliot's dissatisfaction with any attempt, even a relatively conservative attempt like Arnold's, to rescue religious faith through the identification of divine with human power. Throughout his work, Arnold relates notions like the "best self" or "a human nature perfect on all sides" with poetry, and for Eliot, this is simply untenable. Rather, at best poetry comes, as he writes in *The Use of Poetry and the Use of Criticism*, as "the sudden lifting of the burden of anxiety and fear which presses upon our daily life so steadily that we are unaware of it. . . . The accompanying feeling is less like what we know as positive pleasure, than a sudden relief from an intolerable burden" (144–45). Because poets, like the rest of modern society, are ordinarily beset by a spiritual malaise of which they are hardly conscious, the poem comes to them, and then passes to their readers, not as an instance of the humanly perfect, but as an instance of psychic awareness: "It may make us from time to time a little more aware of the deeper, unnamed feelings which form the substratum of our being, to which we rarely penetrate; for our lives are mostly a constant evasion of ourselves, and an evasion of the visible and sensible world" (*Use of Poetry* 155).

Committed, in Frank Kermode's words, "to external authority against the inner voice; to the surrender of self to something greater; to permanence as the opposite and measure of change; to the intemporal as opposed to mere sequential time and history" ("Introduction" 19), Eliot's working through of the modern spiritual crisis—both intensely personal and, simultaneously, of enormous literary significance—produces the least compromising, least *negotiable* understanding of poetry's relationship to belief available to our study. Needless to say, it also represents the greatest challenge to the Emersonian tradition, and serves, to a greater or lesser extent, as its counterforce in shaping the religious sensibilities of many recent poets. Its influence, both in criticism and poetry, may not be as strong as it was through, say, the 1960s, but there is no question that it literally haunts at least some of the poets we will examine in subsequent chapters. "Pieces of the past arising out of the rubble," cries a horrified Jack Spicer at the beginning of his last work, the *Book of Magazine Verse* (1965); "Which evokes Eliot and then evokes Suspicion. Ghosts all of them. Doers of no good" (*My Vocabulary* 406). Beneath the irony is the dawning recognition that Spicer may have inadvertently become a more Eliotic poet than he could have consciously imagined, not only in his work's relation to tradition and the past (that is, "the rubble"), but in its relation to religious belief as well.

One of the most focused discussions of this matter in Eliot's criticism is found in the essay "Religion and Literature" (1935), which begins with a proposition that Eliot refined over many years: "Literary criticism should be completed by criticism from a definite ethical and theological standpoint" (*Selected Prose* 97). For Eliot, this standpoint is, of course, Anglo-Catholicism, and by the time he writes the essay, he has, for the most part, an Anglo-Catholic audience in mind. This is the audience that would be most receptive to his affirmation that "modern literature is corrupted by what I call Secularism, that it is simply unaware, simply cannot understand the meaning of, the primacy of the supernatural over the natural life: of something which I assume to be our primary concern" (*Selected Prose* 105). A Christian awareness of "the primacy of the supernatural" in turn produces "standards and criteria of criticism over and above those applied by the rest of the world," which must be used to judge work "written by people who not only have no such belief, but are even ignorant of the fact that there are still people in the world so 'backward' or so 'eccentric' as to continue to believe" (105–6).

Most readers of poetry, then and now, would have a great deal of difficulty with Eliot's position here, though they might admire the uncompromising way in which Eliot refuses to separate literary from moral and religious judgments. It is worth reading Eliot's remarks, however, not only from the standpoint of his particular faith, but as a modern paradigm for the subordination of aesthetic to religious principles in the consideration of poetry. As one of the greatest—and surely the most orthodox—of poet-critics of the twentieth century, Eliot seeks to produce both a poetry that expresses (however "impersonally") his religious vision, and a criticism that rigorously evaluates poetry according to his religious beliefs. None of the other poets or critics discussed or cited in this book give themselves to such a task. Harold Bloom may occasionally call himself a "Jewish Gnostic" (*Agon* 4), but despite his fascination with "the American religion," what he asserts throughout his work is the supreme power of the aesthetic imagination, which governs religion and poetry both. Among the poets, Duncan comes the closest to producing a body of literary criticism that completes itself in a criticism of a spiritual, if not what Eliot would deem a "theological" standpoint, but his avowed syncretism, the fact that, like Blake and Yeats before him, he is a sect of one, makes the distinction between poetry and religion in his writing nearly beside the point. As Peter O'Leary observes in *Gnostic Contagion*, "When I refer to Duncan, H.D. or [Nathaniel] Mackey as religious poets, I do not mean they have religious aspirations outside of the poem. They devote themselves to the 'orders' of poetry, to the 'trouble of the unbound reference' (as Duncan calls it) with a religious fervor, because only in poetry do they find the revelation that gives order to creation and cosmos" (25). Eliot, by contrast, certainly has religious aspirations both inside and outside the poem, and by subordinating himself, and most particularly, his poetic genius, so fully to a religious authority outside of himself, he achieves those aspirations.

The cultural aspirations that accompany them are a different matter. "The cultural triumph of the Anglo-American form of modernism," writes Poirier, "was largely, almost exclusively Eliot's personal triumph. He had the promotional genius to insist that not personal despairs but unique historical cause and effect relationships explain his poetic practice" (22). That poetic practice, reaching its acme in the *Four Quartets* (1943), consists of a sort of musical mysticism, "a raid on the inarticulate" (*Complete Poems* 128) striving toward Incarnation:

> These are only hints and guesses,
> Hints followed by guesses; and the rest
> Is prayer, observance, discipline, thought and action.
> The hint half guessed, the gift half understood, is Incarnation. (136)

[handwritten marginal note: " the rest / is prayer "]

For Eliot, as he tells us in "Burnt Norton," "Words, after speech, reach / Into the silence" (121), yet such are the limitations of human language that they are always assailed, just as "The Word in the desert / is most attacked by voices of temptation" (122). The model for poetic discipline, therefore, is spiritual discipline, out which may come a verbal pattern that hints at the divine pattern. Awareness of this pattern leads to a devotional stance that is the only bulwark against the dark angel and the chaos of modern history.

Or is it? "Tell X that speech is not dirty silence / Clarified. It is silence made still dirtier" (Stevens, *Palm* 251). Wallace Stevens's "X" in "The Creations of Sound" (from *Transport to Summer*, 1947) is usually assumed to be Eliot or some composite figure including him, and it would seem that in these lines at least, Stevens may be directly responding to what Eliot writes about speech and silence in "Burnt Norton." Speech—that is, poetry—makes silence dirtier rather than clearer because "It is more than an imitation for the ear," a mystical emulation of a preordained divine pattern. It is, rather, a fundamental part of the human process of world making, a seeking after the Emersonian *fact*, in which Stevens has been engaged throughout his poetic career. If poetry is music, it is not music that comes to X "of its own, / Without understanding," in some rapturous state; rather, it is a made thing, like the song of the woman on the beach in "Idea of Order at Key West." X "lacks this venerable complication" (251) and thus "is an obstruction, a man / Too exactly himself" (250). So much for Eliot's vaunted impersonality! What is needed instead is

> a separate author, a different poet,
> An accretion from ourselves, intelligent
> Beyond intelligence, an artificial man
>
> At a distance, a secondary expositor,
> A being of sound, whom one does not approach
> Through any exaggeration. From him, we collect. (251)

An "artificial man" is an artificer or maker of the self, and his self is an "accretion" of the human. For Eliot in "The Dry Salvages," "you are the music / While the music lasts" (*Complete Poems* 136), but for Stevens, the poet is a "being of sound" who is his own music, "intelligent / Beyond intelligence." Here, in a rare instance, Stevens polemicizes against a version of modernism that, according to Poirier, caused him (along with Frost) to appear "rusticated by being made to seem, by a kind of modernist raid on the rest of American literature, like country cousins" (22). "By writing *The Creations of Sound*," Harold Bloom observes, "Stevens commits himself to an even more intense Emersonian than before" (*Wallace Stevens* 237).[10]

Stevens's Emersonian perspective on the relation of poetry to the sacred is, to be sure, a career-long commitment, and here we can only consider it briefly. In his "Adagia" (1934–1940?), he states in prose many of the formulas that have bearing on this issue, including those most pure of Emersonian utterances, "God is in me or else is not at all (does not exist)" and "it is the belief and not the god that counts" (*Opus Posthumous* 188, 198). In both of these statements, the god-term is not discounted, nor is it precisely "humanized"; rather, it is redirected into and through the self. Again we are at the point to which Poirier takes us regarding Emerson and his contemporary followers, where "words like 'soul' or 'God' or 'Divinity' designate for him the very limitations which human desire must always want to transcend" (15). But

Stevens also states that "after one has abandoned a belief in god, poetry is that essence which takes its place as life's redemption" (*Opus Posthumous* 185). Why is this the case, and why would Stevens preserve a patently religious term like "redemption" just at the point when he seems to embrace a wholly secular world-view?

An answer may be found in one of Stevens's later personae, Professor Eucalyptus of *An Ordinary Evening in New Haven*, the metaphysician who seeks

> God in the object itself, without much choice.
> It is a choice of the commodious adjective
> For what he sees, it comes in the end to that:
>
> The description that makes it divinity, still speech
> As it touches the point of reverberation—not grim
> Reality but reality grimly seen
>
> And spoken in paradisal parlance new
> And in any case never grim, the human grim
> That is part of the indifference of the eye
>
> Indifferent to what it sees. (*Palm* 340)

Looking for God in but not beyond reality, the Professor realizes that what counts is the "commodious adjective" applied to the object, that it is always "the description that makes it divinity." In confronting reality, the poet/metaphysician does not accept "the human grim / That is part of the indifference of the eye," but rather addresses reality "in paradisal parlance new." The redemption of life, of reality, is achieved through poetry, which is to say that the poet becomes a sort of redeemer, showing us how to view and describe grim reality so that it becomes divine. Stevens cannot dispense with this religious terminology because it remains crucial in his rethinking of poetry and the sacred. This is why, as Professor Eucalyptus says later in the poem,

> "The search
> For reality is as momentous as
> The search for god." It is the philosopher's search
>
> For an interior made exterior
> And the poet's search for the same exterior made
> Interior: breathless things broodingly abreath

> With the inhalations of original cold
> And of original earliness. Yet the sense
> Of cold and earliness is a daily sense,
>
> Not the predicate of bright origin. (345)

The metaphysical hungers of the philosopher and the poet mirror each other. The exteriority of reality and interiority of the divine inspire both figures to go on searches that are equally "momentous," with the search for reality now recognized as the successor to the search for God. Both searches involve what Stevens calls "cold" and "earliness," but these qualities may be experienced daily, not as "the predicate of bright origin." This is "to say of the evening star, / The most ancient light in the most ancient sky,"

> That it is wholly an inner light, that it shines
> From the sleepy bosom of the real, re-creates,
> Searches a possible for its possibleness. (345)

The ancient light is an inner light, but it is not the light of divine origin. It shines from the real, seeking the "possibleness" of reality.

Thus, "we keep coming back and coming back / To the real: to the hotel instead of the hymns" (336). What we hear in the Hotel Reality are hymns of a different sort, though hymns nonetheless. One wonders if it is in such a hotel that the poet offers his "Final Soliloquy of the Interior Paramour," in which "we say God and the imagination are one" (*Palm* 368). The union of the poet and his muse, "a single shawl / Wrapped tightly round us," counteracts the poverty of a reality without poetry and produces "a light, a power, the miraculous influence." In the grip of that power, the lovers "feel the obscurity of an order, a whole, / A knowledge, that which arranged the rendezvous, // Within its vital boundary, in the mind." Presumably, that godlike power is the imagination, for it can vouchsafe a vision of the cosmic order in the human mind. For Stevens, this achievement "out of the central mind" is sufficient for the poet and his muse, for "we make a dwelling in the evening air, / In which being there together is enough" (369).

The remarkable self-sufficiency at which Stevens arrives by the end of his career has yet to be duplicated by later American poets, which is why, in regard to poetry as a spiritual quest, he has had few followers. More typical in the intention of his poetry, if not the intensity of its style, is Hart Crane.

Crane speaks for a number of recent poets when he calls to his muse in the last line of "To Brooklyn Bridge" to *"lend a myth to God"* (*Complete Poems of Hart Crane* 44). But what exactly does that mean for poetry's relation to the sacred? On the one hand, myths are human creations; therefore, poets have always lent myths to God, for it was only through such myths that the sacred could be apprehended. As an instrument of the sacred, however unstable and subversive, poetry engages in myth making. On the other hand, Crane understands, apropos of his romance with modernity, that the mere acknowledgment of the poet's myth-making function is insufficient. Unlike Eliot, he cannot subordinate himself to old myths and recycle them; in this regard, he is closer to Stevens. Yet Crane's search is for transcendence, not Stevens's sense of "reality." Although Crane argues in his "General Aims and Theories" that the "deliberate program, then, of a 'break' with the past or tradition seems to me to be a sentimental fallacy" (*Complete Poems and Selected Letters* 218), he insists nevertheless that "new conditions of life germinate new forms of spiritual articulation" (222). According to Allen Grossman, in Crane's poetry these new forms appear as "'Orphic machines'—the bridge, the tower, the airplane, the carillon, the hurdy-gurdy, the phonograph, the camera—[that] function like poetic forms in that they produce experience and are burdened and deformed by desire" ("On Communicative Difficulty" 102). Yet as Grossman accurately observes, for Crane these "myths or machines of access to origins . . . were always colored by consciousness . . . of their impossibility" (103).

Thus, in "Atlantis" (positioned at the end of *The Bridge* but composed before the rest of the poem), the Brooklyn Bridge may be an "intrinsic Myth," "Deity's glittering Pledge," an "Everpresence, beyond time" (107), but the insistently metaphorizing spirit of the orphic poet must strain mightily in order to keep his modern vision of transcendence in view. In the end, Crane's understanding of poetry, and of the poetic identity, is more purely *sacrificial* than that of any other American poet. "The Broken Tower," always read as his "death poem," marks the completion of his gnostic initiation ("And so it was I entered the broken world / To trace the visionary company of love"), but just as importantly, it indicates how the "word" of such an extreme orphic desire for cosmic unity is bound to prove incommensurate with a "Word" that is forever apart and beyond:

My word I poured. But was it cognate, scored
Of that tribunal monarch of the air
Whose thigh embronzes earth, strikes crystal Word
In wounds pledged once to hope,—cleft to despair? (*Complete Poems of Hart Crane* 160)

At the broken tower, "that tribunal monarch of the air," the poet who has poured his word is wounded unto despair and death by the indifferent Word, the untranslatable utterance of a deity that the visionary company, a "corps / Of shadows in the tower"—Crane's imagined precursors—likewise failed to speak. The sheer verbal intensity of Crane's Orphism, his desire for cosmic harmony in a broken world, remains unprecedented. Whether the poets of cosmos who come after (in our case, Duncan and Johnson) are more capable of maintaining their psychic integrity remains to be seen.

In discussing the problem of genre in Crane's poetry, Harold Bloom notes that there is "no authentic distinction to be made between the lyric and the epic Crane" ("Introduction" xvii), and that "what allied Eliot and Crane (despite Crane's desires) were their common ambitions for making the lyric mode perform the work of the epic" (xviii). In the same discussion, Bloom also distinguishes "Wallace Stevens' long meditative sequences," but still insists that "The transformation of lyric into epic was a Romantic *praxis* long before it was Modernist" (xviii). Generic distinctions in regard to long poems become increasingly difficult in both Romantic and Modernist poetry, and this especially true in regard to American poetry, where the lyric sequences of Whitman and Dickinson break traditional generic categories from the start. *The Waste Land* and *The Bridge* may be understood as brief, fragmented epics permeated by lyricism; *Four Quartets, Notes toward a Supreme Fiction*, and *An Ordinary Evening in New Haven* are meditative sequences that likewise rise to great lyric heights; while Pound's *Cantos* and Williams's *Paterson*, with their concern for either global or local history, more obviously attempt to perform the traditional cultural work of the epic. One modernist work, however, stands apart from all of these poems, and though lyrical meditation is crucial to its design, its religious dimension in particular leads us to reconsider poetic genre and discourse yet again. The work is H.D.'s *Trilogy*, which Robert Duncan, coming upon it in the years following World War II, saw as "a gospel of Poetry," leading him to "read everything in a new light" (*H.D. Book* 25).

What Duncan learns from H.D. and transfers to his own poetry has everything to do with this notion of poetry as gospel, keeping in mind that Duncan's use of the term "gospel" can be taken quite literally. On the one hand, it means that poetry contains, brings forward, or enacts spiritual truth. On the other hand, it means that poetry as a scripture unto itself *is* that truth.[11] Raised in the mystical tradition of the Moravian Church, a lifelong student of the occult, and an analysand of Freud from 1933 to 1934, H.D. gradually evolves from her patriarchally imposed identity as a prominent "Imagiste" to achieve her greatest poetic potential as a visionary medium, prophetess, and scribe. *Trilogy* and the other long poems of her later career are full-blown counter-scriptures, sacred texts that both reclaim and revise the occult and religious traditions in which she is immersed. What H.D. calls "spiritual realism" in *The Walls Do Not Fall* requires a commitment to "substitute enchantment / for sentiment" (537); through magical practice, poets must seek for occult truth without settling for mere personal expression. At a time of extreme historical crisis (the poem is written in London during the Blitz), H.D. insists that her colleagues "re-value / our secret hoard" of wisdom—"talismans, records or parchments." For, as H.D. continues,

> explicitly, we are told
> it contains
>
> *for every scribe*
> *which is instructed,*
>
> *things new*
> *and old.* (538)

The poet-scribe rewrites the ancient traditions, and in doing so, prophetically reveals new truths. Poets are therefore "bearers of the secret wisdom, / living remnant // of the inner band / of the sanctuaries initiate" (517); their goddess, as revealed in *Tribute to the Angels*, is the Lady who "carries a book but it is not / the tome of the ancient wisdom, // the pages, I imagine, are the blank pages / of the unwritten volume of the new" (570).

H.D.'s poetry anticipates more recent developments in the ongoing history of poetry and the sacred. Her understanding of poets as a "living remnant" conflates a biblical concept, that of the saving remnant of the righteous and God-fearing, with the gnostic concept of initiation into a select order with special access to secret wisdom. Remarkably, in *Trilogy* these traditional ideas are sustained in tandem with an explicit modernism that celebrates "the unwritten volume of the new." Whether more recent poets are able to maintain this balance between traditional models of belief and unwritten newness is a question I will explore at some length. But in any case, as Hölderlin writes in his poem *Andenken* ("Remembrance"), "*Was bleibet aber, stiften die Dichter*" ("But poets establish what remains") (qtd. in Santner 140). For Eric L. Santner, the idea that poetry opens us to "what remains" is crucial, because in doing so, poetry partakes in the discourse that Santner names "psychotheology." According to Santner, the remnant, in terms of both psyche and society, "is not a part of a whole but rather the opening beyond the 'police order' of parts and wholes. What poets establish is not some sort of vision or consciousness of the All; rather they introduce into the relational totality of social existence—into the social body divided into parts—the perspective of 'non-all'" (142). Here, as in H.D. and those who come after her, what poets reveal may renew or redeem human potential when the social order has become overbearing, too full of what Santner calls "undeadness." In this way, poetry's foundational relationship to the sacred, to a source of life that is both apart from and within us, surely remains.

Robert Duncan

FROM POETRY TO SCRIPTURE

A poem always runs the risk of being meaningless, and would be nothing without this risk... (Derrida, *Writing and Difference* 74)

Is the root charge of poetry a power to partake of a Gnostic "version" of things, catastrophic events wherein we know truth by its downward turn?
(Mackey, *Paracritical Hinge* 135)

Confronted with Robert Duncan's last two volumes of poetry, *Ground Work: Before the War* (1984) and *Ground Work II: In the Dark* (1987), readers of Duncan's oeuvre face a troubling situation, that some may be reluctant to acknowledge: *Ground Work* represents what appears to be a significant transformation in Duncan's verse, which some may see as a decline in its lyric qualities. This is not to say that these books are failures: there are individual poems and even sequences in both volumes that are as compelling and rhapsodic as anything Duncan wrote earlier. But something strange happens in the last phases of Duncan's work. An unmaking or a passage beyond the bounds even of open form poetry, combined with a shift in what was previously the poet's centering sense of prophetic vocation, results in an unprecedented kind of writing that no longer seems to be lyric poetry in any conventional sense of the term. It is this writing—this scripture—that I hope to describe and account for here.

Critics of Duncan have certainly intuited this situation.[1] Peter O'Leary, for instance, proposes that the four Duncan poems which are "arguably his best work" are "Often I Am Permitted to Return to a Meadow," "Poem Beginning with a Line by Pindar" (both from *The Opening of the Field*), "Apprehensions" (from *Roots and Branches*), and "My Mother Would Be a Falconress" (from *Bending the Bow*). For O'Leary, these "stand out from the rest of his writing, but in a way that supports the achievement of his serial poems and the projective imagination that inspired him in that poetic mode. The four poems can be imagined as pillars holding up the roof that shelter the temple. To these four poems I would add three 'Passages': 'The Fire, Passages 13' from *Bending the Bow* and two late visionary *Passages* that Duncan left unnumbered: 'The Dignities' and 'In Blood's Domaine,' both from *Ground Work II: In the Dark*" (*Gnostic Contagion* 73–74). I would have to agree with O'Leary's assessment, though I would also add the brilliant revisionary lyric "This Place Rumord to Be Sodom," two or three more of the earlier Passages, and two more pieces from the *Ground Work* volumes, the magnificent "Circulations of the Song" and Duncan's very last poem, "After a Long Illness."[2] Even so, we are still faced with a disappointing falling off of achievement, especially when one recalls how Duncan dramatically refused to publish his work for fifteen years, from about 1968 (when *Bending the Bow* came out) to 1984, saving this accumulation until he felt the time was right for its appearance. What, we may rightfully ask, is happening in Duncan's poetry from the period of *Bending the Bow* to his death in 1988?

We prefer to think of great poets (and there is no question in my mind that Duncan is a great poet) as growing ever stronger and more determined in their utterances, and this is especially true of poets like Duncan who directly emerge from a visionary tradition of the sublime. But Duncan is more than a visionary poet, and even more than that singular American figure who, in the second half of the twentieth century, successfully synthesizes romantic and modernist modes of poetic discourse to produce what he terms a "grand collage" (*Bending the Bow* vii) of uncanny beauty and mystery. He is a *religious* poet: for him, poetry is a religion and the prophetic poet inherits from the religious and philosophical traditions of the past all that is necessary to bring spiritual insight or *gnosis* (which includes a renewed understanding of the social and political conditions of history and of one's own time) to his readers. In "The Truth and Life of Myth," perhaps his greatest testament, Duncan gives witness to "a Creation by Creative Will that realizes Itself in Form evolving in the play of primordial patterns" (*Fictive Certainties* 34). Yet always in this work, as in his other prose, "what I speak of here in the terms of a theology is a poetics. Back of each poet's concept of the poem is his concept of the meaning of form itself; and his concept of form in turn where it is serious at all arises from his concept of the nature of the universe, its lifetime or form, or even, for some, its lifelessness or formlessness" (16). Duncan's own concept of form derives from a syncretic theosophical tradition that includes Neoplatonism, Christian and Jewish kabbalism, and gnosticism, all of which share an emanational vision of being and creation. Yet at the same time, this tradition leads to a vision of *decreation* too: "Chaos, the Yawning Abyss, is First Person of Form. And the Poet too, like the Son, in this myth of Love or Form, must go deep into the reality of His own Nature, into the Fathering Chaos or Wrath, to suffer His own Nature. In this mystery of the art, the Son's cry to the Father might be too the cry of the artist to the form he obeys" (15–16).

This suffering of the Son as he returns into the Chaos of the Father is fundamental to an understanding of Duncan's later poetry, for in this work, the form-making poet, the devotee of Eros whose power brings forth the "form of forms" (*Fictive Certainties* 38), must confront the fathering formlessness of the Abyss that has paradoxically served as the hidden *ground* of his earlier achievements.[3] To endure this return is to engage in a ritual of dis-ease, of psychic (and ultimately, physical) pain and dissolution. In O'Leary's formula, "the religious dimension of Duncan's maturity is an intensely narcissistic, mystical, and personal theosophy whose major mode of expression and meaning is a language of illness, in which he suspends himself and through which he engages in poetic, creative production. In short: to use a language of illness in poetry is to live in illness and give meaning to illness" (*Gnostic Contagion* 22–23). The shamanistic ritual of illness that O'Leary defines here and details throughout his study of Duncan comes to a head during the period when Duncan is writing the *Ground Work* volumes, and it is late in this period that Duncan develops the kidney disease that eventually leads to his death. But death haunts the late work even before Duncan becomes seriously ill;[4] it is elemental to the psychic and discursive transformations the poet undergoes as he fulfills what is in effect his destiny, or what the gnostics would call his *heimarmene*. Hans Jonas defines this notion as the "tyrannical world-rule" of the Archons, the demonic lords of the seven planetary spheres who would keep the gnostic's spirit (*pneuma*) from leaving the fallen Creation of the Demiurge and reuniting with the alien God of the Abyss.[5] It is "universal Fate, a concept taken over from astrology but now tinged with the gnostic anti-cosmic spirit. In its physical aspect, which includes for instance the institution and enforcement of the Mosaic Law, it aims at the enslavement of man" (43). Thus Duncan's late work is not only a shamanistic ritual of psychic dis-ease, but it is also the necessarily disjointed and increasingly *chaotic* account of the *pneuma*, as it struggles in a final crisis against its star-born fate, so that it may return to its home beyond the stars.

Another reader who recognizes an increasing sense of crisis in Duncan's late work is Nathaniel Mackey, whom O'Leary interprets as having contracted from the older poet the "gnostic contagion" that constitutes the soul of the shaman/poet. In his essay "Uroboros: Robert Duncan's *Dante* and *A Seventeenth Century Suite*," Mackey observes that "a sense of exhaustion and limitation, along with a somewhat confessional note, enters these works, a sense that is contrapuntal to [Duncan's] poetics' promise of an escape from closure" (*Discrepant Engagement* 91). Mackey relates this sense to Duncan's increasingly obsessive use of other poets' material to generate his own, as may be seen in the sequences he discusses, based on selections of Dante's prose and of seventeenth-century English poems. This appropriation of earlier poetry, based on Duncan's communal belief in a "poetry of all poetries" (*Bending the Bow* vii) or a "form of forms" operates dialectically. It "deepens the sense of exhaustion and limitation that enters these works. . . . What is interesting is that this should have occurred in the context of works given over to variations upon the works of others. It underscores Duncan's insistence upon calling himself a derivative poet, pointing up the fact that the self upon which he feeds has been largely constituted of his borrowings from others, his feeding upon others" (Mackey, *Discrepant Engagement* 95). Mackey's final move is to relate these sequences from *Ground Work: Before the War* to a Derridean notion of the "trace": "'a kind of writing before writing as we know it', an inscription prior to, 'fiercely beyond', presence" (103). What Duncan produces in his late work is thus a sort of spirit writing, mediumistic "in the compound, conjunctive sense of channeling voices from the past and engaging the medium qua medium, consciously and self-reflexively engaging issues pertaining to poetics and poetic tradition" (99).[6]

Drawing on these observations, what I wish to argue is that given Duncan's psychic and discursive trajectories, his later poetry ritualistically turns upon itself, becoming an increasingly attenuated, self-diminishing, even self-sacrificing body of writing. The further this process extends, the more the writing feeds on both the poet himself and on other poetries. Yet this ascesis is simultaneously an apotheosis. The figure of the poet is both dispersed and centralized, curtailed and inflated, becoming, to an unprecedented extent, a sort of Primordial Man or Adam Kadmon out of the gnostic and kabbalistic traditions that Duncan knew so well.[7] As for the text or body of writing, despite its possible weakening or lessening as *poetry* in any normative sense, it actually grows and blossoms into a strange, postmodern *scripture*, as occult, hermetic, and theosophical as any of the spiritual traditions that shaped Duncan's early sensibility or mature verse.

::::

My use of the term *scripture* in relation to this late poetry needs careful explanation. Duncan's primary mode in his early poetry is decidedly post-romantic, as seen in such works as "The Years as Catches," "Berkeley Poems," "Heavenly City, Earthly City," and *Medieval Scenes*. Of course, he also assimilates a complex and to some extent contradictory set of modernist principles, especially through Ezra Pound—though arguably Duncan's Pound is also a post-romantic, the author of *The Spirit of Romance*, whose *Cantos* is "a work pervaded by the invocations of ghosts, time travel, esoteric philosophy, and superstition" (Johnston 11).[8] However, from the late thirties to the early fifties, Duncan is also deeply engaged with the work of Gertrude Stein, an heir not of romanticism but of realism,[9] an unequivocal modernist for whom writing, as Marjorie Perloff puts it, continually produces a "tension between reference and compositional game, between a pointing system and a self-ordering system" (*Poetics of Indeterminacy* 72). Duncan's engagement with Stein takes various forms, including many imitations, and culminates in the volume *Writing Writing* (1952–1953). In her definitive essay on Duncan and Stein, Jayne L. Walker observes that these texts

> are not simply extensions of his search for freer, more discontinuous poetic structures; they entail a far more radical assault on the structures and functions of language. Abandoning the discursive function of language as a means to a conclusion, they enact a surrender to the substantial qualities of the medium, to associations of sound and rhythm which subvert and resist rational ordering.
> . . . In his imitations of Stein, Duncan turns his back on writing as self-expression, political commentary, or spiritual exploration. No longer a communication *about* or directed *toward* some object or idea, writing is its own subject, object, and

end—a serious play on the surface of language. The medium is dense—almost, but never entirely, opaque. The writer is free to follow associations of sound and rhythm into the realm of "non sense." (28)

To turn one's back on "writing as self-expression, political commentary, or spiritual exploration" is to turn one's back on the romantic heritage.[10] As we see from this passage, Walker goes some way in explaining Duncan's motives for this uncharacteristic move; she also points out that "Duncan was never totally committed to Stein's project. Even while imitating her style, he was often straining against some of her theoretical and epistemological presuppositions" (22–23).

These presuppositions include what could be termed Stein's anti-mimetic realism: as Perloff puts it, "she resolutely opposes mimesis, the notion that the verbal or visual construct can replicate the external world of nature" (*Poetic License* 148), while at the same time subscribing to what Lyn Hejinian describes as a belief "that language is an order of reality itself and not a mere mediating medium" (90). In working through Stein (both compositionally and psychologically), Duncan appropriates but also undermines her principles. Hejinian points out that Stein, following William James, "proposes the act of writing as the organization and location of consciousness in legible units, and not just of consciousness but of the consciousness of consciousness, the perceiving of perception" (143–44). This pragmatic, positivistic philosophy at the base of Stein's writing practice is antithetical to Duncan's idealist, spiritualist, and theosophical worldview.[11] Thus, Walker is right to conclude that while Duncan's "apprenticeship to Stein taught him a new attention to the substantiality of words, an obedience to their sound associations, and a commitment to writing as a temporal, sequential process," he nevertheless "after 1955 . . . left behind Stein's materialistic, deconstructive project in favor of his own search for the secret harmonies hidden in language and in (the Book of) nature" (34).

For Duncan, as for Stein, language as "an order of reality" means that language is fundamental to our comprehension of the objective world around us. To defamiliarize language using the techniques that Stein and other modernists develop is to comprehend reality anew, freed of repetitive habits and a fixed view of how the world operates moment to moment, day to day. From Stein, Duncan learns that language is both an autonomous entity following its own grammatical and semiological codes, and one of the interrelated orders of reality—but "reality" for Duncan means something more than it does for Stein. Consider, for instance, this passage from Duncan's "Writing as Writing":

> Poetry made up of sentences of words. Poetry in its regular irregular lines and divisions. Poetry in its steady revisions of its original vision, an accurate eye correcting its accuracies, an image of a man made in his own image inaccurately. I endeavor in delivering to deliver the speech from all truth spoken into its true form. I strive in inscribing in its different lengths the lengths of description I would go to, the lasts of all passages of literal understandings. I arrive in the reiteration of all the relations at lengthy vacations of ordinary prose in poses of poetry. (*Derivations* 45)

Readers familiar with Stein's work will certainly notice both the similarities and differences in Duncan's "imitation." Technically, it resembles what Perloff, in her anatomy of Stein's various styles, describes as "narration-as-permutation of phrasal repetitions, each reappearance of the word or phrase giving us a new view" (*Poetic License* 158). This particular instance of Duncan's "writing as writing" owes a good deal to a work such as "Composition as Explanation": an explanation of the techniques and principles of composition that self-reflexively demonstrates or embodies those techniques and principles as well. In "Composition as Explanation," Stein addresses the psychological relationship of composition to time and change ("after that what changes what changes after that, after that what changes and what changes after that . . ." [*Selected Writings* 519]), in order to account for the presence of time in a work, even though she does not believe that there is change in time: "If the time in the composition is very troublesome it is because there must even if there is no time at all in the composition there must be time in the composition which is in its quality of distribution and equilibration" (522). Writing, especially writing in sentences, is a continual engagement with ongoing acts of perception in a Bergsonian temporal continuum (*durée*) that Stein herself calls "a continuous present" (518).

By contrast, Duncan's "sentences of words" operate self-reflexively on the conditions of perception and language, but also move continually toward a spiritual dimension of being that is noticeably absent in his pragmatist precursor. In the passage from "Writing as Writing" quoted above, we find, on the one hand, the sense of continuous process or change conveyed through an equally continuous act of perception. On the other hand, there is the sense of an ideal order behind the flux of change. Hence the tension or even contradiction in "Poetry in its regular irregular lines and divisions" and "Poetry in its steady revisions of its original vision, an accurate eye correcting its accuracies." Note also how that sentence ends with "an image of a man made in his own image inaccurately," indicating Duncan's fascination with the creation and fall of Primal Man, "the Adam" or "the Anthropos," which will become a central concern in his next book, *Letters*.[12] In "Writing as Writing," Duncan's peculiar concern with accuracy and inaccuracy indicates how his Platonic, gnostic, and kabbalistic worldviews always lead him back to the creation and catastrophe myth that underlies so much of his poetry. Either a previously perfect creation has been corrupted by forces of imperfection, or creation itself is an imperfect, fallen, inaccurate parody of the true spirit by an ignorant demiurgical power. In either case, writing in this inaccurate world requires "steady revisions of its original vision."

Unlike Stein, whose writing practices are in the service of an empiricist and positivistic worldview, Duncan composes his ostensibly Stein-like sentences because "I endeavor in delivering to deliver the speech from all truth spoken into its true form. I strive in inscribing in its different lengths the lengths of description I would go to, the last of all passages of literal understandings." Here again, we find a tension between Duncan's and Stein's philosophical perspectives as Duncan appropriates Stein's techniques. True to the romantic tradition, Duncan views the poet as a prophet, a spiritual messenger, one who "delivers" divine speech—that is, brings this speech to others—and in doing so, "delivers" them—that is, frees them—to know truth. But to accomplish this mission, the poet must distinguish "all truth spoken into its true form" from mere "speech" or "passages of literal understandings." Therefore, in order to determine and deliver the truth, the poet must engage himself in—or, like a savior in gnostic myth, descend into—the linguistic processes of the fallen world, its "literal understandings." Hence, "I arrive in the reiteration of all the relations at lengthy vacations of ordinary prose in poses of poetry." The "lengthy vacations" of ordinary prose posing as poetry (or is it poetry posing as ordinary prose?) constitute a spell during which the poet learns the ways of language in the mundane world.

But for Duncan, language does not merely play a role, however important, in mundane affairs. If poetry is "made up of sentences of words," then the words of these "sentences"—judgments pronounced by the powers of cosmic law—must in themselves be judged by being "made up"—invented—by the poet. "Not in believing, but in pretending. Not in knowing, but in pretending. Not in understanding, but in pretending" (*Derivations* 42): in these phrases from "Imagining in Writing," Duncan insists that it is through "pretending" or making things up (as in the child's beginning to play a game by saying "Let's pretend . . .") that we apprehend the truth in the reality we perceive around us.[13] Only then do words become "fictive certainties." As he tells us in "The Truth and Life of Myth": "Facts or ideas or images are not true for me until in them I begin to feel the patterning they are true to, the melody they belong to. Once this feeling of a patterning begins, the work comes to one's hand; the form of the whole can be felt emerging in the fittingness of each passage" (*Fictive Certainties* 31). Truth is found not in facts or ideas or images in themselves, or even in the subject's perception of them. Rather, their truth lies beyond, in the patterning and melody that the poet learns to command through his writing, which in turn connects him to what Duncan, following Rudolf Otto in *The Idea of the Holy*, calls "the Numen." Otto's conception of the numinous is complicated and difficult to summarize, since most of *The Idea of the Holy* consists of an elaborate working through of this one notion. To a great extent, terms such as "the holy" and "the sacred" are synonyms for "the numinous," and are all ultimately related to the Hebrew *kadosh*, though Otto understands the concept as fundamental to all religious systems and believes its most highly developed form is to be found in Christianity. The numinous relates in turn to the individual's experience of "creature-feeling" in the presence of divinity's "mysterium tremendum," a term Otto unpacks at length. Duncan's interest in *The Idea of the Holy* seems less connected to specific creeds and systems, and instead focuses on the idea of a spiritual *presence* in all Creation. For Duncan, "the numen of the universe is its awful and overwhelming reality as an entity, its *genius*. . . . The Numen Itself shakes the very language, the words I hope might be no more than words. Speaking of a thing I call upon its name, and the Name takes over from the story I would tell, if I let the dimmest realization of that power enter here. . . . The Word, as we refer to It, undoes all the bounds of semantics we would draw in Its creative need to realize Its true Self" (*Fictive Certainties* 33).

In a certain respect, we are still not too far from Stein, who declares that "poetry is doing nothing but using losing refusing and pleasing and betraying and caressing nouns. That is what poetry does, that is what poetry has to do no matter what kind of poetry it is" (*Lectures in America* 231). For Stein, poetry's exclusive concern for nouns (that is, names) and the things they represent produces semantic and generic limitations, since "nouns as I say even by definition are completely not interesting" (211). But for Duncan, a sense of the numinous in words and in things *saves* poetry from "all the bounds of semantics," producing the *polysemous* potential of poetry he later celebrates in the introduction to *Bending the Bow* (ix). This redemptive power of poetry may be seen even in the titles in *Writing Writing*—"The Beginning of Writing," "Imagining in Writing," "Writing as Writing," "Possible Poetries" and so on. Thematically and philosophically, the "possible poetries" that Duncan imagines are quite different from Stein's portraits and object poems, with their "cubist" concern for the perceptible world.[14] Nevertheless, Duncan, as an aspiring mage, apprentices himself to Gertrude Stein, a worldly writing teacher, a teacher of composition whose techniques he can, through his own prophetic acts of inscription, ultimately usurp and deliver to "all truth spoken into its true form."

The self-consciousness with which Duncan "imitates" and spiritually revises Stein in *Writing Writing* remains with him throughout his career. It is this same self-consciousness that leads me to apply the term *scripture*—writing in the religious sense and in the overlapping poststructuralist sense of *écriture*—to Duncan's late work, though scriptural qualities begin to manifest themselves much earlier and grow increasingly pronounced. I have already noted Duncan's assertion "what I speak of here [in "The Truth and Life of Myth"] in the terms of a theology is a poetics" (*Fictive Certainties* 34). Years later, in his essay "The Delirium of Meaning: Edmond Jabès" (1985), Duncan again derives a poetics by conflating linguistic and religious dimensions of writing. Meditating on the textuality of *The Book of Questions*, Duncan associates Jabès's poetry with Ferdinand de Saussure, founder of structuralist linguistics, and Moses de León, the author of the *Zohar*: "Saussure, Moses of León, whatever be the redirection of each in linguistics or in the creative reading of the Torah—I return to them as if their professions were but screens that allowed a deep reworking in Poetics" (*Selected Prose* 212).[15] Indeed, from the late thirties, when he first reads Stein, to the mid-eighties, when he is reading Jabès—in other words, across the length of his career—linguistic self-consciousness and religious revisionism together yield a poetics.

Once Duncan completes his apprenticeship with Stein, he is ready to enter the major phase of his work as religious poet, which will begin with the premonitions of *Letters*, emerge as full-blown prophecy in *The Opening of the Field*, reach its crisis point in *Bending the Bow*, and come to its long, torturous conclusion in the two volumes of *Ground Work*.[16] By the time he begins "Passages," the second of his two open-ended serial poems, his understanding of his poetic/prophetic vocation is completely congruent with his process-oriented methods of composition, which are ramified through such influences as his relationship with Charles Olson, his reading of Whitehead's *Process and Reality,* and his study of Erwin Schrödinger's biophysics.[17] Drawing on the poststructuralism of such figures as Roland Barthes (whom Duncan read with great care) and Umberto Eco, Joseph Conte defines the "infinite serial form" of "Passages," typical of late Duncan, as "a work without bounds: having no beginning and no end; a limitless interrelation of parts; the absence of an externally imposed schema; mobility; and an intentionally incomplete condition of form" (49). Conte's insightful analysis of the formal operations in "Passages" demonstrates how fully Duncan's mature style conforms to a model of poetry as scripture, that is, as *écriture.* Indeed, his description of the series as "ahierarchical, autonomous sections which are nevertheless interrelated in the constant movement of an aperiodic structure. . . . a condition of form which is both deliberately incomplete and in a state of disequilibrium, unbound and uneven" (69) can be extended to include all of Duncan's poetry starting with that in *Bending the Bow,* and also may account for Duncan's ceasing to number his "Passages" poems midway through *Ground Work: Before the War.* In reading this poetry, one is naturally reminded of Barthes's work on textuality, especially in such essays as "From Work to Text," with its emphasis on the plural nature of the Text: "The Text is not a co-existence of meanings but a passage, an overcrossing; thus it answers not to an interpretation, even a liberal one, but to an explosion, a dissemination" (159).[18]

The further one reads in Duncan's last books, the greater one's sense that the boundaries between individual poems and sequences are dissolving (or as Barthes puts it, "exploding"), leaving instead a multiphasic open work, allusive, variegated, and kaleidoscopic, but also strangely homogeneous, end-lessly moving back upon itself as it simultaneously reaches outward toward a constantly receding horizon of transcendence. Here I again have recourse to Duncan's late, deep reading of Jabès, and to that of another poetic thinker enamored with *The Book of Questions*, Jacques Derrida—for in both Dun-can's and Derrida's interpretations of Jabès, I find descriptions that apply to Duncan's late poetry as well. Throughout *The Book of Questions*, writes Dun-can, "there is at work this presence of a voice of the writing itself and of voices within voice in the writing. . . . This voice of the writing itself is the threshold of a presence/absence in which the creation of person and narrative, melodic unfolding and sounding of chords, can take place" (*Selected Prose* 210). Der-rida similarly detects this scriptural "voice of the writing itself" that propels the poetry into a state of "presence/absence." As he puts it,

> The poet, in the very experience of his freedom, finds himself both bound to language and delivered from it by a speech whose master, nonetheless, he himself is. . . .
>
> The poet is thus indeed the *subject* of the book, its substance and its master, its servant and its theme. And the book is indeed the subject of the poet, the speak-ing and know being who *in* the book writes *on* the book. This movement through the book, *articulated* by the voice of the poet, is folded and bound to itself, the movement through which the book becomes a subject in itself and for itself. . . . For in its representation of itself the subject is shattered and opened. Writing is itself written, but also ruined, made into an abyss, in its own representation. (*Writing and Difference* 65)

As the substance and master, servant and theme of his poetry, Duncan ex-periences a shattering and an opening in his late work that produces a ruin and an abyss. In gnostic terms, the poet as Primal Man catastrophically falls apart, leaving the poem as the ruin of a new creation. But at the same time, the poet as *pneuma* makes his way back to the original Abyss, leaving the poem as the record of his return. The poem is thus both a making and an un-making, a beginning and an end, and the Word is both bound and unbound to the limit of the poetic imagination. The self-referentiality of this writing (which, as Mackey recognizes, is paradoxically dependent on the work of other authors) confirms Duncan's uncanny prophecy in the introduction to *Bending the Bow*: "In the poem, this very lighted room is dark, and the dark alight with love's intentions. *It* is striving to come into existence in these things, or, all striving to come into existence is It—in this realm of men's languages a poetry of all poetries, *grand collage* I name It, having only the immediate event of words to speak for It" (vii). The Numen or "It" strives to come into being through both words and things, in the former case shaping Itself into Duncan's *grand collage*, "a process that represents primarily itself as a quest; more than anything else, it enacts the different paths a search for knowledge may follow, and so, just as there is no one master tradition, so there is no single collage that stands in a privileged relationship to the other possible efforts" (Bernstein 189).

:::

As Duncan enters further into the final stages of his work, this "process that represents primarily itself as a quest" assumes increasingly drastic forms. Like "Brancusi's towering column" in "Transmissions, Passages 33," Duncan's poetry may be read as

> moving into its true power,
> into an imagined "endlessness",   each stage of the form
>   dying upward,   giving way
> measures moving   in eternity   unmoving (*Ground Work I* 19)

"Endlessness" is equated with a process of "dying upward," which in turn produces a text that moves progressively in temporal stages but paradoxically finds itself "in eternity unmoving." Both the intertextual weave of tradition and the aperiodic, paratactic, and polysemic mode of composition are pushed to extremes by the spiritual urgency of Duncan's "transformative illness," a shamanistic "psychosis." Writing of the initiatory ritual that Duncan enacts in "My Mother Would Be a Falconress," O'Leary describes his condition as "a beatified state of poetry, and as such, positive not negative. Without the error of creation, there is no restorative gnosis. In the grip of transformative illness, psychosis or poetic disturbance takes on an entirely different character" (*Gnostic Contagion* 148). After "My Mother Would Be a Falconress" (begun at 2:00 A.M. on August 1, 1964, and positioned almost at the center of the poems that make up *Bending the Bow*), Duncan enters a condition of gnosis that, for this poet/shaman, is the culminating experience of a lifetime in poetry—or more than a lifetime. In "Man's Fulfillment in Order and Strife," Duncan describes how, in becoming a poet, "I came to be concerned not with poems in themselves but with the life of poems as part of the evolving and continuing work of a poetry I could never complete—a poetry that had begun long before I was born and that extended beyond my own work in it" (*Fictive Certainties* 113). The "order and strife" that constitute the internal dynamics of Duncan's career finally result in poems that are indeed less and less "complete." They are unlike anything Duncan writes in his earlier work (though they are certainly anticipated there), and are unprecedented in American poetry (despite Duncan's many acknowledged precursors). They include all of "Passages," which become more dæmonic after the crisis of "My Mother Would Be a Falconress," though they are already moving away from their relatively benign utopian beginnings in "Shadows, Passages 11" ("Was it / sign of a venereal infection raging in the blood? For poetry / is a contagion" [*Bending the Bow* 32]) and "The Fire, Passages 13."[19] As Duncan tells us in "Transmissions," these texts are to be read as "death-throes":

> scenes of the life
> dying come forward,   foreword
> to the texts of Hell and Heaven,   transient
> and transitional poems (*Ground Work I* 23)

"[T]ransient / and transitional," a "foreword / to the texts of Hell and Heaven," these poems are neither a Divine Comedy (that is, a tour of the afterlife written as a critique of this life) nor a Marriage of Heaven and Hell (that is, an ironic revision of normative religious thought). Though such poets as Dante and Blake remain, as always, crucial to Duncan's sense of his prophetic vocation, the poems of this period are not visions per se. They are, instead, as the title of this particular poem indicates, *transmissions* that create the conditions of vision during the last movements ("death-throes," with a pun on "throe" and "throw") of the poetic spirit,

> The "I" passing into sIght,
> the Mind   wherever
>   it touches   blindly
> forming this eye at the boundaries it knows . . . (20)

The concerns for imaginative boundaries and linguistic "Passages" across them are connected to the concern for death, for death is the boundary that the poet must cross, passing from form into formlessness. He must open himself to death and dissolution, his own physical and psychic death as well as the death-dealing powers he witnesses in the political and social realms, for paradoxically,

> A million reapers come to cut down
> the leaves of grass we hoped to live by
>   except we give ourselves utterly over to the
>   end of things. (24)

Duncan's crucial allusion to the major work of Walt Whitman here at the end of "Transmissions" (it is the only reference to Whitman in a text bristling with allusions) points to a network of contradictions and ambivalences that informs his work of this period. Duncan subscribes to Whitman's vision of the United States as "essentially the greatest poem" (5) and of democracy as the social power that "seeks to bind, all nations, all men, of however various and distant lands, into a brotherhood, a family" (948–49). Yet here, "the leaves of grass we hoped to live by"—the poetic scripture that promises life—will fail, will be cut down by the (grim?) reapers, unless we give ourselves to the end of things, some unnamed apocalypse. Duncan assures us that "we are in apocalyptic times. But this crisis is not at some particular time or place; it is the condition of man and we find it wherever men have been awake to that condition" (*Fictive Certainties* 114). Whitman is preeminently a man awake to that condition; hence his "oracular mode enters poetry and history where profound contradictions come into play. In the widening of what we call the credibility gap, incredible transformations may come into the statement of the truth" (170). This observation emerges at a point in Duncan's "Changing Perspectives in Reading Whitman" at which he is discussing his own writing of "The Soldiers, Passages 26," for Whitman is perhaps Duncan's most important model of a poet of *kosmos* who must necessarily endure the strife and dissolution of his ordered, universalizing, democratic vision. For Whitman, the historical event that precipitates this crisis is the Civil War; for Duncan, it is Vietnam, perhaps the single most important concern of the "Passages" sequence from the midsixties through the early seventies. The "end of things" to which Duncan claims we must utterly give ourselves over takes shape for him in those years with unprecedented—and immensely contradictory—imaginative force.

Duncan's opening to these forces during the years of the Vietnam War is well documented, especially in Nathaniel Mackey's remarkable essay "Gassire's Lute."[20] Mackey, who reads both with and against Duncan in his criticism and his poetry,[21] observes that in the Vietnam War poems, "Duncan is caught between morality and cosmology, between outrage at human evil and a 'higher' understanding of evil's place in the scheme of things. . . . The tug between morality and cosmology, ideology and poetry, bears the brunt of the troublesome impact. The ages-old sense of inspiration as an inspiriting, an invasion of a human vessel by a non-human daimon or spirit, carries the danger of a loss of touch with human realities and feelings" (*Paracritical Hinge* 82, 83). Duncan's elevated tone and his tendency toward oracular pronouncement become particularly troublesome, for as Mackey understands, Duncan longs "to have it both ways. The charge the poem is given is not one of abdicating the exalted mode but of bringing it to bear on more resistant matters. . . . We hear the pathos of an upward aspiration we both identify with and are put off by, hearing the echo of our own resistance in Duncan's inability to keep the godly voice aloft. The aspiration caves in itself as if to confess to what it wants immunity from" (80, 85–86). The afflatus that so elevates Duncan leads him to speak simultaneously from human and divine perspectives, and these perspectives, as manifested in the form and tone of the verse, simultaneously critique each other. As Mackey recognizes, this is precisely what Duncan desires for his poetry, regardless of the particular issue or event it may address. As Duncan declares in "Man's Fulfillment in Order and Strife," "each of us must be at strife with our own conviction on behalf of the multiplicity of convictions at work in poetry in order to give ourselves over to the art, to come to the idea of what the world of worlds or the order of orders might be" (*Fictive Certainties* 111–12).

Within Duncan's own multiplicity of convictions, the political outrage found in such poems as "The Multiversity, Passages 21," "Up Rising, Passages 25," and "The Soldiers, Passages 26," gradually passes, for as Duncan cautions himself in "Before the Judgment, Passages 35," "Where one's own / hatred enters   Hell   gets out of hand" (*Ground Work I* 28). Although his righteous anger "against the works of unworthy men, unfeeling judgments, and cruel deeds" (35) never truly dissipates, we find that eventually "the forces of Speech give way to the Language beyond Speech" (30). What does Duncan mean by a "Language beyond Speech"? Recall that much earlier in

"Writing as Writing," Duncan tells us that "I endeavor in delivering to deliver the speech from all truth spoken into its true form." In both instances, the poet suggests that there is a "beyondness" in poetry that surpasses contradictory human truths as they are articulated in speech. This linguistic condition corresponds to the poet's spiritual condition. "Before the Judgment" comes from a set of Passages subtitled *Tribunals* (31–36), and they are almost the last in the Passages series that Duncan chooses to number, before the series dissolves to an even greater extent into the single, ongoing act of writing with which Duncan is engaged.[22] Who sits upon these Tribunals, and who stands before them? In each case, it is the poet himself. As we have seen, the poet partakes, however contradictorily, of both the human and cosmic (or from a gnostic viewpoint, hypercosmic) orders. To be sure, Duncan feels that the poet is empowered to judge the misdeeds of others, and in the Vietnam poems in particular, he takes that upon himself. But for the poet to go beyond speech is for him to go before the judgment as well, which is precisely what this poem enacts.

"Before the Judgment" is a highly allusive and extravagantly disjunctive text, even by Duncan's standards: Dante's *Inferno* as translated by John Carlyle, his brother Thomas's *The Hero as Poet*, Hesiod's *Works and Days*, Pound's *Spirit of Romance* and Hell Cantos intermingle with contemporary references to global pollution and the Vietnam War, President Lyndon Johnson (whose escalation of the war infuriated Duncan) and Joseph Alioto (who as mayor of San Francisco, despite his relative liberalism, was intolerant of potentially violent antiwar protests). The text lacks the musicality and rhythmic charm of the earlier "Passages" in *Bending the Bow* or the rhetorical vigor of the best of the political "Passages," such as "Up Rising." An unsympathetic reader might regard "Before the Judgment" as incoherent, and assume that Duncan simply loses control of his material. Yet the very first words of the text are "Discontent with that first draft" (*Ground Work I* 28), indicating that the poet is highly conscious of his method of composition and the significance of his references. As Duncan makes clear in "The Truth and Life of Myth," "my purpose here has been to give some idea of how little a matter of 'free' association and how much a matter of an enduring design in which the actual living consciousness arises, how much a matter of actual times and actual objects, the living reality of the myth is for the poet" (*Fictive Certainties* 13). There is no reason to doubt that Duncan's belief in writing as the design of consciousness alters as he grows older, or that he changes his mind on the subject of "free association."[23] Rather, a poem such as "Before the Judgment" attains to "the Language beyond Speech" precisely because it is so intent on transforming "actual times and actual objects," the poet's past and present history, the traditions he studies and the texts he reads, into "the living reality of myth," which in turn determines the compelling scriptural quality of the text. "Our engagement with knowing," writes Duncan in "Toward an Open Universe," "with craft and lore, our demand for truth is not to reach a conclusion but to keep our exposure to what we do not know, to confront our wish and our need beyond habit and capability, beyond what we take for granted, at the borderline, the light finger-tip or thought-tip where impulse and novelty spring" (*Fictive Certainties* 87). In the poem Duncan states this more severely:

> This pain you take
>
> is the pain in which Truth turns like a key.

> This Confession that struggles within you   and grows
> this *History of My True Country*   that you have come to acknowledge,
> will not let you alone. And the Eternal Ones of the Dream
> cast you forth from them.

> The Guardian moves as I am moved.

> It is like a movement perceived in a stone. Beyond my will,
> unwilling,   I am moved. (*Ground Work I* 34)

Written at the boundary, the "borderline," in an "unwilling" state, "Before the Judgment" and similar poems in the later work "keep our exposure to what we do not know." "Truth turns like a key," opening a door to spiritual powers that "will not let you alone." These powers, these "Eternal Ones," both possess the poet and cast him forth; like one of the gnostic Aeons, he belongs to them, belongs among them, but at the same time he has been thrown "forth from a raging Absence, even among men" (34). In a similar vein, Duncan alludes to a passage in Hesiod's *Works and Days* that he can "barely read" yet "has long lingerd at the threshold of the poem" (30). In this passage, Hesiod tells of the men of the Golden Age, mortals who lived in peace and content under Kronos, before the Olympian rule:

Now, since the time this happy race was covered up by earth,
As tutelary deities Zeus bids them still go forth
To serve as guardians of men, and at his high behest
Watch over suits and wicked deeds, clothed in a shroud of mist.
Givers of wealth, they roam the world, beneficent and kind—
This is the kingly privilege that they have been assigned. (61)

Duncan refers to these "ancestral spirits" as "the Golden Ones" and significantly includes among them his own mythic "Master of Rime" and "She   whose breast is in language," figures from the Structure of Rime sequence and such lyrics as "Often I am Permitted to Return to a Meadow." Following Hesiod, Duncan writes that "wherever judgment is made   they gather round watching, / what the heart secretly knows   they know" (29). In effect, Duncan confirms that the poet is both the judge of the World-Order and the figure upon whom judgment is passed, since his own creations are privy to the truths of the human heart and judge him as he himself passes judgment. The Structure of Rime sequence is concerned with the Law, the "unyielding Sentence"; the figures that appear in this series allegorize Duncan's ongoing struggle to achieve cosmic justice and balance in his writing so that he can take his place as the rightful arbiter of the World-Order. Thus, in "The Structure of Rime I," he calls on the "Lasting Sentence," for "sentence after sentence I make in your image. In the feet that measure the dance of my pages I hear cosmic intoxications of the man I will be" (*Opening of the Field* 12). Over twenty years later, in "Before the Judgment," the "intoxicated" (that is, poisoned) poet has become the figure he foretold, but his prophetic powers are now exhausted and he himself has been sentenced. He sees "the cops in the street now,   'the law' supplanting the Law" (32), and vindictively "returns to early dreams of just retributions and reprisals inflicted for his injuries" (33). The Law as Platonic "Major Mover," the Law that the poet wrestled as Jacob wrestled with the angel, the Law that "was Syntax" (11) and guided the poet's writing—that Law, and the poet who loved it, are now corrupted, just as the Whitmanian vision of America has become corrupted as well. Duncan's only choice is to condemn himself as he condemns others, and in an act of self-sacrificial dissolution, to suffer the pain of "Truth." All he can do is maintain "the Dream beyond death, / secret of a Life beyond our lives" (*Ground Work I* 34) and hope to escape the cosmic bonds of his fate.

:::

"Poetry!   Would *Poetry* have sustaind us?" Duncan asks this strange question in the first section of "Santa Cruz Propositions" (dated "10PM–1AM, 13–14, October 1968"), the poem written immediately after "Before the Judgment." The tone is unusual for Duncan, caustic and almost patronizing in the face of an untenable situation. The figure Duncan works in the first lines of the text is that of a surfer riding a wave "toward revelation," but threatened by "the depth of an impending failure." Hence the question. As for "*Poetry*":

> It's lovely
>
> —and no more than a wave— to have rise
>   out of the debris, the stink and threat
> —even to life— of daily speech,   the roar
>   of the giants we begin from,
> primordial Strife,   blind Opposition,
>   a current that sweeps all stagnant things up
>   into a torrent of confidence   beyond thought. (*Ground Work I* 36)

Duncan's doubts about the sustainability of poetry as a medium for revelation stem from its ineluctable connection to the "stink and threat" of "daily speech": yet another reason for his striving, as we have seen, for a "Language beyond Speech." For Duncan, "the curve of the poem / withdraws its promise" while "the shores / suck at the glorious sweep of the abyss" and "The voice carries us on to our just rewards, / and leaves us" (36, 37). However much we give ourselves to poetry, however much it (perhaps falsely) promises, its origins in "primordial Strife" will drown us in speech as we are pulled

> into the undertow and night of our species.
> There is no dream in which the high throne
>   of the poet's personal Empire does not finally come
>   to the dark shore of *Her* flood
> and his word-power go out futilely
>   to war with the insolent mob where
>   her boundaries advance. (38)

These lines, with their imagery of the poet as doomed emperor and of a flood governed by a maternal deity, are yet another retelling of Duncan's Atlantis dream, which he first describes in "Occult Matters" (*H.D. Book* 86–89). Of fundamental importance to such poems as "Often I Am Permitted to Return to a Meadow" and "Ode Beginning with a Line by Pindar," this dream provides Duncan with a lifelong myth of *poesis*, of his birth and of his fate as a poet.[24] Here, however, he specifically refers to the futility of his "word-power" in the face of the "insolent mob." Once again, it is poetry's relation to common speech that renders him ineffectual, dethroning him and drowning him in the maternal flood, though he is also forced to acknowledge that this flood is the "*Grande Mer, Atlantique,* first condition / from which I came and all the / generations of me came" (38). Unlike Whitman in "Out of the Cradle Endlessly Rocking," who is inaugurated into poetry by the sea, "the fierce old mother" whispering "death" to the ecstatic boy, Duncan's poetic vocation is threatened by the sea through psychic drowning in a return to the prenatal state. Indeed, Duncan calls the sea "Old Mummummymurmurmur," a name that contains "mummy" (both mother and an embalmed body wrapped in cerements), "mum" (silent), "murmur," and perhaps "murder." Poetry, then, cannot sustain him; because of its very origins in the primal mother and in what Allen Grossman calls the "mother tongue," his word-power will be reduced in the end to the insolence of the mob, to a murmur, to silence, to death.[25]

The notion that poetry itself may lead to psychic drowning recurs in the midst of "A Seventeenth Century Suite" as Duncan plays upon George Herbert's "Jordan (I)," a piece that deals directly with poetic vocation and the question of an appropriate poetic style. "Jordan" is a decidedly paradoxical poem. Herbert is a metaphysical poet who tends toward elaborate conceits to express his deep religious faith and his calling as poet/priest, yet here he wrestles with the need for a direct statement of true belief in a plain and unadorned style: "Who sayes that fictions onely and false hair / Become a verse? Is there in truth no beautie?" (*Ground Work I* 76). The language of the poem is complex and allusive as the poet winds his way to his declaration of faith; he insists that "Shepherds are honest people; let them sing" (76), though his own song employs an elaborate discourse and enters into the most complicated poetic and religious debates of his time.

Duncan, playing on Herbert, is less concerned with the conflict between plain and metaphysical styles in expressing religious truth, and more concerned with the possibility that spiritual truth may not be expressible in language at all:

> Who says that fictions only
> become a verse? Is there no actual heart-beat
> in which these words arise?   no mortal eye
> in whose sight the image must prove true?
> no immediate life in whose assemblies
> Truth in Beauty is verified? May no lines pass
> except they do their duty   not to the heart's unbroken
> melody   but to some model lost at sea
>   where meaning drowns in undertow
>   the mind proposes   and mermaids
>   raise a storm below?
>
> Is there no verse, no deep imagining, except
> the turbulent phantasie pour forth conglomerate
> and ominous things exceeding nightmare,
> disowning what we would think to see,   or speak
> as if from the dumb sub-being mass
> that refuses to yield to the natural will? (*Ground Work I* 77)

Here, poetry's duty is to an inarticulate mental image or model, yet when poetry seeks to articulate its truth, it is overwhelmed, drowned in an undertow of mere invention—mermaids, turbulent phantasie, ominous things exceeding nightmare. It seems that in these lines, the poetic imagination is at odds with the spirit's "natural will," its quest for truth, and speech is related paradoxically to "the dumb sub-being mass" ("dumb" in double sense of silent and stupid) that resists this will. How can the poet fulfill his duty to "My God, My King" (the same phrase with which "Jordan" concludes) when he lives in a fallen world "where Time's a serpent coild / and the witty tongue speaks with Time's sting"? "Whatever I *believe*," Duncan concludes, "my *Art*'s to be true / to what in truth is my Nature, / Imagination's Rule,   and from / the plainness of that intent   I'd sing" (78). But as in Herbert's case (and it's clear how deeply Duncan understands Herbert's dilemma), there is nothing plain in his intent, and "Imagination's Rule" may counteract rather than express "what in truth is my Nature."

There is something deeply troubling about Duncan's turn from a normative attitude toward poetry, though as I have been arguing, it is just this ambiguity toward—if not outright rejection of—the poetic vocation that defines his late work. At the height of his lyric power, Duncan is an orphic singer, a poet of *kosmos* who celebrates the "orders" of being as they come forth out of "primordial Strife."[26] Although always something of a spiritual elitist, one of the poetic and theosophical cognoscenti, he also accepts the common element of social life and speech, as we see in his devotion to such poets as Whitman and Williams. As he declares in "The Truth and Life of Myth," "our poetic task remains to compose the true epithalamium where chastity and lewdness, love and lust, the philosopher king and the monstrous clown dance together in all their human reality" (*Fictive Certainties* 27). Whether Duncan actually writes such an epithalamium remains an open question, but if he does, he is long past it by the time of *Ground Work*, in which the underlying gnosticism of his worldview emerges full-blown.[27] In thinking about this shift in Duncan's vision, I am reminded of Hans Jonas's chapter in *The Gnostic Religion* called "The Cosmos in Greek and Gnostic Evaluation." Given the Gnostics' belief in the terrible power of cosmic fate, *heimarmene*, Jonas notes that

> The change in the emotional content of the term "cosmos" is nowhere better symbolized than in this depreciation of the formerly most divine part of the visible world, the celestial spheres. The starry sky—which from Plato to the Stoics was the purest embodiment of reason in the cosmic hierarchy, the paradigm of intelligibility and therefore of the divine aspect of the sensible realm—now stared man in the face with the fixed glare of alien power and necessity. Its rule is tyranny and not providence.... Under this pitiless sky, which no longer inspires worshipful confidence, man becomes conscious of his utter forlornness, of his being not so much a part of, but unaccountably placed in and exposed to, the enveloping system. (254–55)

The shift that Jonas describes finds a parallel in Duncan's "Coda" to "A Seventeenth Century Suite," which is based on John Norris of Bemerton's "Hymne to Darkness" (1687; *Ground Work I* 89–90).[28] Norris's poem, which seems highly influenced by Milton, celebrates darkness as God's primal essence, prior to the creation of light. Duncan, however, revises Norris's text into a gnostic hymn, and in doing so records the transformation of his thought in regard to the cosmic orders. As he tells us,

> Once in a dream when I was young I dreamd to see into that Well
>   of Harmonies,   or thru invisibilities
>   the ordinate progressions of a solar instrument
>   where planets in folding circles of the sky I saw to sing . . .

But this Neoplatonic and orphic attitude has changed, resulting in a very different attitude toward God the Father and the celestial spheres:

> *Our Father Who Art in Heaven* . . . I begin
> my prayer before the Night, and, gazing in,
> I wonder at the depth that I call *"Him"*.
> For *Heaven* is not that Spring of Lights
> that burns for Heaven's sake but darkens
>   into an emptying of sight.
>
> The stirring of that Harp of Spheres or vaster
>   music of Saints and Stars whirling
> in the ecstatic Rose, unfolding Glory that God knows,
> flows back into a blackness, Ur-ground, In-gathering or . . .
>
>   Now it comes to me.
> Out, out from the First, from the Void,
>   the over-whelming repose of a finality
> overtakes the trembling lives, the sounding
>   energies,
>   and into a Silence I call *Our Father*
>   draws them in. (92–93)

Here, the Father is not the Creator of the "Spring of Lights" or "that Harp of Spheres," and the vision of the Heavenly Rose that is vouchsafed to Dante, one of Duncan's greatest masters, "flows back into a blackness." Instead, Duncan's *pneuma* makes its way toward the Void, the Silence, which Duncan acknowledges as the true Father.

Duncan's change in attitude toward the cosmic orders, from platonic to gnostic, is entirely congruent with his changing attitude toward both writing and the body. As if he himself were an inscribed text, he declares that "darkness overtakes my thought of dark, / rifts of Our Father blot me out. I'm near / extinguisht. Return . . .   return . . ." (93). Likewise, in "Rites of Passage: II" from "Poems from the Margins of Thom Gunn's *Moly*," we hear him sigh "Peace, peace. I've had enough. What can I say / when song's demanded? —I've had my fill of song? / My longing to sing grows full. Time's emptied me" and comes to the conclusion "let my struggling spirit in itself be free" (*Ground Work I* 69). The *Moly* poems, originally written in the margins of Thom Gunn's book, are a particularly acute instance of an ongoing sexual/textual crisis that is part of the fundamental trajectory in the later work. Michael Davidson calls the *Moly* poems a "coincidence of material and textual marginality with a thematics of sexual isolation and desire" (*Ghostlier Demarcations* 181). As I see it, Duncan moves from a redemptive attitude toward writing the sexualized body (as in "The Torso, Passages 18") to a growing horror of the body, both sexual and textual, which he sees as diseased *matter*, fallen and defiled (as in "In Blood's Domaine"). Thus, in the poem "Moly," Duncan calls one of Odysseus's sailors transformed by Circe (or, perhaps, himself in the act of fellatio), a "Dear Beast, dear dumb   *illiterate* / Underbeing of Man" (*Ground Work I* 68; my emphasis). Man as beast, as material, appetitive being, loses his ability to read and write—loses, that is, his textual being altogether—and this awareness is acted out by Duncan on the literal body of Gunn's provocative book of poems. As Davidson notes, "whether writing to another poet or permitting other writings to interrupt his conversation, Duncan saw the boundary between text and margins as a shifting one, in whose instability lay the hope of abolishing the totalized authority of other texts" (*Ghostlier Demarcations* 194). The unstable, shifting boundary of text and margins that Davidson identifies may actually express Duncan's desire to abolish the authority of all textuality, leading, as we have seen, to a general flooding of Duncan's writing. The *body* of the text relinquishes itself to the sea of language and the *spirit* of the text seeks its final release into the void.

This leads us to a section of Passages titled "Jamais" ("Ever" or "Never"), which plays on Mallarmé's *Un Coup de Dés* ("UN COUP DE DÉS JAMAIS N'ABOLIRA LE HASARD" ["A THROW OF THE DICE WILL NEVER ABOLISH CHANCE"]). Mallarmé's revolutionary work is arguably the single greatest precursor of all poems written as "projective verse" or "composition by field," poems that employ the page, including its white space, as a fundamental compositional element. Duncan recognizes this, of course, but he also turns toward *Un Coup de Dés* at this point in his career because the poem, as Henry Weinfield observes, deals with the problem of "how to establish meaning in an essentially meaningless universe—that is, in a universe from which the gods have disappeared, with the result that meaning cannot be transcendentally conferred" ("Commentary" 266). In a certain respect, Duncan is actually less "modern" than Mallarmé, in that he never really abandons the belief that meaning can be transcendentally conferred, that it emanates from a Source that is itself a sort of primal Poem. For Duncan, however, the question is always how one understands or conceives of the transcendental source of meaning, a question that grows extremely urgent in his late work. Recognizing this distinction, we can say of Duncan what Weinfield says of Mallarmé: "Poetry is not only the vehicle but the locus of the sacred for Mallarmé . . . The sacred exists for Mallarmé, but only insofar as it can be experienced phenomenologically; it exists only as an experience, through the concrete medium of language, or, in other words, as Beauty" ("Introduction" xiii–xiv).

But Beauty (or Poetry), given the nature of language, always hovers over the Void, and to fall into the Void is to fall into meaninglessness. *Un Coup de Dés* enacts that hovering; indeed, one of its central images is that of a wing above the Abyss. From Mallarmé's perspective, the poet has no choice but to chance or risk meaninglessness; every poem he writes is such a throw of the dice. But for Duncan, the return to the Void is a return to the *source* of meaning, though with supreme irony, that meaning is ultimately *inexpressible*. Nevertheless, it is there. Hence the opening of his poem:

JAMAIS

must extend   beyond the throw of the dice   "a" just now, yet
          no throw of the dice may   chance IT. (*Ground Work I* 147)

If for Mallarmé a throw of the dice will never abolish chance, then for Duncan, no throw of the dice can abolish "IT," his term, as we have seen, for the Numen or Source of meaning that exists beyond the world of chance. In this context, "jamais" should probably be translated as "ever" rather than "never"—given the nature of IT, such is *ever* the case. Some lines later, Duncan writes:

Lovely, the Dreams and Chance encounters
          but Now   is wedded thruout to   the Intention of a Universe.
               Verse,   linkt to the Idea of that Governance,
moves "beyond" . . . (147)

Phrases such as "the Intentions of a Universe" and "the Idea of that Governance" take us back to the Duncan of *The Opening of the Field* and *Roots and Branches*, the celebrant of the cosmic orders. But faced with Mallarmé's severe challenge—that all is chance and may result in nothingness—Duncan pushes his sense of "Now" or IT to a point "beyond." The text registers an increasing sense of panic and dissolution, leading to a concluding moment of gnosis: "What!   I do not 'know' what I see?" "Love," which Duncan associates with the Son and with the spirit of Form, triumphantly but self-destructively "flings itself forward," a "dark-wingd / creature of the air" (148). The final word of the poem is a single, disconnected "the" in quotation marks: the definite article with no noun or participle following, an indicator of Something, but Something that finally cannot be revealed.[29]

:::

Ground Work: Before the War ends triumphantly with "Circulations of the Song," a poem that uncannily combines deep poignancy with magisterial strength. Addressed to Jess, Duncan's "old companion of the way" (167) (though he is never actually named), "Circulations of the Song" is a love poem written in the certain knowledge of the poet's passage into death, a work in which the cosmic principles of Eros and Thanatos seem, for a moment, to be harmonized and transformed into a single persona through the poet's rhapsodic *melopœia*.[30] It is also Duncan's last great performance as a poet of *kosmos*; as he declares, "I am falling out into that Nature of Me / that includes the Cosmos it believes in" (170). Throughout the poem, the stars shine benevolently, and the dark into which the poet goes is "the wide Universe / emptying Itself into me, thru me, / in the myriad of lights falling" (172). Likewise, sex is "the sweet jet from sleep's loins / night stirrd to arousal" (169), a dark sweetness that spills over into an autumnal harvest "—apple, cherry, plum—deep purple / as night and as sweet—quince and pear—" (170) signifying Duncan's deep pleasure and contentment with the material world from which he will depart.

Yet paradoxically, the poem also profoundly gnostic in its orientation, given that it is written "after Jalāl al-Dīn Rūmī," the great Sufi mystic and poet. As a mystical movement within Islam, Sufism entails, according to Franklin D. Lewis, "gnostic attitudes toward the material world . . . fed prob-

ably by Zoroastrian, Manichaean, Buddhist and Hindu theosophical teach-
ings" (21). Rumi (1207–1273) was already well known and widely translat-
ed in the West by the time Duncan writes "Circulations of the Song." His
popularity culminated in what Lewis calls the "Rumi-mania" of the 1990s,
led by the poet Coleman Barks, who, "more than any other individual, is
responsible for Rumi's current fame" (1). Yet despite various translations of
Rumi's poetry, including those by Barks and of Robert Bly, Lewis observes,
"though not a translation of a specific poem by Rumi, 'Circulations of the
Song' demonstrates a remarkable familiarity with, or intuition about the
spirit, pacing and style of Rumi's ghazals. To my taste, this is the closest and
most satisfying approximation in the English language of the experience of
reading Rumi's ghazals in the original Persian" (585).[31] Extraordinary as this
praise may seem, it makes a great deal of sense given Duncan's theosophi-
cal background and immense learning, as well as his psychic condition at
this point in his life. In Rumi's teachings, "the seeker of God must die to
self before he can shine with the divine light. Dying to self, or even slaying
the self . . . includes learning to accede to God's will, putting out the fires of
ego, training the carnal self and concupiscent soul" (Lewis 417). Thus, when
Duncan declares that "I am falling into an emptiness of Me / every horizon
a brink of this emptying" (*Ground Work I* 171), he understands full well that
as "gnostic revelations / come to me" (174), their source is in the traditions
he intimately shares with this seemingly remote medieval Persian master.

"Circulations of the Song" therefore lends immense pathos to what fol-
lows, since it stands at the threshold of Duncan's last book, *Ground Work II:
In the Dark*, the very title of which indicates a different order of things. The
book begins with "An Alternate Life," a lovely, foreboding set of poems writ-
ten in a style similar to that of "Circulations," but quite uneven, due in part
to the more personal situation it addresses. Duncan uses his personal expe-
rience most effectively when he transforms it into "essential autobiography,"
the subtitle of "The Truth and Life of Myth" but equally applicable to much
of *The H.D. Book* and to his great lyrics, such as "My Mother Would Be a
Falconress." As Michael Davidson tells us, "An Alternate Life" "describes
a love affair with a much younger man." It is out of the "solitude" that the
affair engenders that Duncan "remembers his permanent companion, Jess,
whose permission and acceptance sustain and revivify him, even though
his presence . . . provokes humbling self-reflection" (*Ghostlier Demarcations*

190–91). This self-reflection consists of the intertwining of mundane details (one of the poems is called "The Quotidian") with the mythic register of the poet's "essential" or interior life, and it is on this level that the poet's dark truth takes—or should we say, *loses*—shape:

> The Mind —the fucking Mind!   The stars in Its thought
> shine forth in abysses, "Night" spaces,
> the fucking alone brought us *deep* into. (*Ground Work II* 2)

As the most intense experience of the physical world, sex also has the power to carry us beyond the physical world, into the "abysses, 'Night' spaces" that are knowable only through an act of Mind. What Duncan calls "the fucking Mind" is both the mind that he curses because it brings him this dangerous knowledge, as well as the mind in the act of fucking, through which this knowledge arrives. Note also how "Mind" here is not merely the individual mind but "Its" Mind—the Numen or sacred principle of Creation that has its ultimate source in the Abyss. Oddly dispassionate, the poet notes that "the matter of Love / the Mind knows   has my own particular death in it"—yet "It is not 'Death',   not my own particular time in dying" (3). Love carries Death within it, signified by a loss or diffusion of form; the individual's experience of Love and Death is merely one instance of this transcendental principle, which carries the *pneuma* from the created cosmos to the uncreated Void beyond. The growing reality of this truth upon the aging lover produces the discursive tension in "An Alternate Life" between a language of quotidian detail (reminiscent of Levertov or late Williams) and the dominant mode of the *Ground Work* volumes, its continually mythologizing, dissolving *écriture*.

The latter mode asserts itself strongly near the end of the sequence, as Duncan revises Yeats's Byzantium poems, with which he feels a compelling gnostic kinship. "Sailing to Byzantium," written by the aging Yeats with much the same awareness of mortality as Duncan's poems, presents the poet "sick with desire / And fastened to a dying animal," longing to be gathered "Into the artifice of eternity" (*Collected Poems* 191). Having passed out of nature into the form of an artificial bird, the poet then perches on a "golden bough" in the Emperor's court and sings "To the lords and ladies of Byzantium / Of what is past, or passing, or to come" (192). A similar image recurs in the more abstract "Byzantium," in which the transfigured poet "scorn[s] aloud / In glory of changeless metal / Common bird or petal / And all the complexities of mire or blood" (243). "Byzantium" ends with a vision of reincarnation, as "Astraddle on the dolphin's mire and blood / Spirit after spirit" make their way around the cosmic wheel, unable to escape their fate.

Duncan adopts Yeats's immortal bird on the golden bough, transforming it from a beautifully wrought artifice to what I take to be an ominous, living raven:

> Man's a bird of omen, dark as anthracite, upon that golden bough,
> and all his words, the rapturous reiteration of some vow,
> an animal call in anguish, a summoning of fate,
> in which the strife,   the wearing and the after-glow
> of what was realized,   the total thrust of a life,
>
> charges the contour of a momentary line
> as if throughout we meant but to sign   this place and time. (14)

The words of the poet/raven are "the rapturous reiteration of some vow, / an animal call in anguish, a summoning of fate." Unlike Yeats in the Byzantium poems, we cannot hope to escape the mire and blood of animal life; in the strife of our *heimarmene*, we are arrested in "the total thrust of a life" and trapped in "this place and time." The poem ends with Duncan reasserting his faith in Love that "touches upon a presence that is all" (15), yet given the sense of fate that Duncan describes, Love seems to lose its redemptive power.

As *Ground Work II* proceeds—and as Duncan's health declines—Love literally passes beyond itself into the Void. We find individual poems and further sections of the Passages and the Structure of Rime sequences, but throughout, utterance becomes more diffuse and form grows increasingly fragmentary. "Toward His Malaise," the main poem in the sequence "To Master Baudelaire," is arguably Duncan's last truly sustained and firmly composed lyric, yet another valediction to his bodily existence once "I come to Death's customs, / to the surrender of my nativities" (16). Torn between his continued affection for the material world, expressed in traditional images of the passing seasons, and his growing Baudelairean *ennui*, "plus laid, plus méchant, plus immonde" (more ugly, more nasty, more foul), Duncan is forced to admit that the "unity" of Creation he has previously celebrated is a "grand illusion of what is lovely" (17). Thus, he "gratefully / will let go"

(16), passing into oblivion with what he calls, in the last, devastating phrase of the poem, "the endlessness / of a relentless distaste" (18).

Baudelaire appears again, along with Nietzsche, Swift, and Rilke, in the terrifying section of the Passages sequence called "In Blood's Domaine," which Davidson accurately describes as a "scene of invasion" (*Ghostlier Demarcations* 192). Throughout this *cri de coeur* (or, better, perhaps, *cri de corps*), Duncan declares that the bacilli of syphilis and tuberculosis are angelic "attendants of lives raging within life" who have "come home to thrive in us" (*Ground Work II* 68).[32] Life raging within life breeds death, but the infected writers whom Duncan invokes are possessed of a spiritual "disease" as well: "Swift, Baudelaire, Nietzsche into the heart Eternal of what Poetry is / answer to the genius and science of the Abyss" (68). "As ever for Duncan," O'Leary reminds us, "the experience of disease recreates the experience of language" (93). Disease propels the poet into the eternal heart of poetry, and to enter that space is to answer to—that is, to stand in judgment before—the genius (the spirit) and science (the knowledge or gnosis) of the Abyss. To be released into this knowledge or to practice this science is to go beyond poetry. As Duncan puts it in the even more fragmentary "After Passage" following "In Blood's Domaine," "Mind comes into this language as if into an Abyss" (69).

As if he were already in the Abyss, Duncan can now only compose "A / music / at rest" (70). In "Close" he reveals that

I make my realm this realm in the
     patently irreal—   History
     will disprove my existence.

The Book will not hold this poetry   yet
     all the vain song I've sung comes into it (84)

The voice that is speaking here comes from the "irreal," a place that is not a place, entirely Other than the real. If History is the narrative of what we take to be the real—that is, the *created* world—then the speaker's existence is bound to be disproved. The poet is outside of history because he is outside of the Creation of which history is the account.

In the same vein, he and his poetry are outside of the Book, a figure drawn from Mallarmé, who, like Baudelaire, haunts the late work. In his essay "The Book: A Spiritual Instrument," Mallarmé first declares that "all earthly existence must ultimately be contained in a book," and then proceeds to explain why this is the case: "Man's duty is to observe with the eyes of the divinity; for if his connection with that divinity is to be made clear, it can be expressed only by the pages of the open book in front of him" (*Selected Prose* 24, 25). But Duncan no longer allies himself with "divinity" nor with the earthly existence that divinity oversees. Thus the Book will not hold this poetry because, in effect, this is not "poetry" in the normative sense at all, but a scripture that cannot be contained in a Book. "The idea of the book," notes Derrida, "which always refers to a natural totality, is profoundly alien to the sense of writing. It is the encyclopedic protection of theology and of logocentrism against the disruption of writing, against its aphoristic energy" (*Of Grammatology* 18). As we observed earlier, Duncan reads theology as poetics; as a poet of *kosmos* he is bound to "a natural totality," the "encyclopedic" orders of Creation he invokes so beautifully through much of his career. Now, however, his disruptive *écriture* is set against what he regards as "vain song." In a display of "aphoristic energy" from "Illustrative Lines," his penultimate poem, he instead asserts his gnostic faith:

> What works in me is not mine but
> ancient survivals, how much witheld
> strives unspeakable in the word to speak
> the lips refuse, eyes
> close upon to face what Man is in this.
>
> Child, not of Our Father, but of the Abyss
> where he was. In the fires of that mine
> Love comes to Grief to strike a light
> again, and Dark increases to enhance
> the pathos of a brief humanity time allows
>   not easily. (87)

The halting syntax of these lines indicates the poet's struggle to speak the unspeakable, a dark knowledge of the spirit's paternity that the lips of the created body refuse to utter and its eyes refuse to look upon. But the truth is out: the spirit has gone into the dark that dominates this last book and gives it its title. The book then, is no book; it is, so to speak, unbound, and its pathos is analogous to the human pathos to which Duncan refers.

We turn, then, to "After a Long Illness," Duncan's last poem, a coda that he composed after coming to believe, in his illness, that he was done with poetry, or that poetry was done with him.[33] Much of the poem describes Duncan's symptoms and the psychic effect they have upon him as "My Death attended me" (*Ground Work II* 89), and he anticipates the union with his lover that Death, as "Lord of a Passage" will bring. Then, in two extraordinary stanzas, we are presented with the poet's last testament:

"I have given you a cat in the dark," the voice said.
Everything changed in what has always been there
at work in the Ground   the two titles
        "Before the War",   and now, "In the Dark"
underwrite the grand design.   The magic
        has always been there,   the magnetic purr
        run over me, the feel as of cat's fur
charging the refusal to feel.   That black stone,
        now I see, has its electric familiar.

In the real I have always known myself
        in this realm where no Wind   stirs
        no Night
turns in turn to Day,   the Pool of the motionless water,
        the absolute Stillness.   In the World, death after death.
In this realm,   no last thrall of Life stirs.
        The imagination alone knows this condition.
As if this were before the War,   before
        What Is,   in the dark this state
that knows nor sleep nor waking, nor dream
        —an eternal arrest. (90)

Here, the "grand design" of the *Ground Work* project is revealed to have been "underwritten" by a voice from the Dark, the Abyss, the realm of "absolute Stillness." The fundamental paradox of *Ground Work* has been that the writing continually seeks a ground, a foundation, and yet that ground is actually groundless, for the writing simultaneously constitutes a fall, a *thrownness*, and a return to the acosmic source from which it was thrown, finally resulting in what Duncan calls "an eternal arrest." Scholars of gnosticism frequently quote a famous Valentinian formula: "What liberates is the knowledge of who we were, what we became; where we were, whereinto we have been thrown; whereto we speed, wherefrom we are redeemed, what birth is, and what rebirth" (Jonas 45).[34] In Duncan's lines, the quest for gnosis has reached, if not the fulfillment of liberating gnosis, then at least a great sense of rest.

O'Leary finds this poem "horrifying" because of "Duncan's insistence on persisting with his imperial sense of the imagination even as he is dying and passing into an immense, static eternity" (*Gnostic Contagion* 169). But why should Duncan relinquish the one power that has brought him this far, carried him into this knowledge? O'Leary goes on to write beautifully that "Duncan's final attendance is a vigil at the brink of emptiness" (170). Let us linger for a few more moments with him on the brink.

Why does the voice give the poet "a cat in the dark"? The cat, with its "magnetic purr," is a familiar, a dæmonic spirit attending to a witch or warlock, and Duncan, of course, thought of himself from early on as an "enamord mage," one who knows "How all Forms in Time will grow / And return to their single Source" (*Opening of the Field* 23). Thus it is appropriate that he should have such a familiar, a creature of the dark. But perhaps subconsciously, Duncan may also be referring back to "A Storm of White," another poem in *The Opening of the Field*, in which he mourns a "dear gray cat that died in this cold," who was "born on my chest / six years ago" (74). The cat, born as Duncan is coming into his period of greatest poetic strength, attends the poet and in its death, teaches him a lesson that he must now remember as he faces his own passing. Dying in "gull-white weather" with "trees / ghosts of blackness or verdure / that here are / dark whites in storms," the cat points to the void, an emptiness of either black or white. As Duncan prophetically intones,

> The line of outliving
> in this storm   bounding
> obscurity from obscurity,   the foaming
> —as if half the universe
> (neither sky nor earth, without
> horizon)   were forever
>
> breaking into being another half,
> obscurity   flaring into a surf
> upon an answering obscurity. (74)

If life passing into death is a storm bounding from obscurity to obscurity (in the double sense of darkness and the unknown) then beyond the storm, on the far side of death, is "the Pool of the motionless water" revealed in "After a Long Illness." Here there is no wind, and "no Night / turns in turn to Day," dark and light themselves having gone into a primal nothingness. Likewise, the stormy conflict of war or strife, which Duncan always believed to define the cosmic order, is finally arrested. Hence, as Duncan understands, we are both *before the war* and *in the dark*: at which point the poet's *ground work* can finally end.

:::

"After such knowledge, what forgiveness?" (*Complete Poems* 22). T. S. Eliot's famous question in "Gerontion" inaugurates the best known spiritual quest in modern poetry, indeed, a quest that is paradigmatic of religious poetry in a secular world, in which religion is no longer an assumed cultural dominant. It is a question that Duncan, however, either as a poet of *kosmos* or a poet of *gnosis*, could never ask. Yet spiritual knowledge remains at issue in both poets, and it is worth briefly comparing their enterprises as I conclude this chapter. If Eliot is concerned with forgiveness after knowledge, we must inquire as to Duncan's concern once he has come into the particular spiritual knowledge that he seeks. As I have shown here, Duncan's late work takes the form of a gnostic scripture, an increasingly attenuated writing that paradoxically enacts an increasingly urgent quest for the spiritual truths toward which his entire career as a poet, his lifelong sense of poetic identity, pointed him. From the beginning, he rejects all forms of orthodoxy, including Christian orthodoxy, while at the same time declaring himself a romantic visionary who continually seeks "the truth and life of myth," which are to be found equally in all the religious and literary traditions he studies and assimilates to his own prophetic verse. But he also learns that there is a price to pay for such knowledge, a price exacted in his poetry and from his poetry, until in the end he has nothing more to give. Thus Eliot's question may help us understand the different but still related question that Duncan's late work poses.

In "Orders, Passages 24," Duncan rejects the New Americanist prejudice against Eliot (stemming largely from Charles Olson) in the following terms:

> Down this dark corridor, "this *passage*," the poet reminds me,
>
> > and now that Eliot is dead, Williams and H.D. dead,
> > Ezra alone of my old masters alive,   let me
> > > acknowledge Eliot was one of them,   I was
> > > one of his,   whose   "History has many
> > > cunning passages, contrived corridors"
>
> comes into the chrestomathy. (*Bending the Bow* 78)

A chrestomathy is a selection of literary passages for study, and in this case the term stands for the Passages sequence itself, or even Duncan's whole oeuvre as an instance of the *grand collage*. As part of his chrestomathy, Duncan quotes from the stanza in "Gerontion" that begins with Eliot's question of knowledge and forgiveness, the stanza in which History, gendered female, "has many cunning passages, contrived corridors, / And issues, deceives with whispering ambitions, / Guides us by vanities." For Eliot, History is a seductress, and to be lost in her sexualized passages or labyrinth is to fall into the sins of vanity and fruitless desire. For Duncan, passages of history, myth, lore, and tradition promise an ever-widening vision of spiritual possibility, endless possibilities of redemption, under the mothering gaze of the spirit whom he names in "Tribal Memories, Passages 1," "Her-Without-Bounds" (*Bending the Bow* 9).

Yet Duncan's specific inclusion of Eliot in the chrestomathy among his old masters indicates that he is as sympathetic to Eliot's concerns as he is to those of Pound, Williams, or H.D. Unlike the other modernists whom Duncan mentions, Eliot's concerns are not only specifically Christian, but they are decidedly penitential, related to forgiveness, redemption, and atonement. The knowledge to which Eliot refers is the knowledge that History thrusts upon us: worldly knowledge, experiential knowledge of the vapidity, sin, and corruption adumbrated in "Gerontion" and many of his other early poems. History itself is fallen as well, as the nightmare of modern history that constitutes *The Waste Land* clearly demonstrates. Eliot's need for redemption from history and forgiveness from sin leads him to gradually transform his poetry into a penitential offering placed on the altar of his Anglican God, culminating in the *Four Quartets*, a volume that takes George Herbert, the seventeenth-century poet/priest as its presiding spirit.[35] In short, the trajectory of Eliot's poetic career would seem to be antithetical to that of Duncan, for whom knowledge, as we have seen, is *gnosis*. As Hans Jonas defines it, "gnostic 'knowledge' has an eminently practical aspect. The ultimate 'object' of gnosis is God: its event in the soul transforms the knower himself by making him a partaker in the divine existence (which means more than assimilating him to the divine essence). Thus in the more radical systems like the Valentinian the 'knowledge' is not only an instrument of salvation but itself the very form in which the goal of salvation, i.e., ultimate perfection, is possessed" (35).

Such being the case, Duncan's late work is not only a means of articulating the writer's knowledge of salvation, it is not only a gospel or scripture, it is the form that his salvation takes. This religious poetry, unlike Eliot's, is not merely the expression of spiritual need or longing for salvation. It is not an offering, not a prayer, not an act of sanctification. It *is* his salvation. Eliot seeks forgiveness from his Christian God after his profane descent into history. Whereas for Eliot, the Word is God and the poet emulates God by casting his faith into the words of the poem, for Duncan the Word, moving *through* the poet, is what it speaks and speaks what it is. Let us recall Duncan's explanation from "The Truth and Life of Myth": "The myth we are telling is the myth of the power of the Word. The Word, as we refer to It, undoes all the bounds of semantics we would draw in Its creative need to realize Its true Self. It takes over. Its desire would take over and seem to put out or to drown the individual reality" (*Fictive Certainties* 33). But the realization of the Word means, as we have seen, the dissolution of words, the dissolution of Poetry. In Duncan's case, unlike Eliot's, Poetry, in effect, has been abandoned, left behind in the poet's pursuit of knowledge. And after such knowledge, will poetry forgive the poet?

Unlike Christianity (and for that matter, most versions of the other major Western faiths), Gnosticism believes that the root cause of human failing and unhappiness is not sin but ignorance. "The gnostic movement," argues Elaine Pagels, "shared certain affinities with contemporary methods of exploring the self through psychotherapeutic techniques. Both gnosticism and psychotherapy value, above all, knowledge—the self-knowledge which is insight" (*Gnostic Gospels* 149). A gnostic poet must dedicate himself to overcoming ignorance and gaining insight, which incidentally may account for Duncan's lifelong dedication to Freud. But poetry depends in part upon ignorance, upon the unknown, upon what remains to be uncovered, something that Duncan deeply understood. Pace Olson and "Against Wisdom as Such," Duncan, in his best work, drew on the wisdom traditions he knew so well in order to create an open, processual exploration of the cosmic orders. At the height of his strength he started the Passages series, recognizing that this most radical of unbound works could grant him the full permission that he desired to traverse the realms of matter and spirit, history and myth. But as we know, Duncan was never, like his precursor Whitman, solely or perhaps even primarily a poet of *kosmos*. Following the network of Passages and other late works, we witness the unmaking of the poetic demiurge in Duncan and the eventual loss of Poetry itself.

My claim in this chapter is that there is a dramatic shift in the power and intensity of Duncan's late work, as it is transformed into the testament and enactment of poetic self-sacrifice. If we go to poetry, as I believe we do, to be both challenged and consoled, then we will find our desire amply fulfilled by Duncan, even, strangely, in the ritual undoing of poetry that comes at the end of his career. Duncan's lyrics have earned him a permanent place in the poetic canon. But his scripture compels us to rethink our understanding of the poetic canon, of why and how poetry binds and unbinds our spirits, and what it is we seek when we read the works that constitute each assemblage of that *grand collage.*

Ronald Johnson

THE POETICS OF KOSMOS

The κόσμος of the philosophers, then, is an "arrangement" of all things, in which every natural power has its function and its limits assigned. As in the case of any good arrangement, the term implies a systematic unity in which diverse elements are combined or "composed." (Kahn 222–23)

For those few capable of an extraordinary apprehension of symbols, the concreteness of event is rendered transparent, as a stunning reversal occurs: history itself becomes a symbol, the world itself a theophany, the created universe a glyph to be deciphered. In a sense the glove is tugged inside out as the cosmos becomes myth and myth in turn turns into a cosmos unto itself. In this reversed world, appearance and reality trade places in a strange and perhaps dangerous dance. (Wasserstrom 170–71)

As I suggested in the previous chapter, fundamental to our understanding of Robert Duncan's poetic development is the tension in Duncan's work between an endlessly branching, utopian poetry of *kosmos* and a far darker, self-undoing inscription of *gnosis*. We cannot appreciate Duncan's importance without considering how this dialectic plays itself out through his entire career. Indeed, of the recent poets working in longer serial forms, Duncan engages his spiritual agon most fully and takes it to its furthest extreme. Yet the two terms that constitute this dialectic carry tremendous poetic potential in and of themselves, and it is no accident, I think, that Ronald Johnson and Jack Spicer, two of Duncan's associates from different points in his career, individually embody them in their work. In this chapter I consider the younger of those poets, Ronald Johnson, whose work is related to Duncan's through their shared vision of *kosmos*. In chapter 3, I will treat the far more vexed figure of Jack Spicer, whose gnosticism and Calvinism,

though largely opposed to Duncan's worldview at the time of their associa-
tion, may ultimately have proven more portentous for Duncan than either
poet could have imagined.

Among contemporary American poets—indeed, among American poets
going back, perhaps, as far as Whitman—no two are more concerned with
both the science and metaphysics of cosmology than Duncan and Johnson.
In regard to their long friendship, Peter O'Leary, Johnson's literary execu-
tor, reports that after Duncan's death, Johnson felt "that there was no one left
in San Francisco with whom he could 'talk cosmos'" (e-mail). Their shared
interest in cosmology led me to assume, while I was writing *The Utopian
Moment*, that Duncan had influenced the younger Johnson, both in terms of
what Duncan calls the *grand collage* of form and the equally grand content
of the two poets' projects. But after reading my book, Johnson wrote to me
that influence was one of the "only nits I would pick." "As to Dunc," Johnson
explained, "I can remember well Jonathan Williams' publication of his 'Let-
ters,' which somehow 'gave me permission,' young as I was, to be romantick
in the face of Olson, etc. But living in S.F., Robert and I were always buddys
[*sic*] respecting each others' territories. Our common ground was on the
central childhood myth engendered by the Oz books—he always accepted
me as an equal, not an acolyte" (letter).

The "permission" from older to younger poet to which Johnson alludes
may be the single most important aspect of that uncanny phenomenon we
call influence. Yet "acolyte" is also a highly charged term, and all that John-
son claims does not necessarily preclude what Harold Bloom would call the
anxiety of influence. Clearly, Duncan's famously powerful personality was
something to be resisted by the younger Johnson, however respectful the
friendship. O'Leary, who knew Johnson well during the last years of his life,
states that "my feeling is that was the core of their connection: cosmology
& cosmogony, but also talk. Ron told me another time that he refused to
let Duncan get the upper hand in conversation. Duncan always wanted to
dominate but Ron said he would interject as often as he could" (e-mail).
As we shall see, there is much independently discovered but shared liter-
ary territory in Duncan's and Johnson's work. In addition to the Oz books
of L. Frank Baum, they have many of the same modern poetic precursors
and contemporary influences in common, including (to name only a few)
Pound, Stein, H.D., Zukofsky, and Olson. There are crucial differences to

examine as well. But in treating the relationship between the two poets, I write in the spirit of Duncan when he announces, apropos of Whitman, that "back of our own contemporary arts of the collagist, the assembler of forms, is the ancestral, protean concept, wider and deeper, of the poet as devotée of the ensemble" (*Fictive Certainties* 168). Both Duncan (until the last phase of his career) and Johnson (from beginning to end) are "devotée[s] of the ensemble," and it is toward an understanding of that term that we are bound. The crowning achievement of this devotion is Johnson's *ARK*, and its composition is a sacred practice that both draws on and revises the metaphysical and poetic traditions that we have already observed in Duncan's work.

A convenient starting point for exploring Johnson's poetics of *kosmos* is Beam 10 of *ARK*, and so it is with these two hermetic and yet revealing lines that I begin:

> *daimon* diamond Monad I
> Adam Kadmon in the sky[1]

It is a typically Johnsonian couplet, representing a typically Johnsonian set of strategies. First, consider that Beam 10 consists entirely of this one couplet, making it the shortest section of *ARK*. Johnson celebrates the minimum and the maximum, microcosm and macrocosm; thus, in the note at the end of *ARK*, he names Zukofsky and Olson as his precursors. But even as early as "The Unfoldings" (from *Valley of the Many-Colored Grasses*, 1969), he asks Thoreau's question,

> Who placed us with eyes
> between a microscopic and a telescopic
> world?
> (*To Do as Adam Did* 58)

and answers with a poem moving out from a central axis to offer visionary details of those microscopic and telescopic worlds. We may assume, then, that Beam 10 is the most microcosmic moment of *ARK*, or, as it were, a "Monad" of the poem in its totality. In his *Monadologie*, Leibniz claims that each monad, the most basic substantial unit of the cosmos, reflects the divine order from one or another point of view, ascending in an infinite scale of increasing self-consciousness. In effect, Beam 10 is a monadological reflection of the cosmic order that is *ARK*.

RONALD JOHNSON

The simple substance of *ARK* that is Beam 10 sounds either like a nursery rhyme or Blake's "The Tyger," and this too is a typically Johnsonian move. Johnson's goal of utopian harmony, whether located in a biblical Garden of Eden or an American Oz, is inextricably bound up in his fascination with language play. Through the devices of poetry, such sites may be constructed in the mind, even as Simon Rodia built his towers in Watts and Le Facteur Cheval built his Palais Ideal in Hautrives. As Johnson frequently indicates, he conceives of his long poem as architectural, particularly in comparison to the major works of his precursors: "I had all those big poems in front of me, *A*, and *The Cantos*, and *Maximus*, to look at. And I said, can I do this any differently? Robert Duncan pointed out that I was the only one to make it an architecture" ("Interview" 35). It is no accident that Duncan should point this out to Johnson, since Duncan's serial poems also do not constitute an "architecture" in quite the same way as *ARK*. For Johnson, words literally are building materials, as seen most clearly, perhaps, in those later sections of *ARK* composed entirely from Thoreau's journals or Van Gogh's letters. Yet this is not merely the result of a modernist or postmodernist collage aesthetic. From the simplest invocations borrowed from nursery rhymes to the most sophisticated polysemic verbal structures, language is both the stuff of creation and the means of creation, a kabbalistic notion that leads us back to Duncan's "ancestral, protean concept, wider and deeper, of the poet as devotée of the ensemble."

"Up above the world so high / Like a diamond in the sky" or "Tyger! Tyger! burning bright / In the forests of the night": in either instance, the insistent trochaic tetrameter hammers us into a visionary state, as against the night sky a luminous (super)natural entity seizes our imagination. In Beam 10, that entity is not only a monad out of Leibniz and a gemlike star evoking the child's naïve wonder, but also the *daimon* of Platonic philosophy, the intermediary spirit that moves between the natural and supernatural worlds. Variously associated with wisdom, inspiration, and love, the Platonic *daimon* is yet another figure of cosmic interconnection, integrating the orders of existence and continually bringing the universe into being. Yet this process is not without dialectical tension or conflict. In *The Symposium*, Socrates speaks of Eros as a *daimon*, and to be possessed by Eros is to desire the Beautiful, a desire that leads, in the noblest souls, to creative activity of the highest order, including the creation of poetry. But it is also possible that

Johnson's *daimon* is as much Yeatsian as Platonic. In *Per Amica Silentia Lunæ* (1917), Yeats's extraordinary essay on the metaphysical origins of creativity, "the Daimon comes not as like to like but seeking its own opposite, for man and Daimon feed the hunger in one another's hearts" (335). The Daimon sets us to the great task: "The more insatiable in all desire, the more resolute to refuse deception or an easy victory, the more will be the bond, the more violent and definite the antipathy" (335–36). For the hero and the poet, "the Daimon is our destiny," for it is the Daimon "who would ever set us to the hardest work among those not impossible" (336).

Thus in Beam 10, the "I" is both Monad and daimon, microcosmic reflection of the divine whole as well as antithetical self seeking its destiny in the creation of the poem as world. Again, Duncan on Whitman: "In Whitman there is no ambiguity about the source of *meaning*. It flows from a 'Me myself' that exists in the authenticity of the universe. The poet who exists close to the vital universe then exists close to his Self" (*Fictive Certainties* 191). Scholars have long debated the precise nature of "self" or "I" in Whitman, the psychological and spiritual meaning in the distinctions he makes regarding the "real me," "my soul," and so on. There is no question, however, that one aspect of the self for Whitman is cosmic: "Walt Whitman, a kosmos, of Manhattan the son." In *Song of Myself*, to be a "kosmos" is to be "Turbulent, fleshly, sensual," "no stander above men and women or apart from them" (210). But in the much later poem "Kosmos," from *Autumn Rivulets*, the concept is more defined, and proves even more expansive:

> Who believes not only in our globe with its sun and moon, but in other globes
> with their suns and moons,
> Who, constructing the house of himself or herself, not for a day but for all time,
> sees races, eras, dates, generations,
> The past, the future, dwelling there, like space, inseparable together. (517)

Those who would truly construct the house of the self create themselves as cosmic beings, in whom all of humanity, all of time, and all of space dwell inseparably together. Whitman's " I," like those of Duncan and Johnson, his poetic descendents, partakes in the eternal but also constitutes the eternal, and it is through poetry that this universal identity is confirmed and its potential for the ensemble of humanity is revealed. As Whitman tells us in the ecstatic preface to the 1855 edition of *Leaves of Grass*, "Through the divinity of themselves shall the kosmos and the new breed of poets be interpreters of men and women and of all events and things" (25).

This is why in Beam 10, the Whitmanian "I" becomes "Adam Kadmon in the sky." In Western mystical traditions, especially kabbalistic traditions, Adam Kadmon is cosmic man, the primordial emanation of God out of Nothingness, or as Blake understood, "the human form divine" (12). In the kabbalah of Isaac Luria, Adam Kadmon is God's body, "the first configuration of the divine light. . . . He therefore is the first and highest form in which the divinity began to manifest itself. . . . From his eyes, mouth, ears and nose, the lights of the Sefiroth burst forth" (Scholem 265). God's universal body is made of light, a notion, as Johnson intuits, still to be found obscurely in the nursery rhyme of the little star: the child turned both cosmologist and kabbalist when he chants, "How I wonder what you are." But in the Lurianic creation myth, the vessels intended to contain the Sefiroth, or emanations of the Godhead, could not hold these supernal lights. The "breaking of the vessels" constitutes a cosmic catastrophe, a Fall preceding Adam's fall in the Garden. As Scholem explains, "*Adam Ha-Rishon*, the Adam of the Bible, corresponds on the anthropological plane to *Adam Kadmon*, the ontological primary man. Evidently the human and the mystical man are closely related to each other. . . . The drama of *Adam Kadmon* on the theosophical plane is repeated, and paralleled by that of *Adam Rishon*. The universe falls, Adam falls, everything is affected and disturbed and enters into a 'stage of diminution' as Luria calls it. Original sin repeats the Breaking of the Vessels on a correspondingly lower plane" (279–80).

Originating with the Jewish kabbalists, the mythos of Adam Kadmon, divinity as Primordial Man, makes its way, via the Christian kabbalism of the Renaissance, into the mainstream of western religious, philosophical, and poetic thought, as well as the occult and theosophical systems that have served as their shadowy counterparts. The universal human form celebrated by Blake and Whitman is passed down to Duncan and Johnson, and like the kabbalists before them, poets in this tradition seek to restore the fallen cosmic order through linguistic ritual. In his definitive essay on kabbalah in *Roots and Branches*, Burton Hatlen argues that the poems in Duncan's book do not present "ideas" but "are themselves magical acts that seek to unite opposites and thereby redeem the world" (211). According to Hatlen, Duncan, following kabbalistic teachings, "seeks to recover Adam Kadmon, original man, and thereby to recover, spiritually, the unfallen Garden" (217). Thus, in "Apprehensions," we read that "Theosophists teach that primal man is a vast dispersed being," that "Man / so exclusively defined he is / a figure of light" (*Roots and Branches* 36). Furthermore, the heroic desire for cosmic restoration inspires the poem, producing a verbal form that imitates and also enacts such restoration:

> Then hunger be stem
> from what I am,
> and the hero bloom as he will toward that end
> the poem imitates by admitting a form. (*Roots and Branches* 36)

Like Duncan, Johnson wishes "To do as Adam did" and "build a Garden of the brain" (*ARK*, Beam 30, "The Garden"). The return to the Garden is simultaneously a return to the universal body of the unfallen or redeemed Adam Kadmon. "This is the way the world begins, the word begins," chants "*THE GARDNER*" in Beam 30, "wrestling the old ineffable." Likewise, in the phantasmagoric *ARK* 35, "Spire Called Arm of The Moon," we encounter "the blue-gold scroll of up above," which is also "the Tower of / Bearings," on which in turn is a plaque that reads

> Become Adam, become his sparks and limbs.
> You will see it too.
> Exact as Ezekiel
> amidst the long way back
> *Aurora consurgens*
> "that the inwardes of my head
> be like the sun"
> I build.

In the first chapter of the Book of Ezekiel, the prophet's elaborate description of the *merkabah*, the chariot throne on which is seated a radiant "figure with the appearance of a human being," is the "most graphic account of a vision of God" to be found in the Hebrew Scriptures. According to Daniel C. Matt, even before Ezekiel's "book was canonized as part of the Bible, his vision had become the archetype of Jewish mystical ascent. . . . An entire literature developed recounting the visionary exploits of those who followed Ezekiel's footsteps, among them some of the leading figures of rabbinic Judaism. The journey was arduous and dangerous, requiring intense, ascetic preparation and precise knowledge of secret passwords in order to be admitted to the various heavenly palaces guarded by menacing angels. The final goal was to attain a vision of the divine figure on the throne" (3–4). To be as "[e]xact as Ezekiel," then, is to follow the mystical "long way back" to a vision of union with the original Adam, whose limbs constitute the divine attributes and whose sparks are the fallen aspects of the godhead that remain to be gathered and restored. The building of the poem is a kind of dawn, "*aurora consurgens,*" as the "inwardes" of the poet's head assumes a solar radiance, like the head of Adam Kadmon, from which emanate the Sefiroth.

For both Johnson and Duncan, poetry becomes the modern equivalent of the mystic's ascent to the throne. But although their vision derives from the hermetic traditions of mysticism, what they have to offer is not, finally, esoteric knowledge requiring "ascetic preparation and precise knowledge of secret passwords." Thanks to Whitman, the American Adam Kadmon is truly a figure of the ensemble, or as he says in *Song of Myself,* "the word En-Masse" (209). Because "nothing, not God, is greater to one than one's self is," the material, the immediate, and the democratic all obviate the mystical quest:

Why should I wish to see God better than this day?
I see something of God each hour of the twenty-four, and each moment then,
In the faces of men and women I see God, and in my own face in the glass
I find letters from God dropt in the street, and every one is sign'd by God's name,
And I leave them where they are, for I know that wheresoe'er I go
Others will punctually come for ever and ever. (244)

For Whitman, as for so many other Romantics, poetry takes the place of prophecy, and art fulfills the role previously held by religion. Duncan and Johnson are late adherents to this creed; their projects involve what Duncan variously calls the *grand collage* or "Symposium of the Whole," in which an expansive poetic of open form appropriates and reconfigures mythic and religious materials so that they become "authorities of the Imagination in which Logos is Beginning" (*Bending the Bow* viii). "In the beginning there was the Word," Johnson reiterates at the end of Beam 17 (dedicated to Duncan), "—for each man, magnetized by onrush, is Adam to his Tyger" (*ARK*). The visionary impulse is democratic and constantly renewed: in the power of the Word, "each man" may summon his daimonic self and become a new Adam.

:::

"The *Leaves of Grass* in its nine editions," Duncan observes, "grows, not toward a definitive architecture, but as a man grows, composed and recomposed, in each phase immediate and complete, but unsatisfied" (*Fictive Certainties* 164). It is at this juncture that Duncan and Johnson part company in regard to poetic form. What Joseph Conte calls "infinite serial form" (47) in Duncan's mature work could not have developed without Whitman's guidance: "Once I returned to Whitman, in the course of writing *The Opening of the Field* when *Leaves of Grass* was kept as a bedside book, Williams's language of objects and Pound's ideogrammatic method were transformed in the light of Whitman's hieroglyphic of the ensemble" (*Fictive Certainties* 190–91). At one of the most crucial points in Duncan's career, the constructivist aesthetics of Duncan's immediate precursors are reconditioned by Whitman's romantic organicism, the sense of the poem as a human body, the growth that is "immediate and complete, but unsatisfied." As we noted in chapter 1, Conte sees Duncan's Passages sequence as constituting "a work without bounds: having no beginning and no end; a limitless interrelation of parts; the absence of an externally imposed schema; mobility; and an intentionally incomplete condition of form" (49). I have argued that this description applies to all of Duncan's poetry from *The Opening of the Field* onward, including his first series, the Structure of Rime poems. But only a few of the qualities that Conte notes in Duncan's serial poem may actually be found in Johnson's poetry, particularly the poetry of *ARK*. Duncan distinguishes *ARK* from other twentieth-century long poems—including, perhaps, his own—by claiming it to be an architecture.[2] He certainly saw his own work in more Whitmanian terms, "not a definitive architecture" but an organic human form. In this respect, the figure of Adam Kadmon is not simply thematized in Duncan's poetry: rather, the concept totally *informs* the poetry, "in which the poet seeks to keep alive as a generative possibility a force and intent hidden in the very beginning of things, long before the beginning of the poem" (*Fictive Certainties* 167).

The patterning that occurs in *ARK* remains much more constructivist and less organic, much closer to Johnson's architectural models, such as the buildings of Simon Rodia and Le Facteur Cheval. "Is *ARK* then as well as being a structure, a big body?" asks Peter O'Leary in his interview with

Johnson. Johnson replies: "I had a conversation with Guy Davenport about it. I said, you know, Blake says it's all one big body. And I said, no, I think it's a tree. And Guy Davenport said, 'I think you're right.' I felt it being this, as being a tree. It's one of the great structures: it's got depths and heights, it's got circulation, it goes into streams. It goes into stream patterns, which is what branches do. I think time makes things a tree" (41–42). Here, Johnson rejects the image of the poem as human body but clings to the organic model, invoking the form of a tree.[3] But he still speaks almost architecturally, and reverts to entirely architectural terms in the final note to the poem itself: "The idea of *ARK* came when I was able at last to conceive it a structure rather than diatribe, artifact rather than argument.... Literally an architecture, *ARK* is fitted together with shards of language, in a kind of cement of music."

Given that Johnson worked over twenty years on the poem, his blueprint for *ARK* changed relatively little, and was realized with extraordinary determination. Thirty-three Beams make up the Foundations, thirty-three Spires rise above them, and thirty-three Arches constitute the surrounding Ramparts. Time as well as space is structured, since the first book moves from sunrise to noon, the second from noon to sunset, the third through the night until the great "Lift Off" with which the poem concludes. Thus, *ARK* (to paraphrase Conte on Duncan) is composed according to a conscious schema; it has definite boundaries, and a clear beginning and end. The movement of the verse, in terms of its visual and aural components, is increasingly decisive and measured, from the mix of prose, poetry, concrete verse, and visuals in the Foundations, to the graceful, consistently centered lyrics of the Spires, to the regularity of the Ramparts, with its invariable construction in three-line stanzas. *ARK*, of course, is a work of great flexibility, and, like Duncan's serial poems, "a limitless interrelation of parts." But although the poem's discourse is saturated with organic references, it is far more a building raised up by a kind of orphic music than a body complete but growing incrementally with every passing instant. "With stones of words and mortar of song" (56), says Johnson of the writing of his half-completed poem in the note at the end of *ARK 50*. And so it remains till he finishes the task.

In the note at the end of *ARK*, Johnson, distinguishing his efforts from those of his precursors, writes that "if my confreres wanted to write a work with all history in its maw, I wished, from the beginning, to start all over again, attempting to know nothing but a will to create, and matter at hand." Likewise, he tells O'Leary that "I wanted it to be *without* history, such that it was constructed of things in my time" (33). Johnson is thinking of Pound's idea of the epic as a poem including history, but in addition to *The Cantos*, he has Williams's *Paterson*, Olson's *Maximus*, and Zukofsky's *"A"* in mind as well. And indeed, Johnson writes, in terms of the traditional "matter" of the long poem, the most ahistorical, least didactic or polemical work of them all. What he understands as "things in my time" or "matter at hand" (in the O'Leary interview he calls them "snippets") are observations, word patterns, quotations, and momentary perceptions that are all fitted into the poem's larger structures to achieve an effect of total synchronicity. As Mark Scroggins notes, "when Ronald Johnson devises his 'architectural' form for *ARK* . . . he has left the ideogrammic method of high modernism far behind. . . . [I]n *ARK*, the fragment or quotation is no longer a cultural index, but merely a shiny bit of language that fits into some crucial point in the poem's mosaic" (147, 148).

Yet the shiny bits of language that Johnson fits into his cosmic mosaic are, more often than not, still charged with cultural significance, especially given his predilection for mythic and religious allusion. Following Scroggins, one is led to ask why we should *not* treat these traditional fragments and quotations as Poundian ideograms, or for that matter, as symbols calling for hermeneutical unpacking. Borrowing a term from Steven M. Wasserstrom, I see the building blocks of *ARK* as constituting an immense archive or repository of the "tautegorical sublime." According to Wasserstrom, imaginal forms achieve this status when they are "released from a need to deliver religious phenomena to a meaning outside themselves. . . . The documentary remainder of religious history, the symbolic heritage of the past—angels, *sefirot*, hierophanies—could now successfully resist condescending 'explanations' which read them against their original spirit. They are now allowed to be themselves; they are themselves meaning; they mean themselves. These traditional symbols demand to be read in their own terms" (57). For Wasserstrom, treating religious and mythic material in this way is crucial to understanding of the work of Mircea Eliade, Henry Corbin, and Gershom Scholem, the three great historians of religion who are the subject of his study, and who together produce a complex vision of what Wasserstrom provocatively terms "religion after religion." Given what we know of John-son's intentions regarding *ARK*, it appears that once we enter this text, we are reading not scholarship but *poetry* that employs the tautegorical sublime to achieve its post-religious ends.[4]

Because he declines to write a poem "with all history in its maw," John-son does not interpret human events or phenomena along social, political, or ideological lines, as is variously the case with the long poems of Pound, Williams, Olson, and Zukofsky. Items derived from myth, religion, litera-ture, the arts, and even modern science "tautegorically" replace ideology: the cosmological vision of *ARK*, deliberately lacking any polemical thrust or search for social cause and effect, challenges the notion that literary value is to be found by determining the historicity of the text. As Rachel Blau DuPlessis puts it, "the poem may not exclude social observation, but it eternalizes the conditions it observes; the work—and, as is claimed, the vocation that sustains it—are most poetic when they are outside of histori-cal change and social mediations. Johnson's work presents a universalizing architectural vision, not one linked to the timely wobble of situated specif-ics, but to the resonant sound waves of natural permanence" ("Echological Scales" 109).

Nowhere in *ARK* is this more evident than in the first of the Spires, the magnificent section 34, "Spire on the Death of L.Z.":

this is paradise

this is

happening

on the surface of a bubble

time and again

fire scuplt of notwithstanding

dark

the whole parted world

in choir

when the wind's bright horses

hooves break earth in thunder

that,

that is paradise

This passage is a beautiful homage to Zukofsky as well as a gentle critique. For Zukofsky, the original theorist of Objectivism, poetry is a matter of "thinking with the things as they exist, and of directing them along a line of melody" (12)—a belief to which Johnson certainly subscribes. As we have seen, Johnson thinks of *ARK* as made from the substance of language, words as things, held together by the musical qualities of the verse. In this respect, he is very much an heir of Objectivism, a poet for whom the immediacy of perceived detail is of the utmost importance to the act of composition. "[T]he wind's bright horses / hooves break earth in thunder": the Zukofsky Spire in particular is filled with such phrases, based on natural observations and heightened by the music of assonance and alliteration. One can imagine the lightning and thunder of a wind-driven storm like great horses driven across the Kansas prairie.

But in contrasting *ARK* to *"A,"* Johnson also notes that "Zukofsky put a lot of contemporary history and Marxist politics into his poem" ("Interview" 33), which is just the sort of material that Johnson avoids.[5] The refrain in the Zukofsky Spire is "this is paradise," both parts of which (the demonstrative pronoun "this" plus the verb "is," and the noun "paradise") appear variously throughout. *This*—what is before us at the moment, what we can perceive—is paradise, the fit subject matter of the poem. "[A]ll of history," and an ideological interpretation thereof, need not fill the poem's "maw." Such concerns, presumably, keep the poet from what Johnson elsewhere in the Spire calls the "work of vision / of the word / at hand." Paradise is a synchronous world "based / on the principle / of the intervals between cuckoos / and molecules"; it is "the surface of a bubble / time and again."

With Duncan, we are obviously in a different territory. The *grand collage* of the poetry includes all of Duncan's political concerns. The sexual politics of poems such as "This Place Rumord to Have Been Sodom" or Passages 18, "The Torso" (not to mention the unprecedented frankness of "The Homosexual in Society," the essay he publishes in 1944) prove him to be an important gay activist long before the term or the concept had any popular currency. His early and ongoing interest in various forms of anarchism and communism come to fulfillment in the fury of "Up Rising: Passages 25." His opposition to the Vietnam War and to imperialism in general permeates *Bending the Bow*. Indeed, the cosmological vision he derives in part from Whitman likewise inspires the political content of his verse, and Whitman as a model for the engaged poet appears as early as "A Poem Beginning with a Line by Pindar" and is confirmed in "The Fire: Passages 13." The latter juxtaposes Whitmanian and Poundian rhetorics of political indignation. As in Pound's Hell cantos,

> Satan looks forth from
> men's faces:
> Eisenhower's idiot grin, Nixon's
> black jaw, the sly glare in Goldwater's eye, or
> the look of Stevenson lying in the U.N. that our
> Nation save face • (*Bending the Bow* 43)

Duncan then segues into a quote from Whitman, in which he condemns "swarms of dough-faces, office-vermin, kept editors, clerks, attaches of ten thousand officers and their parties, aware of nothing further than the drip and spoil of politics—ignorant of principles." "My name is Legion," the poet/shaman declares, "and in every nation   I multiply / Over those who would be Great Nations   Great Evils" (44).

Duncan's opus does not constitute an epic in the same way that Pound considered *The Cantos*, but in its weave of serial poems and individual lyrics, it is clearly a poetry that "includes history," that takes not only mythic and religious material but also past and current events as part of its "argument" in every sense of the term. Troping on Pound's definition of poetry as "language charged with meaning to the utmost degree," Duncan derives a visionary politics in which "poetry charged with meaning to the utmost degree must be thought of as being charged with a conscience of order and disorder" (*Fictive Certainties* 129). Appropriately, the "central theme" of this visionary politics is "a Man of all men, multiphasic, beyond what we can know but central. . . . This was the Adam in whom all the species have their identity. In the traditions of the Jewish Kabbala this Adam falls apart into the lives of all men—his identity hidden in our identities" (*Fictive Certainties* 115). Duncan poses the idea of a "World-Order" as a standard against which all political acts, for good or for ill, must be judged. Recall that in *Ground Work: Before the War*, Passages 31–35 are called "Tribunals," and the last of which, "Before the Judgment," draws explicitly on the *Inferno* and the Hell cantos of Pound. But the American poet as legislator of the world does not only sit in judgment. As Duncan explains, with his "Up Rising: Passages 25" in mind, "back of such a sense of moral outrage is the strong sense of belonging to this 'we,' of being American as a condition of being human, so that the crimes of the Nation are properly my own, of having, in other words, a burden of original sin in the history of the Nation. The vital center of my vision of any World-Order is that it must redeem, must be the redemption of, not the rising above, that burden of acknowledged crimes against humanity" (*Fictive Certainties* 130). As we have seen, the World-Order in the form of the Poem judges even the poet, and it is a measure of Duncan's faith in this "vital center" that he can speak of redemption even when the judgment calls for the poet himself to be radically, irredeemably decentered.

This sort of analysis of the American political psyche is simply not found in Johnson's work, which is characterized instead, especially in *ARK*, by what Eric Selinger calls Johnson's "utopian patriotism" ("*ARK* as a Garden of Revelation" 169). Selinger has carefully examined what we could term the problem of evil in Johnson's poetry, as it manifests itself in the theological and in the political registers. Unlike Duncan, Johnson never writes overtly political poetry, even during the period of extreme crisis in the late sixties and early seventies, a period when the visionary intensities of *ARK* are first taking shape. Instead, as Selinger demonstrates, Johnson adopts the view of "balanced dissent" (the phrase comes from Beam 2) as the justification for "the poem's exuberant Americana" ("*ARK* as a Garden of Revelation" 160)—an exuberance, I might add, that could appear politically suspect, or at least naïve, even in less spasmodic historical moments.

In his consideration of Beam 25, "A Bicentennial Hymn," Selinger notes Johnson's presentation of "an American political ideal," not, as Duncan would, through the condemnation of contemporary corruption, but rather through the more typically Johnsonian tactic of collage and excision. "A Bicentennial Hymn" quotes "The Star Spangled Banner" and "The Battle Hymn of the Republic," but as Selinger observes, "Johnson has pruned his chosen texts to eliminate conflict, sadness, and historical pain. . . . [B]y keeping his focus on hope, and not on history, he leaves room for himself to indulge the hope that if the USA is modeled on nature, then all of nature is the sort of America where he, and presumably the reader, feels right at home" (161). Indeed, Beam 25, despite its title and "FIREWORKS MUSIC," is actually less about our country's two hundredth birthday than it is about cellular biology, which is to say, organic life's magical ability to regenerate itself: "prosper / O / cell," as Johnson punningly puts it, before giving us the step-by-step drawing of a cell undergoing meiosis. If this is Johnson's understanding of America's utopian vitalism, then perhaps we can say that his vision complements Duncan's, especially regarding the place of American history and the national psyche in the World-Order both propose.

At root, the difference lies in the two poets' relation to what we have heard Duncan call "a burden of original sin in the history of the Nation." Poets in the romantic tradition do not ordinarily invoke the idea of "original sin," and Duncan's use of the term is rather surprising in this respect—at least until we remind ourselves that Duncan is nearly as much an heir of the modernists, whose pessimism has spiritual origins as profound as the romantic optimism that Duncan usually (and Johnson almost always) displays. T. E. Hulme, whose views strongly influenced those of Eliot and Pound during the formulative period of modernism, describes this classical, pessimistic, reactionary ideology as springing from "the conviction that man is by nature bad or limited, and can consequently only accomplish anything of value by disciplines, ethical, heroic, or political. In other words, it believes in Original Sin. We may define Romantics, then, as all who do not believe in the Fall of Man. It is this opposition which in reality lies at the root of most of the other divisions in social and political thought" (250). Is Duncan, then, not a romantic because of his application of this idea? The kabbalism and theosophy that he spent a lifetime studying certainly involves a notion of Original Sin; as we have seen, he understands fully that the myth of Adam Kadmon is in essence a tale of the Fall before the Fall, which is related in turn to the gnostic myth of the demiurge's catastrophic creation. No, what makes Duncan a romantic is his belief in the *perfectibility* of Man, or as Hulme puts it, "that man, the individual, is an infinite reservoir of possibilities; and if you can so rearrange society by the destruction of oppressive order then these possibilities will have a chance and you will get Progress" (61). The utopian World-Order of which Duncan writes (before succumbing to his "gnostic contagion") will redeem our sinful nature and our sinful nation, acting, in effect, as both a Christian Second Coming and a Jewish *tikkun olam* (redemption of the world).

In its totality, Hulme's definition of a romantic probably is more applicable to Johnson than to Duncan: Johnson, after all, laughingly tells us apropos of "Palms" (made from the biblical Psalms) in the Song of Orpheus, Beams 21, 22, 23 of *ARK*, that "I took out the 'S'; I took out the snake" ("Interview" 44). Excising the snake from the myth of the Garden means eliminating the root of all the trouble, rejecting the notion of the Fall or Original Sin—and in saying he "took out the snake," Johnson may also mean he is exposing the sexual energy that is condemned in most normative religious interpretations of the tale.[6] Johnson is hardly a polemical poet, but as a gay man living in San Francisco during the seventies and eighties, he persistently signifies his resistance to any doctrine that emphasizes human sinfulness through his poem's celebration of the power of phallic Eros.[7] We see this, for instance, in the drawing of the priapic altar to "Mr. Curious Hermes" in Beam 16. Hermes, the god who carries messages between the divine and human worlds, bears the caduceus, the winged staff with two snakes, which Johnson also interprets phallically, with "twin snakes wrapt round our vitals." Likewise, when the "Old Sarpint" appears in *ARK* 44, "The Rod of Aaron," it is, as Selinger notes, "transvalued," become "a snaking branch on the 'everyday Arbor Vitae', or Tree of Life, rather than a tempter dangling from it" (*ARK* as a "Garden of Revelation" 164). In Exodus 7:8–12, the rod of Aaron becomes a serpent that devours those of the Egyptian magicians, an image of divine good literally consuming evil. Furthermore, it is quite likely that, given the "peculiar grace // *that yet / brancht forth*" at the end of *ARK* 44, Johnson also has the "flowering of the rod" imagery from H.D.'s *Trilogy* in mind, where it always symbolizes fertility, rebirth, and resurrection, concepts that are crucial to the cosmic order such poetry proposes.

:::

The archetypal singer of the World-Order is Orpheus, and the importance of the myths surrounding him to the poetry of both Duncan and Johnson has been frequently addressed. Johnson writes more often and more explicitly about him, and he claims that the "central myth" of *ARK* "is that of Orpheus and Euridice, the blessed argument between poet and muse, man and his anima." But although references to Orpheus are generally more diffused in Duncan's work, let us recall that Orpheus plays a significant and troubling role in one of Duncan's most important early poems, "Heavenly City, Earthly City" (1946). There, the argument between Orpheus and Eurydice is anything but blessed: it is violent, guilt-ridden, fraught with ambivalence; and the poet, imagining himself to be Orpheus, experiences his dismemberment at the hands of the Bacchae with something akin to relief:

The Bacchae tear in my fleshly sleep
fleshly ribbons that gleam like gold.
I lie under the weight of the black water.
Eurydice, toward whom I dare not look
—she is the bright spirit that sleeps in my heart—
returns to meet my inward gaze. (*Years as Catches* 89)

Although not as critical of the orphic role as his friend Jack Spicer, Duncan recognizes the danger that the modern poet incurs by identifying with this figure, inevitable as this identification may be if he (and it is primarily a problem for male poets) is inclined toward a mythic perspective. This danger, as Duncan says in his refrain in "Heavenly City, Earthly City," is that "Pity is the wrath in which we walk" (87). The orphic poet, as both Spicer and Duncan know, is in love with himself; the beauty he brings to the world (and the love he brings to Eurydice) ultimately may be condescending; and his patronizing attitude toward his audience (after all, who else can move even stones and trees?) masks "wrath" or aggression.[8] "Remember," says Duncan to Orpheus, "the beauty and charm are hate's machineries, / demonic art that catches the damnation into its disk / and lends to hell its immortal strain" (87–88). Orpheus's self-absorption, his "beauty and charm," are disastrous, fatally entwined with the power of hell. Duncan views the accomplishments of Orpheus much as he views the accomplishments of America: with reservation, ambivalence, and a probing dialectical perspective.

Johnson's orphic stance is somewhat less problematic and, as it were, more wholesome: again, as wholesome and idealistic as his vision of a balanced American democracy. Mallarmé speaks of "the Orphic explanation of the earth, which is the sole duty of the poet," and in our time, we would be hard pressed to find a poet who takes that felicitous phrase more seriously—and more literally—than Johnson.[9] One might even argue that *ARK*, on one level, is his orphic explanation of America. Having read Elizabeth Sewell's *The Orphic Voice: Poetry and Natural History* (1960), Johnson testifies that "I knew I wanted to be of that order of writer she talked about. I'd met my myth: Orpheus and Eurydice, and that proved honeyed terrain" ("From *Hurrah for Euphony*" 25). It is quite understandable that Sewell's book should make such an impression on a young, aspiring poet of Johnson's bent. It begins with the electrifying declaration that "poetry is a form of power. It fell to early thought to make that power visible and human, and the story of Orpheus is that vision and that mortality" (3). But Sewell's understanding of poetry and the Orphic myth is not merely a matter of allegory or of rhetorical power in general. Rather, for Sewell, not only poetry but also the powers of thought that we ordinarily associate with the natural sciences and even with mathematics are all part of a "field of activity or myth, where mind-bodies work and unite with figures in order to learn and discover." This field "is far wider than words, and wider than consciousness. It is a field of all behavior which is not wholly mechanical, in any living thing" (27). Such being the case, she explains that her theme is

> that for the last 400 years, with the coming of what one might call the modern age, poetry has been struggling to evolve and perfect the inclusive mythology on which language works and all thought in words is carried on, and that this type of thinking is the only adequate instrument for thinking about change, process, organisms and life. The history of this struggle and evolution is occasionally explicit, more often implicit. This is where Orpheus comes in: for Orpheus is poetry thinking about itself, and every significant mention of Orpheus by a poet or scientist may bring the working methods a little nearer the surface, make them easier to grasp than they will be when they are bound up with all the other things poets think and write of. (47)

Thus, by choosing the tale of Orpheus as his central myth—keeping in mind that in Sewell's view, the notion of "myth" encompasses modes of thought both poetic and scientific—Johnson places himself directly in the line of thinkers for whom the self-reflexive exploration of natural history is the primary task. The unique methods that he develops over the course of his career, reaching their greatest intensity in *ARK*, involve the continual alignment of mythic/poetic materials with naturalistic/scientific observations. This is the work of the modern orphic poet.

It takes Johnson his entire career to work through his relationship to the orphic myth, as may be observed in the three poems he dedicates to Duncan: "The Different Musics," "Beam 17, *The Book of Orpheus*," and "*ARK* 71, Arches V," subtitled "Death of R.D."[10] These poems confirm what Peter O'Leary tells me, that "Duncan is the Orpheus poet for Ron" (e-mail). But if Duncan is never far from Johnson when the latter is writing about Orpheus, we must also acknowledge that these three pieces, rather evenly spaced along the timeline of Johnson's career, each represent a different stage in the development of his style, and, for that matter, in his thinking about and addressing his older colleague. The earliest poem, "The Different Musics," while definitely Johnson's own and by no means derivative of Duncan (though of course, Duncan himself claimed proudly throughout his career that he was a "derivative poet"), incorporates some of Duncan's signature gestures and tropes in order to achieve what Rachel Blau DuPlessis describes as the orphic "spilling sound of bliss" ("Echological Scales" 104). Despite the strengths of *A Line of Poetry, A Row of Trees* (1964) and *The Book of the Green Man* (1967), it would appear that Johnson, as it were, is still an initiate in the orphic mysteries, and Duncan still serves as a sort of psychopompos. The title evokes a notion similar to that of Duncan's "orders" or levels of being that constitute the cosmos, held together by music and dance. The first part of the poem shares Duncan's etymological interests, as Johnson moves through a series of linked dictionary definitions (DUST, THEISM, FEBRUARY, PERFUME, THYME) dealing with spirit, madness, and ritual. Johnson then segues, via a quote from Charles Ives ("An apparent confusion if lived with long enough / may become orderly" [*To Do as Adam Did* 52]) to an extraordinary passage describing humus on the forest floor—an "apparent confusion" indeed, until one recalls the crucial quote from Thoreau in *The Book of the Green Man*: "Those old books suggested a certain fertility, an Ohio soil, as if they were making a humus of new literatures to spring in" (83). New literatures spring from the poet's engagement with what has come before him, and not only from the self; new growth in art, as in nature, depends on the humus of the past. Furthermore, to hear the orphic song of the earth, the poet must go into the natural world, which is why the next part of the poem, framed against both left and right margins, mentions Sibelius, who "heard // overtones from a rye- // field," and Johnson himself, who "put my ear to / the ground, & heard // the blood / rush to my head // thundering where the roots // drummed" (*To Do as Adam Did* 52, 53). To rapturously give oneself to nature leads to the discovery, in Duncanesque rhetoric, of "New extremities, new labyrinth / & branching, new, inextricable windings. // A new foliage of sensings: / sings & sings . . ." (53). At this most blissfully orphic moment, a chorus of birds joins Johnson, and the poem centers itself, as later in *ARK*, along the page's central axis. In effect, the poem has turned into a tree, as later Johnson will tell us that *ARK* is a tree ("Interview" 41–42)—the Tree of Life, the cosmic tree that in the kabbalah is also the body of Adam Kadmon himself. The orphic and kabbalistic myths shared by the two poets are here combined.[11] And to further this visionary excess, the poem concludes with Duncan's master trope from *The Opening of the Field*:[12]

> And night comes opening its arms like smokes to enfold us:
> THE DANCERS!
> Where their feet touch the earth
> an encircling of plume, diaphanous featherings.
> THE DANCERS!
> (*To Do as Adam Did* 54)

In effect, "The Different Musics" opens itself to Duncan's influence, or perhaps enters its own "place of first permission" by joining its music to that of the older poet.

This is no longer the case by the time Johnson writes "Beam 17, *The Book of Orpheus*," one of the most important of the early sections of *ARK*. The dedication to Duncan is an acknowledgment of a friendship based on shared poetic wisdom and experience, but by this point, Johnson's style is all his own. At certain moments, the poem sounds a bit like Duncan, but it doesn't move like Duncan, nor, for that matter, look like Duncan's work on the page. The text is impersonal, seems to come out of nowhere, and it is worth noting that the preceding Beam poem is subtitled "*The Voices*." Because "Beam 17" is subtitled "*The Book of Orpheus*" rather than what will shortly follow in Beams 21, 22, 23, "*The Song of Orpheus*," its tone is as didactic as it is rhapsodic; it is as much an explanation of the orphic myth and function as a voicing of orphic power.

The poem consists of a set of five nearly discrete units set one after (or upon) the other, like so many building blocks, architecturally rather than organically. The first section, in short prose paragraphs, is an imaginative retelling and interpretation of the tale of Orpheus and Eurydice. We learn that the singer's "music is the art of TIME. Its work is Abstract and Mathematick, but is created in our own image"—once again, an indication of how close the myths of Orpheus and of Adam are for Johnson. Orpheus "crosses the threshold of the unconscious to find Euridice," whom Johnson regards, at this point, as the poet's Jungian anima. Orpheus "was torn apart by irrational women (for, it is said, preaching the love of man for man) so he is only a head now bearing down Being, only a singing": his death, as his life, exemplifies the consuming power of Eros, but the truth of his art endures beyond death. DuPlessis, I believe, is correct when she asserts that "Johnson's myth is not about conjugal love and loss . . . but about scales of knowing and mystery resounding in one's own flesh. Orpheus is finally torn apart by a raging anti-ritual, exactly opposed to the mellifluous cadences of sacred song. Female agency is thereby depicted as destruction in its own right, but also as an act with unintended (and ironic) consequences: the male hero benefits. Trying to destroy him the Maenads induce his painful initiation as a triumphant sufferer and martyr for song" ("Echological Scales" 108).

This is why in the second section of the poem, in verse at the center axis of the page, the second of the two orphic dreams ends with the poet finding "a woman carved of wood, who in my arms / turns carefully yellow daffodils. // A figurehead Euridice / is what I hold." Eurydice, however much she is the poet's anima, is still a figurehead for what is, as DuPlessis puts it, "resounding in one's own flesh." The third section, in imitation of Christopher Smart, is one of many cosmic visions among the Beams of *ARK*, which teaches us that "the action of the universe is metamorphosis—its articulation, metaphor"; that is, cosmic process and its human expression as art are really one and the same. These instances, like the retelling of the Orpheus story in the first section, are, if anything, more like Whitman, with his emphasis on cosmic self-creation, than Duncan, with his worship of "the Lady" who mediates between world and poet while inspiring him and giving him the requisite "permission" for his art. Johnson does not appear to seek this sort of permission at all, for he does not need it: Orpheus *is* Adam Kadmon; thus the orphic poet is "fireshook head to foot" and "shall see the world from scratch." The cosmic bringing-forth of being or song is masturbatory: "Wobble to pole: Great Balls of Fire, exquisite sentiment," a notion that is confirmed in the last lines of the poem, "That clockwise, counterclockwise, as blue bindweed to honeysuckle, the cosmos is an organism spirally closed on itself, into the pull of existence." This last phrase is the only one that appears directly related to Duncan, who ends "A Poem Beginning with a Line by Pindar" with the dancing children "clockwise and counter-clockwise turning" (*Opening of the Field* 69). But even so, the social vision of turning children have been replaced by the turning cosmos "closed on itself," more self-sustaining and grandly totalized.

"*ARK* 71, Arches V," is late Johnson. As I read them, "The Ramparts" poems (*ARK* 67–99), "Blocks to Be Arranged in a Pyramid" (written immediately following *ARK*), and *The Shrubberies* (1994–1998, edited by Peter O'Leary and published posthumously in 2001) all owe their greatest stylistic debt to Louis Zukofsky (whom Duncan was reading late in his career too), particularly the Zukofsky of *"A"*-22 and -23, and *80 Flowers*. Both Zukofsky and Johnson in their last phases employ a highly compressed, syntactically ambiguous phrasing, controlled in part by predetermined numerological rules, such as the five-word line in Zukofsky's work or the three-line stanza in "The Ramparts." Yet in "The Ramparts" particularly, Johnson's cosmological thinking produces a more overtly religious, spiritualized poetry than Zukofsky's, which maintains its strong connections to history and materiality throughout his career. Then again, if Duncan's late poetry continually hesitates on the brink of the void, unmaking itself through disintegrating parataxis and self-dissolving allusion, Johnson's late work, by contrast, insists on its Zukofskyan constructedness, its being as artifact, calling increased attention the poetic maker's analogous relation to that Lord whom Johnson calls earlier, in Beam 30, "a delicate hammerer."

"*ARK* 71" is not an elegy or a *tombeau* in any traditional sense. The passing of Johnson's comrade is simply acknowledged by an italicized headnote (headstone?), "*Death of R.D.*" Though much of the language is vividly cosmic, the steady movement of the three-line stanzas, minimally punctuated, produces a sense of equanimity in the face of death, supported by the references to the spiritual "Swing Low, Sweet Chariot," standing out among the concentrated, paratactic phrasal units. Yet this equanimity does not amount to an acceptance of death. On the contrary, it would appear that the death of Johnson's old friend spurs the poet to get on with the task of completing his poem:

> so, absolute for Citadel
> deny tonight abed
> ends coming for to carry us home
>
> brook no delay, er-
> ect sundry those bones anoint
> sweet pomps used Adam

RONALD JOHNSON

Hanging like a sword
fresh in mind,
poise hand at ultimate potter

back days to one Bang d'time
reeling so atom in
engoldened archipelago

now reft even of what might come
Swing low sweet chariot
no more, mourn not

Only an extended quote such as this can convey the steady, ongoing force of the verse, which, when read carefully, proves remarkably unlike the poetry at the beginning of *ARK*. Though knowledge of mortality is seen "[h]anging like a sword," Johnson remains "absolute for Citadel," determined that he will "er- / ect sundry those bones" that constitute the final sections of *ARK*. In this respect, he fulfills the order he gives himself back in "*ARK* 35": not only to "[b]ecome Adam, become his sparks and limbs," but also to see reality "[e]xact as Ezekiel," the prophet of the chariot and of the valley of dry bones as well. Like the "ultimate potter" Himself, he will go "back days to one Bang d'time," his poem taking him back to the Big Bang itself to become an atom in the "engoldened archipelago" that is the universe. As in earlier sections of the text, here again we observe the orphic dimension of the poet's task, to unite human expression with cosmic process. The resulting sound is "'like silver smiting silver' / H. J. on the harp / behind order, Utopia cut figure," probably a reference to Helen Johnson, the poet's mother, who elsewhere in *ARK*, appropriately, is called "The Dancer." At last, the Orpheus and Eurydice figures merge in the vision of a female harpist who is both "behind order" in the unconscious yet also produces the "Utopia cut figure" of conscious art with her playing and dancing. The feminine and masculine principles that seemed at odds in "Beam 17" now appeared reconciled, as is more often the case in Duncan's work. And so the psalm continues to be sung (David, the masculine harpist perhaps merging with the feminine H. J.), even "[i]n the valley of the shadow of" (with the word "death" remaining unvoiced), "gathering life / a breviary of universe." This is the final gift that Johnson presents to Duncan, a hymnal and prayer book of the cosmic orders.[13]

:::

A breviary summarizes and presents the hymns, prayers, and readings of the canonical hours, so in one respect, any one section, or indeed, the whole of *ARK* can be read as "a breviary of universe." Like a cosmic breviary, *ARK* has its holy scriptures (Blake, Whitman, Dickinson, Thoreau, Baum) and its canon of saints (Ives, Le Facteur Cheval, Simon Rodia, James Hampton). Acknowledging his forebears in the note at the end of his poem, Johnson invokes Pound and Williams, and then "more closely, Zukofsky and Olson, braving new schemes for language—The Minimalist and The Maximus— such opposing poles of influence: parities." *ARK* seems to me a good deal closer to *"A"* than the *Maximus Poems*, though Johnson shares with Olson the desire to imbue his poem with an expansive sense of American space. From Zukofsky, as we have seen, comes an overarching sense of the poem's constructed quality, as well as actual constructive procedures, which differ significantly from the organicism of Olson's—and Duncan's—projective verse. I have already addressed the organic and architectural analogies Johnson uses in describing *ARK*, as well as its "monadological" quality, for it is not merely Beam 10 that serves as a monad reflecting the entire structure, but literally *any* point or passage in the poem that can serve in this capacity. Thus, in *"ARK* 72, Arches VI," when Johnson writes of "legerdemain in the Elaboratory," he is again producing a single instance of the textual totality: the poem is a great act of verbal magic or sleight of hand (the word derives from the Old French *leger de main*, "lightness of hand"), taking place again and again in the portmanteau "Elaboratory," a *laboratory* where the poet conducts his experiments in verbal *elaboration*, making slight words and things more grand.

The poet, then, is both magician and scientist, but he is also a priest, evangelist, and scribe. As Johnson ends *"ARK* 90, Arches XXIV," "if Gods there be to address, / read our *scrapture* / released planet's snare." Here, Johnson calls upon the gods to read the poem itself, "our *scrapture*," another portmanteau word that serves as a monad for the entire poem. Playing on "scripture," it also contains "scrap" (for the fantastic buildings upon which *ARK* is based are built out of scraps or snippets, as whole sections of the poem are built out of other texts) as well as "rapture." To read *ARK* is to experience ecstasy, to be transported heavenward and to be released from the "planet's

snare." On one level, Johnson is referring to the evangelical Christian no-
tion of "the rapture," that Christ will take up all living believers in the body
so they may escape the sinful earth and join him in Heaven, the first event
in the apocalyptic struggle of the End of Days.[14] Johnson, of course, is no
evangelical, though he freely appropriates religious concepts of all variet-
ies to enrich his cosmological vision. Thus, the poet's *scrapture* or scripture
of scraps can release us from the "planet's snare": the poem can help us see
through earthly, material being to perceive the spiritual orders. As Selinger
observes, Johnson "lightly [reverses] Blake's admonition, in 'The Everlast-
ing Gospel', that 'This life's five windows of the soul / Distorts the Heavens
from pole to pole, / And leads you to believe a lie / When you see with, not
thro', the eye'" ("Important Pleasures: Ronald Johnson"). As Johnson puts
it in "Beam 5," "we have always known the eye to be unsleeping, and that all
men are lidless Visionaries through the night." But we are also visionaries
during the day, as Johnson's extraordinary eye for natural detail attests. The
materiality of the "planet's snare" is what holds us bound, but it is also the
only way through to our spiritual release into a visionary state.

This leads us back to the issue of Johnson's visionary optimism in *ARK*,
which, as we have seen, is resolutely opposed to any notion of human sinful-
ness. Yet this does not spare the poet from the inevitable experience of loss.
Immediately after the presentation of the poem as *scrapture* and the release
from the "planet's snare" comes "*ARK* 91, Arches XXVI." Selinger notes that
compared to earlier parts of *ARK*, "there is often a sadder, darker tone to
the Arches," and rightly attributes this tone to the poet's awareness of the
loss of his fellows and his resulting elegiac burden. There is also "perhaps a
certain sadness about the poet's neglect by readers" ("Important Pleasures:
Ronald Johnson"). Johnson is one of the least autobiographical poets, and
his work is certainly not centered around his personal joys and griefs. Be
that as it may, there is no denying the personal pathos of "*ARK* 91," which I
read as Johnson's reflection on his project as it approaches completion, and
on his vocation as a poet of *kosmos*. This consideration is made all the more
poignant by Johnson's tone, which moves, as is often the case in his mature
work, between the prophetic and the colloquial.

Johnson begins

> Off the top of my head
> seed, honeycomb, vine curl

shells, snake on branch

mind in orderly array—
forms molded trial & error
living out suitcase

"Off the top of my head" indicates a spontaneous, improvisatory sort of composition, perhaps the writerly equivalent to "living out [of a] suitcase. Yet although *ARK* presents "forms molded" by "trial and error," we are still aware of the "mind in orderly array," the architectural planner one with the *bricoleur*. The overall sense is Whitmanian, and indeed, Johnson's natural imagery, produced "Off the top of my head," is distinctly reminiscent of "Song of Myself," when Whitman finds that "I incorporate gneiss, coal, long-threaded moss, fruits, grains, esculent roots, / And am stucco'd with quadrupeds and birds all over" (217). Some lines later, Johnson declares that "angels upon ladders / vanish Archimboldo elms." "Archimboldo," or as it is usually spelled, "Arcimboldo," is Giuseppe Arcimboldo (1527–1593), the Milanese painter famous for his bizarre portraits in which elements of the human face are represented by fruits, vegetables, flowers and other natural objects—visual representations of what Whitman and Johnson are doing verbally in their poems. We are, therefore, in *a landscape of Simulars, / where shape sort inked shape / old as the hills.*"

But in Johnson's landscape, the angels upon ladders (Jacob's ladder, no doubt, since *ARK* is a sort of celestial dream) are causing elm trees (which the poet, Arcimboldo-like, sees as resembling the human form) to vanish. This is probably an allusion to the Dutch elm disease that destroyed half the elms in the United States starting in the 1930s, but rather than refer to a physical malady, Johnson sees a spiritual assault on nature. Why? Like the trees that the angels cause to disappear, the poet is also assaulted by the invisible powers, for like Blake and Whitman before him, Johnson stands between the natural and supernatural worlds. The poet's task is "to oar the Uproar" of the cosmos, to navigate among the orders of being. Colloquially speaking, this is his "cross to bear, roe to hoe." Usually good-natured about his visionary task, Johnson, nearing the end of his poem, has some sense of himself as a weary laborer, if not a sacrificial victim.

His marginal status may also come into play here, both as an avant-gardist with relatively few readers, and as a gay man coming from intolerant middle-American Kansas before finding Oz in San Francisco. In section 24 of "Song of Myself," devoted to issues of the body, the appetites, and sexual frankness, Whitman declares that "I speak the pass-word primeval, I give the sign of democracy" (211). Whitman's understanding of democracy is both poetic and homosocial, and in both instances, the initiate must recognize a password or sign. Similarly, Johnson indicates that he may be recognized by reader or lover "yet only by secret handshake / under the Mallorn trees, / and get out fast." Johnson is referring either to a furtive poetic or a furtive homosexual encounter under the Mallorn trees, which makes this one of the most delightfully transgressive moments in *ARK*. In Tolkien's *The Lord of the Rings*, the undying Mallorn trees (in contrast to the dying elms) are found in Lothlorien, the forest kingdom of the Elves.[15] Ruled by the Lady Galadriel, whose power comes from one of the Three Rings of the Elves, Lothlorien is a kind of Earthly Paradise, but with the coming of Frodo and the One Ring, it is doomed: either Frodo's quest will fail, the Dark Lord will regain the Ring, and Lorien will be destroyed; or Frodo will succeed, the Ring will be destroyed, and the magic of Lorien will fade away, along with the benign influence of the Elves in Middle Earth. In short, one cannot dwell forever in Lorien (just as Dorothy cannot remain in Oz): we are driven from the earthly Paradise but not through any fault of our own, and in the midst of our pleasure we have to "get out fast."[16]

Poetry, then, can grant us a glimpse of Paradise, but poets themselves cannot linger there. Johnson ends "*ARK* 91" with "Unfolding worlds before us," but still shuttles back and forth between the immortality of the poem and the mortality of the poets. Thus, "Seasons taken for a ride // gallop," which is to say that those who possess a "winged imagination" and take flight with Pegasus must also "cement horsesense, / no fall of an apple unforseen," and in a commonsensical fashion accept their mortal limits. Thinking again, perhaps, of *Leaves of Grass* and of the continuous exchanges in such cosmic poetry between world and text, Johnson declares that "'these trees will be my books' / *over my dead leaves*." Yet despite their mortality, poets may leave "bold Aurora Borealis / all in an opening of a drawer"—a reference, I think, to Emily Dickinson, whose poems of boreal vision were to be found by the world only after her death, upon opening her desk drawer. Moving toward the end of his poem, Johnson longs to offer his readers "stars through unmeasured / heights of pendant atmosphere," as poets such as Whitman and Dickinson did before him. But to do so, they must accompany him on his journey to the earthly Paradise, however brief the visit.

ARK, then, is simultaneously the vessel for that trip ("the good ship *Praxis*" as he says in "*ARK* 81") and an account of that place, both the voyage and the destination. In other words, to read the poem is to make a journey or cosmic ascent toward a spiritualized utopian space (Paradise or Oz) *and* to be in that space, or at least to have some inkling of what it would be like to inhabit it. In his autobiographical "Legend," Johnson writes of *ARK* that "This structure was in the form of a space ship, to carry mankind, along with the wonder of old earth, to the stars." Thus, the poem is as much a spaceship as a "Walled Demesne" (the phrase comes from "*ARK* 70, Arches IV)"—a *merkabah*, or chariot-throne, which in kabbalah is related in turn to the Ark of the Covenant. There is also the sense that it is another Noah's Ark: "Noah on board," begins "*ARK* 81"; "agenda: eternal purr // aardvark to zebu, two by two," with "*ARK* 83, Arches XVII," the ramp, consisting of a grand listing of grouped birds and animals that are presumably coming aboard.

"*ARK* 99, Arches XXXIII," the last section of the poem, may be read as a confirmation of the text as cosmic vehicle. But that is only one among a number of such motifs informing *ARK* that come together as the poem concludes. This last section names itself a "mosaic of Cosmos," much like Johnson's beloved Watts Towers of Simon Rodia. The writing throughout is almost entirely paratactic, phrase set next to phrase, each a tautegorical "snippet" for its own sake but also combined to "remake mankind, / a joyous noise into the void." Here at last is revealed the "portal system Milky Way // as Unmoved Mover" and the "organism omnipotent // poised in flesh": God, man, and *kosmos* as one. In the last lines—the very end of the poem—Johnson invokes

Origins great aorta

Leaved from the wrist up, but
Yet to attain the skies

all arrowed a rainbow midair;
ad astra per aspera
countdown to Lift Off

Here nearly all the major motifs in the poem are united. The aorta sends blood out from the heart to the entire arterial system, so "Origin[']s great aorta" pumps the cosmic force of Adam Kadmon throughout the *kosmos* of the poem, out even to the wrists. These extremities are "Leaved," for in *ARK*, the body of Primal Man, as we have seen, may also be the Tree of Life, producing, as it were, another *Book of the Green Man*, grander than the first. As spaceship, the poem has counted down to "Lift Off" and is about to "attain the skies"—but as in the story of Noah's Ark, we are also given a rainbow (an *arc de ciel*) as heaven's promise to earth of purification and renewal. Somewhere over the rainbow, of course, is the Land of Oz, but as Dorothy learns at the end of the film, Oz magically coincides with Kansas, Johnson's home state, where he was born and raised, and to which he returned during his final bout with brain cancer. The state motto of Kansas is *Ad astra per aspera*, "to the stars through difficulties," a perfectly appropriate motto for *ARK* as well. For *ARK* has taken its readers through a long and difficult journey, a journey that is also a continual arrival in the welcoming stars.

3

Jack Spicer

A REASON TO BE-/LEAVE

It must already be clear, in any case, that there is a link between text and spirit when textual incidents, in the form of fragments, are like a voice falling into us, taking hold of us. (Hartman, "Text and Spirit" 197)

Having considered the vision of *kosmos* that Ronald Johnson shared with his friend Robert Duncan, we now proceed to the darker vision of *gnosis* in Jack Spicer, with whom Duncan had a far more combative relationship, from 1945, when they first met at the University of California, Berkeley, until Spicer's death in 1965. The gnostic ascent from poetry to scripture that we have witnessed in Duncan's late work is surely one of the most radical developments in recent American poetry. Only Spicer equals him in the act of poetic unmaking. But Spicer, whose gnostic sensibility is more pure, and therefore even more volatile, than Duncan's, and whose personal life was far more self-destructive, presents a tragically abbreviated poetic trajectory. We cannot speak of "late Spicer" as we speak of "late Duncan" (or even "late Johnson"): dead at forty, Spicer, throughout his short life as a writer, is possessed of a kind of horror of poetry that Duncan only betrays much further along in his career. The very concentration and wrenching intensity of the seriality in Spicer's work, together with Spicer's absolutism in regard to dictation (which Duncan does not share), enact a dichotomy between poetry and religious belief that operates in all his major works.

One would be hard-pressed to find a more God-haunted poet in the second half of the twentieth century than Jack Spicer. From the triumphant beginning of his career to its bitter end, he never ceases thinking about God and quoting him, which is to say that he never ceases to use religious discourse, however irreverent or even profane he may sound. "That two-eyed monster God" (*My Vocabulary* 49) rules over the world of the *Imaginary Elegies* (1950–1959) and remains a continual presence (or present absence) up through His appearance as the "big white baseball" (416) that makes all the poet-ballplayers look silly in the *Book of Magazine Verse* (1966). Equally important is the fact that the struggle for religious faith in Spicer, or to be more precise, the dialectical tension between poetry and religious faith that unfolds in his writing, determines not only the content or matter of the work, but its form as well. The various innovative procedures that Spicer develops or refines (dictation, correspondence, the serial poem, the "book," and so forth) are all intended to turn the poet into a *medium*, an empty vessel, a vehicle or instrument (car or radio, as in *Heads of the Town*) designed to convey messages from the "sweet Platonic spiritland" (27) first unveiled in the *Imaginary Elegies*. Form and content are inextricable in Spicer's work, and though this may be said about all poetry, it is still relatively rare to encounter a poet who believes so *religiously* in poetry's metapoetical dimension. What I mean by "metapoetical" here is that for Spicer, poetry is about nothing but messages: the message is the reception of the message, and the less poets manage to intervene with the delivery, the more true to their poems, and to their vocation, they will be.[1]

Perhaps all bodies of poetry imply a poetics, but Spicer's work is unique in that it becomes a set of poetic—read: spiritual—exercises. Virtually all of Spicer's poetry constitutes, as it were, "a textbook of poetry," and to read Spicer is to take religious instruction. The question regarding Spicer's work, therefore, is to what extent his "Practice of Outside" (to borrow the title of Robin Blaser's groundbreaking essay) is a *means* of religious expression and to what extent it actually *replaces* religion. This question hovers above the work of other figures who share something of Spicer's poetic sensibility. In *Gnostic Contagion*, his superb book on Robert Duncan (and the title could apply to Spicer equally well), Peter O'Leary writes that "When I refer to Duncan, H.D. or [Nathaniel] Mackey as religious poets, I do not mean they have religious aspirations outside of the poem. They devote themselves to the 'orders' of poetry, to the 'trouble of the unbound reference' (as Duncan calls it) with a religious fervor, because only in poetry do they find the revelation that gives order to creation and cosmos" (25).

Could the same be said of Spicer? My answer would have to be both yes and no: as I have stated elsewhere, "Duncan is a genuinely prophetic poet, a voice of *kosmos*; his magian aspirations scandalized Spicer, for whom dictation, or inspiration, is always a matter of demonic possession rather than the theurgic invocation it is in Duncan" (*Lyrical Interference* 89). Even after Duncan abandons a poetry of *kosmos*, his stance remains that of prophet or mage. Reading Duncan's "Pages from a Notebook," Charles Olson believed that Duncan was falsely courting religion and betraying his poetic principles, and felt compelled to write "Against Wisdom as Such" in response (13–22). Spicer detested the notion of the poet-as-mage even more strongly; his work *in its entirety* could be called "Against Wisdom as Such." As for the Whitmanian vision of *kosmos* so important to Duncan and Johnson, it is debatable whether Spicer believes in a cosmic order, either in the poem or outside it: if such an order does indeed exist, it is in a (probably irredeemably) fallen condition.[2] To return to O'Leary's observation, this is why Spicer may be a religious poet in the sense of, say, Herbert or Vaughan (or perhaps in our time, Geoffrey Hill), rather than Duncan or Mackey (or Johnson), since for Spicer, the religion of poetry in and of itself is always inadequate. Nevertheless, like Duncan and Mackey, Spicer suffers from a disease of the spirit, and poetry is the name of that disease, if not, as O'Leary would argue, the cure.[3] "He was addicted to Poetry as he was to alcohol," Duncan observes, "sick unto death with it" ("Preface" xiv). And if Spicer himself sees poetry, as Ross Feld concludes, as "an inescapably sentimental illness—but one with roots in salvation" ("Apostle's Grudge" 194), then the etiology of this illness remains to be explored.[4]

Consider, for instance, the fourth poem in the section of *Language* ironically called "Love Poems." Poignant, nasty, and brutally funny, the "Love Poems" section is quite typical of Spicer's later writing, and number 4 is no exception:

> "If you don't believe in a god, don't quote him," Valery once
>   said when he was about ready to give up poetry. The
>   purposeful suspension of disbelief has about the chance of
>   a snowball in hell.
> Lamias maybe, or succubi but they are about as real in
>   California as night-crawlers
> Gods or stars or totems are not game-animals. Snark-hunting is
>   not like discussing baseball.

Against wisdom as such. Such
Tired wisdoms as the game-hunters develop
Shooting Zeus, Alpha Centauri, wolf with the same toy gun.
It is deadly hard to worship god, star, and totem. Deadly easy
To use them like worn-out condoms spattered by your own
      gleeful, crass, and unworshiping
Wisdom (*My Vocabulary* 383)

This poem is not only one of the more significant moments in the long de-
bate between Spicer and Duncan, but one of the most revealing texts in re-
gard to Spicer's religious sensibility. Spicer knows that in "Against Wisdom
as Such," Olson had already chastised Duncan for his tendency to appropri-
ate religious terminology. Suspicious of Duncan's search for wisdom in vari-
ous religious traditions, Olson declares that the poet "is not free to be part
of, or to be any, sect; that there are no symbols to him, there are only his own
composed forms, and each one solely the issue of the time of the moment
of its creation, not any ultimate except what he in his heat and that instant
in its solidity yield. That the poet cannot afford to traffick in any other 'sign'
than his one, his self, the man or woman he is. Otherwise God does rush in.
And art is washed away, turned into that second force, religion" (261–62).
Duncan, who was willing to accept Olson as a mentor, duly acknowledges
Olson's criticism in the prose poem "Reflections" (*Bending the Bow* 38–39),
but nowhere, to my knowledge, does he mention Spicer's much harsher cri-
tique. Compared to Olson's concern for a fellow poet whom he genuinely
admires, there seems to be a certain gratuitous animosity in Spicer's depic-
tion of his old friend as a "game-hunter" of gods, stars and totems, easily
exploiting religious phenomena for the sake of his own "gleeful, crass, and
unworshiping / Wisdom."[5] The attack is even uglier due to the image of the
condoms: appropriating religious ideas in which one does not believe for
poetic purposes (which involves the "purposeful suspension of disbelief")
is equivalent to sexual exploitation, or perhaps (because the condoms are
"worn-out") to what was once a meaningful encounter but is no longer.[6] By
contrast, genuine worship (like true love) is "deadly hard," presumably be-
cause it involves a commitment of faith and an attitude of belief that has
nothing to do with the making of poetic fictions, however they may be "spat-
tered" with religious symbols or allusions to wisdom traditions. In other
words, for Spicer, religious belief is congruent with writing poetry insofar as

they are both expressions of the individual's search for metaphysical truth, which is entirely different from the narcissistic, self-gratifying notion of the poem as a source of wisdom.

In Spicer's poem, Valéry is invoked "when he was about ready to give up poetry" because for this exemplary modernist, losing faith in poetry also involves losing faith in some concept of the sacred, so that to continue to quote what Spicer in *The Holy Grail* calls "God-language" (*My Vocabulary* 358) in one's poems would result in an intolerable act of bad faith. Conversely, the continued act of writing poetry implies a continued awareness of the sacred, a sense that on some level, the poet's relationship to the divine is not only viable but also necessary. Recall Henry Weinfield's observation about Valéry's mentor, Mallarmé: "Poetry is thus not only the vehicle but the locus of the sacred for Mallarmé, and in a sense, he remains a religious poet even though he loses his belief. The sacred exists for Mallarmé, but only insofar as it can be experienced phenomenologically; it exists only as an experience, through the concrete medium of language, or, in other words, as Beauty" ("Introduction" xiii–xiv). Spicer, who is deeply invested in the French symbolist tradition, cannot go as far as Mallarmé or Valéry: for him, faith in poetry alone, the concrete experience of language as beauty, is never sufficient.[7]

This is why, I believe, his attack on Duncan is so severe: he is addressing himself as much as his colleague when he questions the poet's integrity in "quoting" a god, for if the poet fails to maintain a relationship to the divine, he will no longer be able to write poetry. This in turn implies that he must continually interrogate the condition of his faith even as he employs the "God-language" that drives his work forward. A latter-day Puritan, Spicer conceives of writing as an ongoing examination of one's spiritual state. Consider the description of the serial poem from Spicer's second Vancouver Lecture: "Robin [Blaser] once said, in talking about a serial poem, that it's as if you go into a room, a dark room. A light is turned on for a minute. Then it's turned off again and you go into a different room where a light is turned on and turned off" (*House That Jack Built* 55). Like the entry in a Puritan's daybook, each poem in the series is a moment of illumination, an opportunity to see the soul's situation in a light that comes from the Outside: an experience that Spicer ironically calls "dictation." Furthermore, as Feld observes, "the only other 'person' Spicer speaks with relaxed confidence of and to in his poem is God. Other humans he cajoles, hectors, admonishes, shakes his head over–but only God is the entity that cannot disappoint. . . . Only in reference to God can the poet, or anyone, be dispensed from 'the big lie of the personal'" ("Apostle's Grudge" 188–89). But though God cannot disappoint, he cannot necessarily provide succor. More often than not, He chastises, and the poem, with all its ghostly interventions, is an enactment of that spiritual scourging.

:::

Much has been made of Spicer's "Calvinism." Taking their cues from Spicer himself—both his personal remarks and what they knew of his studies—both Blaser and Duncan, the two poets who, with Spicer, are the main figures of the "Berkeley Renaissance" of the late forties, have constructed imprecise, sometimes contradictory, but nonetheless important testaments to this dimension of Spicer's belief. In "The Practice of Outside" (1975), Blaser notes, among Spicer's various readings and affinities, "the early time he spent over Calvin's *Institutes*" (313). More importantly, Blaser argues that "Jack's oppositions and contrariness look destructive, even despairing, but they tend to bring forward a language that holds. We may read this as an aspect of his sure-footed Americanness—a Puritanism, a Calvinism at the heart of his experience. And certainly, his life-long interest in Hawthorne comes to mind. Such a reading could be useful, but it would, I think, lead to a misreading" (283). Misreading or not, Calvinism remains a crucial category in Blaser's ongoing assessment of Spicer's work, for he returns to the subject in an interview conducted by Lewis Ellingham (1983), parts of which appear in *Poet Be Like God*. Here, Blaser asserts that "by 1965 the issue [of Calvinism in American letters] had been posed in the wrong terms. One is no longer within the Calvinist-Puritan tradition at all. One is now caught in the entire wreckage of whatever that tradition was. I thought that [the question of Spicer's relation to Calvinism in literature] was posed in such a way that there was not an answer to it" (327). But even in the wreckage of that tradition, its power could be felt in Spicer's work. Thus, as Blaser puts it, "Calvinism supposes over and over again a dualism. . . . Which is to say, the absolute otherness of complete meaning. It divides the world in such a way that you have a dualism: a godhead, and the created world, separate from Him. One may trace this throughout Jack. He was fascinated by it; he knew a lot about it; he is, essentially, quarreling with it. In order to find *not* dualism, finally—though he kept, it's true, feeling the world as dualistic in some way—he so modernizes it that it becomes modern condition rather than Calvinistic condition. And then the search is to find the way in which we are dealing with—what? with contraries, with opposites; not, simply, with dualism" (329).

However sketchy and provisional these remarks may be, I find them worth highlighting, for the Calvinistic dualism of God and the created world, God and humanity, even when revised or modernized, is fundamental to Spicer's poetic. Duncan, who explicitly links Calvinism to gnosticism in Spicer's work, is very clear on this point: "What he sought in Calvinist and gnostic theologies was an ideogram in which God's betrayal and Man's love would never change but co-exist" ("Preface" xxiv). If such is indeed the case, then the coexistence of these unchanging conditions could certainly account for Spicer's increasingly bleak worldview, the knowledge, as he tells Allen Ginsberg in his very last poem, that "we both know how shitty the world is" (*My Vocabulary* 426). In Spicer's writing, the "shitty" fallen world, depraved and unredeemable except for a momentary sense of grace experienced by the few elect, adumbrates both a theology and a poetics. Duncan relates this belief to Spicer's homosexuality and to his lifelong love of games (chess, bridge, baseball): it is "a curse, a trick in the game of a God who predestined such love of man for man to damnation" ("Preface" xiv). For Duncan, "The God who appears in Spicer's poetry is that Creator—the Designer of the Game and of the Rules and of our Winning or Losing—who has projected upon Man the predestination of a Hell along with the agony of a sexual compulsion, a poetic compulsion, an alcoholic compulsion, a gaming compulsion, a psychodramatic compulsion that leads him deep into the defeat rooted in his given nature" (xx). This has all the neatness of psychobiography, and given Duncan's vexed friendship with Spicer, we can regard it as plausible without necessarily accepting it as the last word. Blaser, who was at least as close to Spicer as Duncan, refutes the idea that Spicer's Calvinism can be directly connected to either his homosexuality or his alcoholism: "Don't think Spicer spent much of his energy on the *guilt* of it." As Blaser would have it, theology in and of itself is crucial to the work of all three poets, however bound up religious thought may be with the conditions of their personal lives (Ellingham and Killian 327). Given their backgrounds, this meant theosophy for Duncan, Catholicism for Blaser, and Calvinism for Spicer. In the "Poems and Documents" section that Blaser appended to the *Collected Books*, Blaser adds: "He was clearly drawn to the bipolarity of Calvin's thought and to that passionate sense of god as 'entirely Other', in which contemporary thought may see the word, god, fill again with extraordinary contents—so to speak, at the beginning and the end of our sentences" (367).

How then does "that passionate sense of god as 'entirely Other'" fill again with "extraordinary contents" in Jack Spicer's poetry? As Duncan understood, Spicer's conception of divine Otherness tends to vacillate between gnosticism and Calvinism.[8] In the *Imaginary Elegies*, for instance, the two eyes of God (or the Demiurge) are the moon and the sun. The former remembers "What we have lost or never thought," and we are cautioned to "Fear its inhuman mirror blankness / Luring lovers" (*My Vocabulary* 27, 28). The latter is "good and gold," yet what appears to be divine goodness actually "is / A black and blinding cannibal with sunny teeth / That only eats itself." "Deny the light," Spicer tells us, a particularly gnostic formulation (29). Whether in the blankness of his lunar distance, or even worse, the light of his presence, God is perceived as an overwhelming threat. If the poet is to "be like God" (and it would appear that no one has acknowledged this, despite the now common association of this phrase with Spicer's work in general), the poet must then *consume himself through poetry* in the same way that this demiurgic God eternally consumes Himself through his Creation. But because he is human, the poet cannot do this. Invoking Lewis Carroll's Alice, the *Imaginary Elegies* ends as follows:

Po-etery. Po-etery. The eaxtra slyllables in unimportant.
        because the poem said Drink Me. I'll find a substitute
For all your long –
Ing.
And that little door with all those wheels in it
Be –
       leave in it
Like God. (232)

The puns and visual hijinks cannot hide Spicer's gnostic dread. Like Alice, the obedient poet follows the demiurgic command to "Drink Me," goes through the little door, and finds himself in the Garden in Wonderland—

which is to say, he commences to write poetry. But writing poetry, or "po-etery," is a form of cannibalism, and unfortunately, the poet's limited cre-ation is not God's; it cannot be infinitely consumed.[9] Caught in a double bind, the poet wishes to "Be – / Leave" in God, to simultaneously hold to Him and depart from Him. Either way, He is inescapable. As John Vincent notes, "This poem ends in a knot that cannot be untied" (164).[10]

Spicer completed the *Elegies* in 1959; by then, he had also written *Fifteen False Propositions against God* (1958), an ironic celebration of the "joyful mys-teries" of the Christian godhead, in which the poet's idealistic devotion to beauty ("'Beauty is so rare a thing', Pound sings / 'So few drink at my foun-tain'"), to God, and to his human lover are all seen as equally impossible:

> Dear Sir:
> In these poems I tried to find the three-headed God I believed in
>   sometimes both when talking with you and living with you.
>   The abysmal toyshop
> Intrudes. (*My Vocabulary* 202)[11]

"The abysmal toyshop" produces "Millions of meaningless toys"; they are the toys we build while waiting for the Christ Child to appear, the toys we would give to Him when we come to adore Him. Yet "No one / Knows how to play with them," which is why there is no point in making them. "Kneel / At his birth / Meaningless / As he is," commands the poet; "They are not his toys or our toys we must play with. They are / Our toys" (200). Christ is "meaningless" *to us*; that is, he is beyond both our comprehension and our ability to reach him, and any effort we make in this regard is tantamount to playing with toys.

Here, I am reminded of the Calvinist distinction between a Covenant of Works and a Covenant of Grace, a distinction that accords with Spicer's Puritan view of our general culpability and depravity. Since the Fall, and Adam's failure to adhere to the original Covenant of Works, only the Cov-enant of Grace has obtained: though we, like Adam, are still called upon to love God and to obey his Law, no human works can lead us to salvation, but only the extension of divine grace. Yet misguided humanity still persists in believing that what it does makes any difference to a God who has predeter-mined its spiritual condition, both here and hereafter.[12] In the *Fifteen False Propositions*, Spicer describes "The joy that descends on you when all the

trees are cut down and all the fountains polluted and you are still alive wait-
ing for an absent savior" (201). Here, he is already very close to the religious
perspective articulated in the later works, including his masterpiece, *The
Heads of the Town up to the Aether*, and the intermittently brilliant *Language*
and *Book of Magazine Verse*.

Spicer's concern with the notion of grace is to be understood in these
books as twofold: both as a serious religious doctrine, and as a complex
metaphor for poetry and the descent of poetic inspiration. Like grace, po-
etry is extended to us from above, coming down from Mars, or Heaven:
hence in the *Book of Magazine Verse*, we read of "Love / For God or man
transformed to distance. / This is the third heresy. Dante / Was the first
writer of science fiction. Beatrice / Shimmering in infinite space" (411).
Faced with that impossible distance, the poet becomes a writer of "science
fiction," positing a figure that can somehow bridge the gap, telling the poet
what he needs to hear. As Ross Feld notes, "especially in these later books,
Spicer is convinced that what poets ought to report is only what God al-
ready knows. And that what God only ought to hear is something other than
a poetry, other than the fervid vehemence of an art-making person. It's the
kind of nominalism that eventually leads to speechlessness, unwordedness"
("Apostle's Grudge" 189). Or as Spicer affirms at the end of *The Holy Grail*,
"Something in God-language. In spite of all this horseshit, this uncomfort-
able music" (*My Vocabulary* 358). Increasingly weary of the "horseshit" of
mere poetry, Spicer also becomes increasingly troubled and exhausted by
the "God-language," an uncomfortable music to say the least. The degree
of threat it holds in the later works is matched by the weariness of the poet
and the perverse pleasure he takes in being what he describes in the painful
and magnificent "Sporting Life" as "a counterpunching radio." Spicer ends
the poem with a sort of exhausted masochism: "And those messages (God
would not damn them) do not even know they are champions" (374). Why
would God not damn the messages that beat up the poet in that poem? Be-
cause, like a battered Old Testament prophet, Spicer believes that they come
from God Himself.

Or at least he would like to believe it. "Is spirituality, then," asks Geof-
frey Hartman, "linked to the sense of the individual as such being found, or
found out? That those affected feel directly called or addressed is probably
more important than recognizing whose voice it is or the exact content of

the call. A sudden, mysterious utterance outflanks the resistance to being identified or known too well" ("Text and Spirit" 196). In Spicer, the messages always manage to find and identify the recipient, but the recipient in turn can never be sure of the source of the utterance he hears. It is a kind of grace that could leave the elect longing for damnation: "If this is dictation," he writes near the very end, "it is driving / Me wild" (*My Vocabulary* 423).

:::

Spicer's notorious crankiness, the sheer frustration he increasingly displays at the failings not merely of readers or of fellow poets, but of the poetic medium itself, comes closest to a still point in *The Heads of the Town Up to the Aether*, particularly in its last section, its *Paradiso, A Textbook of Poetry*. Feld, who calls *Heads of the Town* "this daring and disturbing and least lovable of American masterpieces" ("Lowghost to Lowghost" 447), argues that Spicer's "scorn for the 'big lie of the personal' has by this time been thaumaturged and become sublimely beside the point. If there's any triunity about this book, it is in the stripped-down annexing of poetry, poetry, and poetry—divined, discovered, and defined—and nothing else" (442). By some thaumaturgy, or miracle working, poetry has for once been "annexed" to Spicer's obsessive concern with "triunity," the mystery at the heart of his idiosyncratic Christian vision. In other words, nowhere else in the poet's opus do we find such a seamless discursive fabric, such an instance of poetry so completely connected to Spicer's rebarbative theological sensibility. For Duncan, Spicer "was puritan in his ethos of the poem and hostile to the 'poetic', the charm or luxury of the poem. Increasingly his work would take on an apotropaic magic against the seduction of words" ("Preface" xiii–xiv). Is the *Textbook* a miraculous exception to the "apotropaic magic" or its clearest representation? Is this encounter with the Word a sign that he need no longer fear "the seduction of words" (that is, the Beautiful), or is it in itself the most subtle of seductions?

Part of the problem in reading the *Textbook* lies simply in the fact that, like *A Fake Novel about the Life of Arthur Rimbaud*, which precedes it, it is written in prose. This in itself would appear to indicate that Spicer is placing it apart, distinguishing it, from its subject. It is *about* poetry but refuses to partake of it, because, as is amply clear throughout, it does indeed seem to hold poetry under the most severe suspicion. According to Peter Riley,

"Spicer played out verse to its own absurdity in 'Homage to Creeley' (the upper text of the first part of *Heads*) and thereafter abandoned it, needing the textures of prose to create the book's tension of detachment and immersion" (164). Likewise, Feld observes that "after this book, Spicer did not again use prose, as if satisfied that it had laid a strong enough foundation for his kind of poem, the one that's come to a profound peace with being 'the noises alive people wear' and nothing more" ("Lowghost to Lowghost" 447).[13] I'm not so sure that Spicer's kind of poem ever comes near such a profound peace, but the tone of the writing in the *Textbook* has an unprecedented confidence and ease to it, a sense, if you will, of *grace*—"To magic the whole thing toward what they called God" (*My Vocabulary* 306).[14]

Yet Spicer's unshakable Puritanism is such that even under what he may feel to be some dispensation, and regardless of the form, putting words in the service of the Word is still a risky, if not futile business. This is why "the poet thinks continually of strategies, of how he can win out against the poem" (301). The poem, made out of words, corresponds to the real, a lesson Spicer first learns in *After Lorca*. But by the time he writes *Heads of the Town*, Spicer has grown disenchanted with the real, the fallen world full of "mortal creature[s]" (as he says in *Homage to Creeley*) who make "Mistakes" every time they speak, since language is as debased as those who make use of it. In our search for God, however, all we have is language. Furthermore, we know, as John Vincent observes in his reading of section 17 of the *Textbook*, that only the "magical materialization of a divine love object is the sign of a lyric's success" (167). Hence the remarkable series of statements that constitute section 8:

> Descends to the real. By a rope ladder. The soul also goes there. Solely—not love, beyond the thought of God.
> I mean the thought of thinking about God. Naturally. I mean the real God.
> Disregards all other images as you disregard the parts of words in a poem. The Logos, crying to be healed from his godhead. His dismay.
> Disappears within the flatiron of existence. That smoothes out all the words in the poem. Imparts them. Makes them real like the next day.
> And as the words heal, I did not mean the real God. (*My Vocabulary* 302)

The self-deconstructing sleight-of-hand that Spicer first teaches himself in *A Book of Music* is fully operative here. At first, the soul's ineluctable "thought of thinking about God" involves an impossible distance, a distance that only God can traverse by means of a rope ladder, a conjuror's trick ("The Indian rope trick" of section 10) that nevertheless comes into being because of "The Logos, crying to be healed from his godhead." Above and beyond the real, or existence, the Logos is also above and beyond any image, just as the truth of a poem is above and beyond its words. Yet, miraculously, the Logos enters existence, disappears into the real. Existence smoothes out God as it "smoothes out all the words in the poem," imparts fixed meaning both to God and to the words, makes them real and predictable. Words about God, like words in a poem, have the power to "heal"; they are a consolation in the face of the unknowable. But as Spicer's deconstructive flourish indicates, as soon as the words are articulated, it is no longer "the real God."

Spicer's concern for "the real God" points to the gnosticism at work throughout *The Heads of the Town*, especially the *Textbook*. At the heart of the Gnostic religion is the question of the "real God"—who He is, where He resides, and how He may be *known*. Blaser tells us that Spicer borrowed the title *The Heads of the Town up to the Aether* from that of a work of the Peratae, a gnostic sect, about which he read in *The Secret Books of the Egyptian Gnostics*, by Jean Doresse (322–23).[15] According to Blaser, "The words found or discovered in a book are one level of a dictation. Here they rang a bell, though there is no systematic relation in Jack's poem to what we know about the contents of that mysterious book. However, the source and the title open for us Jack's concern with the extremity of thought common to all gnosticism, an opposition of light and dark and extensions of these in metaphor and experience" (323).

But a sustained look at Doresse indicates that there may be more of a "systematic relation" of the Peratae to *The Heads of the Town*, and especially the *Textbook*, than Blaser believes. Doresse notes that according to the Peratae,

> the universe is composed of the Father, the Son and of Matter. Each of these three principles possesses within itself an infinity of powers. Between Matter and the Father resides the Son—Word and Spirit—a median principle always in movement, either towards the immobile Father or towards Matter, which is moved. Sometimes it turns towards the Father and, in its own person, takes on his powers; sometimes, having taken these powers, it returns towards Matter: and Matter, being without form or quality, receives from the Son the imprint of the forms of which the Son himself has received the imprints from the Father. (50–51)

Thus the Son—the Word or Logos—is capable of moving down into Matter (becoming "the Lowghost when he is pinned down to words" [Spicer, *My Vocabulary* 308]) or up toward the inexpressible truth of the Father. This movement is seen throughout the *Textbook*: it is what Spicer calls in section 5 "The motion of the afterlife. The afterlife of the poem," the result of "An argument between the dead and the living" (301). In the *Textbook*, it is the Son, the Word, moving between Heaven and Earth, God and humanity, death and life, who is the focus of this argument.

The Word longs to be put into words, just as God longs to be put on flesh and enter the realm of human experience. But what is the truth of that Incarnation, whether in poetry or in religious belief? Regarding words and the Word, Spicer tells us that "It is up to us to astonish them and Him. To draw forth answers deep from the caverns of objects or from the Word Himself. Whatever that is" (308). Furthermore, "Whatever That is is not a play on words but a play between words, meaning come down to hang on a little cross for a while. In play." Here, Spicer may allude to various gnostic Christian beliefs that Jesus was a purely spiritual being who therefore could not experience crucifixion and death; hence Christ, or "Whatever That is" hanging on a little cross does so in play.[16] This "play," of course, is utterly serious, yet it is also play in the sense of the useless toys we have observed in the *Fifteen False Propositions*. Also, as the linguist Spicer realizes (without having read deconstructive theory), language is always "in play," an endless chain of signifiers, none of which are able to capture the transcendental signified. The poet is called upon to "astonish" the Word, but all he has is the inadequacy of words. "Where we are is in a sentence" (305) declares Spicer, and the pathos of that statement, like the earlier command in the *Imaginary Elegies* to "Be like God," remains to be acknowledged. Furthermore, as Spicer is always quick to point out, "The poet wants to take up all the marbles and put them in his pocket. Wants marbles. Where the poem is like winning the game" (310). No wonder then that the Logos becomes "the Lowghost when he is pinned down to words" (308).

:::

The Heads of the Town, culminating in the *Textbook*, takes the metapoetic and religious dimensions of Spicer's work as far as they can go. The poet's growing distrust of his medium, codified in the *Textbook*, will paradoxically spur him to the extraordinary inventions of *The Holy Grail, Language,* and *Book of Magazine Verse,* but his understanding that "The real poetry is beyond us" (313) can never be put aside or unlearned. In this respect, "real poetry" is like the Logos Himself, beyond and unknowable, except perhaps through gnosis or election. Thus Spicer's poetry despairs of itself because of its inescapably verbal condition. To use Duncan's terms again, a poetry premised on apotropaic magic, aimed at defending against the seduction of words, ultimately leads not to a chastened language (as is the case with Objectivism, which, through Williams, influenced Spicer early on) but to a total distrust of words, a Grand Refusal of poetry as an expression of the irredeemably fallen human order. Just as individual poems unmake themselves and shut themselves down, so too do whole books, and ultimately the project of the poetry itself. Arguably, the entire trajectory of Spicer's work leads to this conclusion, for the nature of his religious thought renders the consolations of poetry too easy and its defamiliarizations never unsettling enough. "The dark forest of words lets in some light from its branches," he tells us at the end of *Language;* "Mocking them, the deep leaves / That time leaves us / Words, loves" (402). The pronouns and syntax are obscure (unfortunately, Spicer gets increasingly sloppy about such matters, but then, given his point of view, verbal precision is both impossible and beside the point). Nevertheless, we get the gist of these lines: just as the Logos becomes the Lowghost, the light coming down through the word forest mockingly, punningly, "leaves" us only "Words, loves." The former are wholly inadequate; the latter, directed toward God (who else is worthy?), are always bound to fall short.[17]

But can devotion to God remain utterly wordless? And if language is a gift of the Word, are we not obliged to make use of it? *"Give me Christ, I seeke not for graces, but for Christ, I seeke not for promises, but for Christ, I seeke not for sanctification, but for Christ, tell me not of meditation and duties, but tell me of Christ"* (Caldwell 349). Thus said Anne Hutchinson in the midst of the Antinomian Controversy, and to me, Spicer increasingly appears as a spiritual or poetic descendant of Hutchinson, at least as antinomian as Emily Dickinson or, in our time, Susan Howe.

Here I have recourse to an essay rightly praised by Howe (*Birth-mark* ix–x), Patricia Caldwell's "The Antinomian Language Controversy." Caldwell's meticulous analysis of Anne Hutchinson's attitude toward language as demonstrated during her trial bears an uncanny resemblance to Spicer's view of language in his later work. In general, the Puritans "were deeply convinced of the reliability of language" (358), but in Hutchinson's case, "merely human language is not to be trusted" (348). Far and away the most extreme adherent to the Covenant of Grace and to the idea that the Holy Spirit resides irrefutably in a justified individual, Hutchinson holds all forms of verbal expression (including scriptural interpretation) under suspicion because for her and her followers, "everything fades before the inexpressible and everything human is annihilated before the divine" (351). In particular, Caldwell notes that Hutchinson's testimony is marked "by her tendency to separate words from their referents" (353)—or as Spicer would have it, "words / Turn mysteriously against those who use them" (*My Vocabulary* 257). Caldwell elaborates: "Distancing herself from her own words and from her hearers, she conveys a sense that verbal expressions are independent objects which may be acted upon and which are not inevitably 'connected' to the will although they may be aligned with it. Words are part of what one has, not part of what one is. They can be set askew, can change or disintegrate, because fundamentally they *are* things, while the ground or object—the thought or conception or insight itself—is, like that other Object [Christ], fixed and immutable" (356).

Obviously this is not the ground on which one might wish to build a poetic, or, as Hutchinson tragically learned, a theology either. Yet the idea that "verbal expressions are independent objects," that words "are part of what one has," sounds remarkably like Spicer in the first Vancouver Lecture (which he presented along with a reading of *A Textbook of Poetry*). There, he speaks of language as a set of building blocks that the "Martians" arrange into a poem (though the blocks "are always resisting it"), or as "part of the furniture in the room" (*House That Jack Built* 8–9). Indeed, as he declares in the course of the discussion, "words are things which just happen to be in your head instead of someone else's head" (29). Dictation, then, is in some respects quite a pragmatic affair: because the words, or things in one's head, are bound to be arranged with at best partial success, it could even be true that "an uneducated person often can write a better poem than an educated person, simply because there are only so many building blocks, so many ways of arranging them, and after that, you're through. . . . And sometimes for great poetry, an infinitely small vocabulary is what you want. Perhaps that would be the ideal, except for the fact that it's pretty hard to write a poem that way" (8).[18] The ideal poem, therefore, can never be written, and it is only a matter of grace—and not of works—that a true poem comes to us in the first place.

"Poetry unsettles our scrawled defense," writes Howe, sounding *almost* as antinomian as Hutchinson or Spicer; "unapprehensible but dear nevertheless" (*Birth-mark* 2). The subterranean tradition of antinomianism in America consists of "isolate voices devoted to writing as a physical event of immediate revelation" (1). In *The Birth-mark*, Howe casts a wide net in her use of the term "antinomian." She relates it as much to her own modern historical and textual materialist reading of power relations as to the earlier American revelation—unmediated, enthusiastic, and individualistic—of writers and prophetic figures who stand apart from social consensus and religious authority. Then again, given the nature of the original Antinomian Controversy, with Hutchinson's defiance of the patriarchal Puritan theocracy, such a range of definitions may be unavoidable.[19] In any case, for Howe, like Dickinson before her, poetry remains "dear" despite being "unapprehensible" because poetry is the privileged, indeed, the revealed site of spiritual as well as social struggle. Howe and Dickinson maintain a faith in language, and a faith in their own inspired (that is, dictated) use of words, a faith that Spicer, by contrast, slowly but surely loses.

Howe makes this distinction fairly clear in an interview with Edward Foster, in which Foster engages Howe on the subject of Spicer and dictation. Although Howe says "I do believe that Spicer radio-dictation thing," she also argues that "the outside is also a space-time phenomenon. I think the outside, or East Mars, partly consists of other people's struggles and their voices. Sounds and spirits (ghosts if you like) leave traces in a geography" (*Birth-mark* 156). Indeed, this is a position that Spicer probably would not accept. Unlike Howe, his antinomianism does not lead to historical investigation; rather, it drives a continually greater wedge between language and faith, poetry and belief. In the midst of *Language*, his most wildly heterogeneous book, he tells us that

> ... dream is not enough. We waking hear the call of the
> In-
> Visible world

Not seen. Hinted at only. By some vorpals, some sea-lions, some scraggs.
Almost too big to get used to, its dimensions amaze us, who are blind to
Whatever
Is rising and falling with us. (*My Vocabulary* 380)

By the time Spicer writes this, he surely hears the call of the invisible world
in waking life, but the hints it offers come to the aid of neither his poetry
nor his belief. "Vorpals" is a nonce word that Spicer borrows from Lewis
Carroll's "Jabberwocky": "He took his vorpal sword in hand." An adjective,
the word seems to mean, as the *OED* puts it, "keen, deadly," and I think
Spicer too intends that meaning when he turns the word into a plural noun.
Vorpals (and for that matter, scraggs as well) seem to be deadly in the way
they hint at the immensity of the Unseen, which Spicer further suggests is
like a *sea*, "rising and falling with us"—hence the sea lions, grouped with
the vorpals and scraggs. The poet's vision of the Unseen, the invisible world,
is simply incommensurate with our normative sense of being, our waking
life. And yet the Unseen is always with us, however blind we might be. Thus,
Spicer writes in the *Book of Magazine Verse* of

> . . . Accepting divinity as Jesus accepted
>> humanness. Grudgingly, without passion, but the most
>> important point to see in the world.
> We do not believe this. God is palpably untrue. Things
>> spreading over the universe like lessons.
> But Jesus dies and comes back again with holes in his hands.
>> Like the weather.
> And is, I hope, to be reached, and is something to pray to
> And is the Son of God. (412)

Duncan comments that "the sentence 'God is palpably untrue' might be read
at first take to mean that the proposition of God is false; but the statement
remains that God is Himself untrue, as a lover is untrue. He is untrue to us
who are His creatures as a poet is untrue to his poems, untrue in love. Then
there follows [in the lines quoted above] what I can barely keep at the level of
belonging to the poem but it breaches that understanding and sounds like a
confession of a rueful faith" ("Preface" xxiii). If Spicer were only able to rest
in that "rueful faith," suffering an untrue God and proving equally untrue to
his poems, then he may have been able to continue writing imperfect poetry

as long as his precarious health permitted him. But the pervasiveness, the ubiquity of a paradoxically unreachable, alien God—a God that like a sea, or like the weather, is all around us—turns out to be unacceptable. In the end, Spicer's Calvinism grows monstrous and inescapable:

> Mechanicly we move
> In God's Universe, Unable to do
> Without the grace or hatred of Him.
> The center of being. Like almost, without grace, a computer
>   center. Without His hatred
> A barren world. (*My Vocabulary* 413)

We have returned to the God of the *Imaginary Elegies*, a God Whose light and darkness, grace and hatred, are equally intolerable in the fallen world. When last seen in Spicer's poetry, He is the "big white baseball that has nothing to do but go in a curve or a straight line." As the poet tells us,

> ... Off seasons
> I often thought of praying to him but could not stand the thought of that big, white,
>   round, omnipotent bastard.
> Yet he's there. As the game follows rules he makes them.
> I know
> I was not the only one who felt these things. (416)

Spicer's insistence on his election, the feeling he shares with his fellow saints of "that big, white, round, omnipotent bastard" bearing down upon him, remains a source of both humor and terror to the end. In this sublimely imperfect poem, they are a measure of the distance that ball must travel.

4

Susan Howe

Is a poetics of intervening absence an oxymoron? (Howe, *Birth-mark* 27)

In the preceding chapter, I suggest that the tradition of antinomianism as it has passed from American religion into American poetry takes two different directions in the work of Jack Spicer and then in the work of Susan Howe. Spicer is the more extreme: no form of authority, no authority of form, can successfully mediate between the poet and a God who is both a totally inaccessible source of meaning and a capricious correspondent, a sender of messages that the poet can neither translate nor convey to an increasingly indifferent audience. Howe negotiates this spiritual distance somewhat differently. Rather than assume Spicer's abject posture (thinly disguised by his biting sense of humor), Howe declares that "In the machinery of Injustice / my whole being is Vision" (*Singularities* 49). At its most radical, Howe's stance is that of prophetic defiance; following in the matriarchal line of Anne Hutchinson and Emily Dickinson, her struggle is less with God per se than with patriarchal forms of social, religious, and scholarly authority. This struggle manifests itself in her obsession with history, an obsession that Spicer for the most part lacks. Frequently, the site of the struggle is the archive, where conflicting ideologies are expressed both *in* texts, often antique and obscure, and *as* texts, born again into new poems from the suppressions and detritus of the past.[1] "If antinomian vision in North America is gendered feminine," asks Howe, "then what will save it from print misfortune?" (*Birth-mark* 4).

In Howe's work, "print misfortune," the stultifying literary and editorial conventions, the patriarchal authority of normative print culture, may be circumvented not only through antinomianism (or what Stephen Collis calls Howe's "anarcho-scholasticism") but specifically through textual practices intended, as Howe famously puts it, to "tenderly lift from the dark side of history, voices that are anonymous, slighted—inarticulate" (*Europe of Trusts* 14). Helping these anonymous, slighted voices to articulate themselves involves, in effect, communication with the spirit world. Howe's poetry is haunted by ghosts and spirits seeking expression after having long been silenced. "And what is left when spirits have fled from holy places?" (*Singularities* 41) wonders the poet in the beginning of *Thorow*, one of her most prophetic works. The premise of much of Howe's poetry is that the spirits have fled or have been driven away; the *space* of the writing has been desanctified and must again be made, if not holy, then at least welcoming and open to the spirits' return. Howe's writing, therefore, becomes a latter-day version of spiritualism, and her poems may be read as ghostly textual enactments, literary equivalents of the spiritualist practice of the séance.

Few of Howe's commentators have considered this aspect of her work,[2] and though Howe herself refers frequently to ghosts, haunted houses, possession, and so forth, to my knowledge she never *explicitly* writes about séances. Nevertheless, the arrangement and construction of the poems, their defamiliarizing, disjunctive techniques, and their spatial and visual conception of the page, produce a theatrical, even ritualized style. Howe's early training was in acting and in the visual arts, her readings are highly performative, and she is steeped in the literature and cultural history of mid-nineteenth-century America, when the spiritualist movement was at its height. Most importantly, her relationship to history, to the idea that the past is a lost world and that the dead need to be rescued, all make the idea of the séance a tempting one for the analysis of her work.[3]

Traditionally, a séance is a carefully structured event intended to create a space, an environment in which the dead can manifest themselves, enter *materially* into the world of the living. The goal of the séance is communion between the present and the past, the living and the dead; it is a ritual designed to blur the boundary that orders time and nature, providing the participants with intimate psychic knowledge that is kept from them in the course of their daily lives. Through the person of the medium (usually a woman) who is capable of losing herself in a trance and opening herself to the spirit world, participants in the séance (they are not an audience in the

passive sense) attempt to construct meaning from the array of sounds, voic-
es, sensations, levitating objects, and visual materializations that present
themselves to the group. Despite the fact that, historically, the séances that
were investigated eventually proved to be hoaxes, con games that at worst
were intended to take advantage of gullible, often bereaved individuals, they
remain, nevertheless, gripping participatory performances, popular works
of art that could assume great psychic power. They have everything to do
with a society's practices of mourning and its search for consolation after
historical trauma. It is no accident that séances were popular in the United
States in the years after the Civil War, and in England during and following
World War I.

Throughout the nineteenth and early twentieth centuries in both coun-
tries, séances commanded huge and diverse followings. The "spirit rapping"
of the Fox sisters, which first began in 1848, set off a tremendous response to
spiritualist phenomena and beliefs. Given Howe's own roots and affinities,
which serve as focal points for many of her works, I find it suggestive that
American spiritualism "arose in western New York, which had for a genera-
tion experienced emotional religious revivalism and evangelical fervor. The
region was populated mainly by New Englanders, many of whom sought a
better world both here and hereafter, giving their ardent support to an amaz-
ing variety of religious and reform movements" (Isaacs 80). New England
enthusiasm—to use a crucial word in Howe's lexicon, which she relates di-
rectly to antinomianism[4]—was at the heart of this rapidly spreading move-
ment. Indeed, "by 1855 probably one million Americans—out of a popula-
tion of twenty-eight million—identified themselves with the new religion,
at least to the extent of giving credence to the phenomena and to the reality
of spiritual communication. Well-known, respectable converts—judges,
senators, scientists—proclaimed the new revelation" (95).

Furthermore, "spiritualism prided itself on its democratic appeal and
practice, emphasizing that a talent for communicating with the spirits was
the prerogative of all. It was also extremely catholic in its attitude toward
conventional religious belief. . . . It did not require faith in any orthodox
sense but equally did nothing to injure the concept of divine intervention"
(Owen 18–19). In other words, spiritualism appealed both to the masses and
to the intellectual elite, and while spiritualists were frequently condemned
by scientific and religious authorities, they themselves sought to combine

the scientific and supernatural perspectives of the entire spectrum of social classes and groups. Many spiritualists subscribed to the most progressive ideas of the nineteenth century. Andrew Jackson Davis, a prolific writer and lecturer who claimed that his first work, *The Principles of Nature, Her Divine Revelations, and A Voice to Mankind, by and through Andrew Jackson Davis, the "Poughkeepsie Seer" and "Clairvoyant"* (1847), was dictated to him from the spirit world, went on to argue "that to rid society of slavery, drunkenness, racial injustice, oppression, and war, it was necessary to reject the concept of sin and to insist that humans follow the harmonious principles of nature in order to reach the successively higher stages of development that were inherent in each individual" (Isaacs 81). Spiritualism in the United States tended toward a kind of enthusiastic liberalism, a passion for reform with which Howe continues to identify.

Yet there are darker forces at work as well. The closest Howe comes to discussing her writing in terms of a séance is in her interview with Lynn Keller:

> Q. Earlier in this interview and several times during your stay here you have said that as a poet you feel you're taking dictation. This would be at the opposite extreme from the biographical, I think—your sense that as a poet you act as a medium. Can you elaborate on that a little bit? When you talk about dictation, it's not that there are voices.
>
> A. No, no. I don't hear voices (though I'm always scared I might). You don't hear voices, but yes, you're hearing something. You're hearing something you see. And there's the mystery of the eye-hand connection: when it's your work, it's your hand writing. Your hand is receiving orders from somewhere. Yes, it could be your brain, your superego giving orders; on the other hand, they are orders. I guess it must seem strange that I say poetry is free when I also say I'm getting orders. It can become very frightening. That's what Melville's so good on in *Pierre* and *Moby-Dick* and elsewhere, that once you're driven onto this hunt, you can't stop until you're told to stop. It connects to blasphemy and to the sacred for me. It connects to God. (33)

In Howe's work, the visual and aural elements are equally important, which is why "you're hearing something you see." Indeed, the strangely "unreadable" print collages found in most of her poems could be viewed as ghostly materializations of dead voices, both from old books and historical personages, which partially reveal themselves through the "medium" of the text. Her reference to her "hand receiving orders from somewhere" also points to the poem as séance: spirit writing, taking written dictation from spirits guiding one's pen, was a specialty of many mediums and a favored mode of communication with the dead.[5]

But most importantly, Howe connects this frightening act of taking dictation—that is, of writing poetry—to God, who is in no respect a benign deity. The poetic "hunt" to which the poet is driven is related ambivalently to both blasphemy and to the sacred, since an antinomian sensibility involves a continuous wavering between the two.[6] In regard to Howe's antinomianism, Rachel Tzvia Back argues that "the antinomian writer, as I read her, is situated firmly *within* a tradition as much as she is in defiance of that tradition" (124). Therefore, any blasphemous act that violates a sacred order or tradition, any intervention or disturbance such as the prophetic hearing and articulation of poetry, of Howe's "getting orders" from the beyond, may be as sacred as the tradition that is violated. Indeed, the sacred may be understood as containing within itself the notion of blasphemy or transgression. At such moments—and they are ubiquitous in Howe's work—the poet approaches what René Girard calls "the two faces of the sacred—the interplay of order and disorder, of difference lost and retrieved" (*Violence* 257).

Girard's theory of sacrificial violence sheds a good deal of light on the historical episodes about which Howe writes. Rituals of ostracism, of scapegoating, of expulsion, and of the regicidal sacrifice of the god-king echo hauntingly in her poems. The fate of Hope Atherton after the Falls Fight and the banishment of Anne Hutchinson from the Massachusetts Bay Colony at the climax of the Antinomian Controversy (*Articulation of Sound Forms in Time* [1987]); the pamphlet wars following the decision of the Puritans to execute Charles I (*A Bibliography of the King's Book or, Eikon Basilike* [1989]); even, on a smaller scale, the marginalization of Clarence Mangan (*Melville's Marginalia* [1993]) and of Jonathan Swift's companion Stella (*The Liberties* [1983])—all are instances of social institutions engaged in organized acts of violence intended to secure authority and impose order over potentially disruptive individuals and circumstances. The conflicts at the heart of such events are both religious and judicial in nature, if one can even make such a distinction, given the nature of the societies in which they take place, such as that of the seventeenth-century Puritans. In her essay "Incloser," Howe asserts that "Anne Hutchinson was the community scapegoat" (*Birth-mark* 52), citing both Girard and Kenneth Burke in order to substantiate her argument.[7] Girard tends to focus on ancient or tribal social orders, but he also explains the religious and sacrificial underpinnings of more modern judicial systems. "*Religion* in its broadest sense," he writes, "must be another term for that obscurity that surrounds man's efforts to defend himself by curative or preventative means against his own violence. It is that enigmatic quality that pervades the judicial system when that system replaces sacrifice. This obscurity coincides with the transcendental effectiveness of a violence that is holy, legal, and legitimate successfully opposed to a violence that is unjust, illegal, and illegitimate" (*Violence* 23). Yet this duality is never stable; hence the recurrence throughout history of the *sacrificial crisis*, "the disappearance of the difference between impure violence and purifying violence. . . . The sacrificial crisis can be defined, therefore, as a crisis of distinctions—that is, a crisis affecting the cultural order. This cultural order is nothing more than a regulated system of distinctions in which the differences among individuals are used to establish their 'identity' and their mutual relationships" (49).

Howe's work engages such moments of sacrificial crisis, moments when violence breaks forth and the regulatory systems of society, of religious, legal, and civic authority, cannot contain it. At times, her awareness of the tenuousness and volatility of such systems can expressed personally, as in the autobiographical introduction to *The Europe of Trusts*, writing of her memories of the outbreak of World War II: "Our law-professor father, a man of pure principles, quickly included violence in his principles, put on a soldier suit and disappeared with the others into the thick of the threat to the east called West" (10).[8] In most of her texts, however, these moments are simultaneously experienced as both intimate and remote. The mediumistic form of the poem produces a theatrical distancing of time and space, while simultaneously opening itself to abrupt, jarring materializations of violence or the intrusion of strained, agonized voices. Howe's understanding of language accords perfectly with Girard's observation that "no matter how diligently language attempts to catch hold of it, the reality of the sacrificial crisis invariably slips through its grasp. It invites anecdotal history on the one hand, and on the other, a visitation of monsters and grotesques" (*Violence* 64). What is often labeled the "indeterminacy" of Howe's language, the free play of the signifier, is certainly palpable word for word, line for line, in her work. But on a deeper structural level, considering the poem in its totality, this indeterminacy does not apply to anywhere near the same extent.[9] Indeed, it could be argued that most of Howe's poems can be read as moving, often wildly, between the determinate Girardian poles of "anecdotal history" and monstrous, grotesque "visitation"—the latter term being especially appropriate when one thinks of the poem as séance.[10]

Frequently beginning with seemingly expository prose that presents personal, familial or historical anecdotes, and then moving to highly elliptical, fragmented, multivoiced lyric sequences and textual collages, Howe's poems of the last thirty years follow a ritualized pattern or order, as if they were the idiosyncratic religious services of a soul, like Dickinson's, that selects her own society. They form, in other words, sacred precincts or *enclosures*, hermetic, requiring initiation or election in order to be entered, while at the same time open for all to view. As Howe observes of her procedure at the beginning of her essay "Incloser" (and this observation applies to all her writing, since she continually assaults the boundary between essay and poem), "by choosing to install certain narratives somewhere between history, mystic speech, and poetry, I have enclosed them in an organization, although I know there are places no classificatory procedure can reach, where connections between words and things we thought existed break off" (*Birth-mark* 45). And yet she also insists that "a poem is an invocation, rebellious return to the blessedness of beginning again, wandering free in pure process of forgetting and finding"; that "a lyric poet hunts after some still unmutilated musical wild of Mind's world" (*My Emily Dickinson* 98, 105).

There is something powerfully, compellingly contradictory about Howe's understanding of poetic form, which may be observed in nearly all her major work. This is not to fault her: contradiction in poetic composition operates differently than in argumentative prose; in poetry, contradiction is *generative* of form, expressive of an otherwise inarticulate desire. Form itself, as Howe indicates in the quote from "Incloser" above, cannot come into being except through a process of enclosure, organization, and classification. But language, by its very nature, strains to escape these bounds in its desire to wander free. The poem is thus an enclosed space but also "the wild," a place of origin to which the poet would return. Like Robert Duncan, one of her most important modern precursors, Howe conceives of the poem as "a place of first permission" (*Opening of the Field* 7). But unlike Duncan's field or meadow ruled by the "Queen Under The Hill / whose hosts are a disturbance of words within words," a desired destination "that certain bounds hold against chaos" (7), Howe's space is an untamed, feminized forest that must be "taken" by the masculinized hunter-poet, as in "Taking the Forest," the third section of *Articulation of Sound Forms in Time*. More overtly threatening than Duncan's meadow, Howe's forest is a place where "Cries open to the words inside them / Cries hurled through the Woods" (*Singularities* 23).

Like Dickinson, ironically looking back on the bloody history of the American frontier in "My Life had stood – a Loaded Gun –," Howe, as antinomian, both (re)enacts and criticizes sacrificial and regenerative violence, making the poem a "nonconformist's memorial," both reverent and subversive. In *The Scapegoat*, shortly after the passage Howe quotes in "Incloser," Girard states that "beyond a certain threshold of belief, the effect of the scapegoat is to reverse the relationship between persecutors and their victims, thereby producing the sacred, the founding ancestors and the divinities" (44). Because of the constitution of the sacred as a violent series of reversals and substitutions, belief in Howe's poetry can never be stable. Entering her poems, we are suspended between the sacred and secular worlds. The sacred seems to be a living, palpable phenomenon to which we are subject; it is also an object we may scrutinize and comprehend through historical analysis. We stand apart from the violence of history, attending to loss and pain through the poem's theatrical materializations. But we are also inside those events, which is also to say they live inside us. They live again, because they have never truly died.

:::

Howe's *Bibliography of the King's Book or, Eikon Basilike* (1989) is one of the clearest examples of her poems-as-séance. In this work, the poet's task is "To write against the Ghost" (*Nonconformist's Memorial* 61)—though in doing so, she finds herself "MAKING THE GHOST WALK ABOUT AGAIN AND AGAIN" (47). These contradictory phrases (is the ghost to be laid to rest or brought back from the beyond?) indicate a larger pattern of contradictory ideas that constitute the sacred. Order and disorder, observance and transgression, lawful sacrifice and profane bloodshed—these are among the defining polarities that Howe reenacts through her writing, which presents itself as both scholarship ("bibliography") and ritual. Even the very phrase "To write against the Ghost" may be more ambiguous than it appears. As

Rachel Tzvia Back notes, the phrase "uses the preposition not in its standard sense of being 'in opposition to', but rather in the sense of being in close contact with . . . or having as a backdrop. . . . In all her writings, and in the *Eikon* in particular, Howe emphasizes this 'leaning against' the ghost of previous texts" (136). Haunted by previous texts, Howe attempts to commune with the past that they embody, but their fragmentary, palimpsestic appearance in her poem points to the violence that produced them, and that they continue to encode. The spirits with which the poet is in contact, such as the ghost of the executed Charles I, are both opposed and supported, represented and erased. The ghosts are what remain of sacrificial victims and of the perpetrators of sacrificial violence as well.[11]

In her detailed commentary on Howe's poem, Back observes that "visually and thematically, it is a tremendously *crowded* text—with words, ideas, and images vying for space on the page and in the book, abutting on and, at times, overtaking and obscuring each other" (128). Yet as Howe tells us at the end of the poem's introduction, "The absent center is the ghost of a king" (*Nonconformist's Memorial* 50). The absent center, not only of the poem, but of the events and texts from which the poem comes, paradoxically generates this *"crowded"* condition. The original absence is the result of the execution of Charles I, a great act of sacrificial violence at the center of one of the most momentous sociopolitical crises in English history. The subsequent publication of the *Eikon Basilike* in its numerous editions, of Milton's *Eikonoklastes*, and eventually, of Almack's *A Bibliography of the King's Book*, of Madan's *A New Bibliography of the Eikon Basilike*—all become part of the crowd of words, ideas, and images that constitute Howe's poem. Her antinomian or anarcho-scholastic sensibility reaches beyond the death of the king and the Puritan revolution, leading her to see historical and mythic parallels and crosscurrents unavailable to conventional archival and historiographical methods.

Functioning as a medium, Howe in effect channels the controversies and debates, the accusations and denials, the spilled blood and spilled ink, and finally, the centuries of chronicles and scholarly research. The poem restages an already highly theatrical chain of events. "I felt when I finished the poem that it was so unclear, so random," she says in her interview with Edward Foster, "that I was crossing into visual art in some sections and that I had unleashed a picture of violence I needed to explain to myself" (*Birth-*

mark 165). Like a medium emerging from her trance, the poet is confused by and cannot objectively understand the ghostly violence that has been "unleashed," made manifest in and through her work. Her "crossing into visual art" indicates how much the impact of the poem depends on the materialization of language, the apparently incomprehensible and therefore frightening appearances and multiple voicings of palimpsestic texts. The poem is a matter of sight and sound in equal measure, embodying and performing "the impossibility of putting into print what the mind really sees" (175). But what does the mind really see? Referring to Milton's involvement in the original controversy over the *Eikon Basilike*, Howe insists that "behind Milton's beautiful words borrowed from other traditions is a rage to destroy and tear down. He hoped *Eikonoklastes* would erase the *Eikon Basilike* or at least show it to be a forgery. But *Comus* is a masque and a theatrical performance also. An elaborate façade, a forgery. A poem is an icon" (177). And as Howe understands, especially in regard to King Charles, both in life and death "an icon is an image that is worshipped. It's a sacred image" (176).[12]

The poem, then, is a sacred image, an unveiling or revelation of the slain god-king, whose deconsecration by the Puritans and their chief apologist is also a reconsecration in a society splintered by the sacrificial crisis. As a séance, an elaborate communication with history as spirit-world, the poem presents itself as both a ritual and a scholarly reconstruction of ritual. As an act of documentation that is also a reanimating theatrical performance, it positions us inside and outside the original events, which continue to reverberate in texts lost and retrieved:

C * R and skull on covers
MADESTIE
More than Conqueror, &c.
King on the binding
1 blank leaf
The lip of truth
A lying tongue
Great Caesar's ghost
She is the blank page
writing ghost writing (*Nonconformist's Memorial* 68)

This passage is one of a number in Howe's *Bibliography* that condenses (or perhaps *encloses*) but also opens historical events via textual remnants or remains. The first line probably refers to the original *Eikon Basilike*, with Caroli Regis (King Charles) and the sign of his death on its cover. "MADESTIE" is one of the innumerable typographical deviations that appear throughout the poem, in both the textual collages and in the seemingly more conventional passages of verse. The word suggests "majestie" or "majesty," but also "modesty," indicating the humility and piety with which the king, seen as a martyr by the Royalists, went to his death. He was, in this respect, *"More than Conqueror, &c.,"* which is to say that in death his status changed, becoming not merely the ruler of an earthly state, but a saint, a sacrificial victim and type of Christ. But the next four lines destabilize this view of Charles. "King on the binding / 1 blank leaf" continues to refer to the original book *Eikon Basilike*. But it is almost as if the king is becoming the book dedicated to his memory; he is "bound" into the material text, yet also perhaps erased, disappearing into the blank leaf. "The lip of truth / A lying tongue" further calls the king's status into doubt. We are reminded of Milton's presentation of the king in *Eikonoklastes*, as quoted by Howe in her introduction: "a deep dissembler, not of his affections onely, but of religion" (48). Are the devout words attributed to Charles in the *Eikon Basilike* really his? Much of Howe's poem, like the history and scholarship that precedes it, hinges on the probability that the book is a forgery, actually written by Bishop John Gauden, who claimed authorship and after the Restoration "was advanced to the see of Worcester in recognition of this service to the Crown, because Lord Clarendon and Charles II believed him" (48). Whose is the lip of truth, whose the lying tongue? How successfully does Milton refute the *Eikon Basilike* in *Eikonoklastes*? How successfully does the scholarship in Francis A. Maden's *A New Bibliography of the Eikon Basilike of King Charles the First, with a Note on the Authorship* (1950) refute the research of Edward Almack's *A Bibliography of the King's Book; or, Eikon Basilike* (1896), the work that serves as a sort of template for Howe's poem? Who possesses, and is in turned possessed, by "Great Caesar's ghost"? As Howe makes quite clear later in her poem,

Dominant ideologies drift
Charles I who is "Caesar"

Restless Cromwell who is "Caesar"
Disembodied beyond language
in those copies are copies (80)

As "Dominant ideologies drift" and political power shifts between op-
posing parties, sovereignty (and the mark of sacrifice it always bears) like-
wise changes polarity. Charles and Cromwell are both regarded as "Caesar"
by their followers and eventually become "Great Caesar's ghost" insofar as
they are literally "disembodied." But just as importantly, they are "Disem-
bodied beyond language": who they are and what they stand for disintegrate
over time, as does the scholarship that attempts to track the historical events
through contemporary accounts and later records. Thus, "in those copies
are copies." Because of Howe's view of the indeterminacy of language, as
she writes in the introduction, "Only by going back to the pre-scriptive level
of thought process can 'authorial intention' finally be located, and then the
material object has become immaterial" (50).

But can the poet or scholar really go back "to the pre-scriptive level of
thought process"? To do so requires a *rematerialization* of the material ob-
ject, those dubious and conflicted texts through which Howe stages her
poem. Summoning the ghosts from the disputes of the past, Howe as me-
dium becomes as dubious a figure as the political activists, apologists, and
polemicists whom she invokes. She too, in other words, leads us to wonder
about "The lip of truth / A lying tongue," which of course is always the case
when one attends a séance. And Howe understands this: "She is the blank
page / writing ghost writing." A blank page, she paradoxically writes and is
written. According to Back, "the reader is to understand that this nondes-
ignated female pronoun—an amorphic 'writing[-]ghost' and she who does
'ghost[-]writing' both—is as much the 'absent center' of this poem as is 'the
ghost of a king'" (150). Back then connects this ghost-writing, ghost-written
female to a variety of historical and mythic figures who hover at the margins
or thread their way almost imperceptibly through the poem.[13] As is often
the case in Howe's work, marginalized or occluded women have access to
historical and spiritual counter-truths; their antinomian resistance to the
patriarchal rule of law transforms them into prophets and scapegoats. In
their victimage lies their power, and vice versa: "Throughout history / this is
the counter-plot" (*Nonconformist's Memorial* 66). These figures—and there

should be no doubt that Howe counts herself among them—constitute "The Foundation of hearsay / Horrifying drift errancy / A form and nearby form" (66). "Hearsay" is rumor, uncertain whispers that may or may not be true. In these lines, however, it is difficult not to also misread "hearsay" as "heresy," which from the perspective of authority is always "Horrifying drift errancy." To engage in errancy is to err, to be mistaken, but also to wander, as does a spirit that seeks to impart a lost or suppressed truth. Every custom, rule, law, or set form attracts a "nearby form," an errant ghost of itself, its spiritual double. According to Girard, in traditional societies structured by the idea of the sacred, doubles are perceived as monstrous and must be ritually destroyed. Such monsters often take the form of malignant spirits. As Girard explains,

> The subject feels that the most intimate regions of his being have been invaded by a supernatural creature who also besieges him without. Horrified, he finds himself the victim of a double assault to which he cannot respond. Indeed, how can one defend oneself against an enemy who blithely ignores all barriers between inside and outside? This extraordinary freedom of movement permits the god—or spirit or demon—to seize souls at will. The condition called "possession" is in fact but one particular manifestation of the monstrous double. (*Violence* 165)

All forms of authority are potentially haunted in this fashion, and the shaman, prophet, cult leader or poet who would open herself to the whispered hearsay/heresy of the counterplot always runs the risk of psychic, if not actual, violence. Ritual possession and violence are part of a single phenomenon: "Ritual possession seems inseparable at first from the sacrificial rites that serve as its culmination" (*Violence* 166). Thus, in a passage that also alludes to the execution of King Charles, Howe tells us that "To walk side by side with / this chapter was Tumult // sacrosanct veils liturgies" (*Nonconformist's Memorial* 72). Walking side by side with—becoming the double of—the lingering spirits around this chapter in history is to experience "Tumult," defined by the OED as "commotion of a multitude, usually with confused speech or uproar; public disturbance; disorderly or riotous proceeding." What results is an experience of "sacrosanct veils liturgies," supposedly sacred, inviolable barriers that both hide and reveal. Through these veils the spirits freely move, between the past and the present, inside and outside the possessed subject. "[L]iturgies,"—public prayer services or rituals of devotion, including the sacrificial mass—may or may not placate the spirits. In effect, Howe's poem in itself, the séance she conducts, must become the ritual that both reenacts and hopefully exorcizes the possessing ghosts.

"Regicide," Howe tells Edward Foster. "I love that word. It's of the devil's party. Kings and crosses, blasphemy, and homicide are all packed into it. This was the killing of the king, and the king was holy" (*Birth-mark* 175). Howe loves the word as she loves her vocation, for regicide and all that it represents is fundamental to her calling as a poet. It is the quintessential act of sacrificial violence, which the poet-medium channels. In *The Marriage of Heaven and Hell*, Blake declares that "the reason Milton wrote in fetters when he wrote of Angels & God, and at liberty when of Devils & Hell, is because he was a true Poet and of the Devils party without knowing it" (35). No doubt Howe, like Blake before her, believes that all true poets are of the Devil's party, and must engage in blasphemy in order to write their poems. The antinomian *gnosis* for which she seeks, through the wilds of linguistic form and through centuries of archived texts, carries a price, as does her idealistic and explicitly redemptive notion that "Poetry shelters other voices" (*Birth-mark* 47). Unlike Milton, who was nearly executed for his participation in the Puritan regime; unlike Blake, who was mocked by literary authorities and harassed by the state; unlike Anne Hutchinson, who was silenced by the Puritan elders and exiled, leading to her death; and unlike Dickinson, who chose obscurity rather than compromise her "White Election"—Howe enjoys a serious (if occasionally baffled) readership, with defenders and explicators ready to leap into the poetic fray on her behalf. Be that as it may, at the heart of her work is a vision of sacred violence that may trouble even her most sympathetic readers, and it is no accident that one of her most obscure poems is called *Scattering as Behavior toward Risk*, a title I take to be emblematic of her work in its entirety. The "scattering" of form for which she is famous is indeed a risky behavior. It is no accident that the title page of that poem is marked with an antique image of a coffin.

Near the end of *A Bibliography of the King's Book* are the following lines:

Who is not a wild Enthusiast

in a green meadow

furious and fell

Arriving on the stage of history

I saw madness of the world

Stripped of falsification
and corruption

anthems were singing
in Authorem

Father and the Father
by my words will I be justified

Autobiography I saw

Legal righteousness makes us servants
All good hearers

Opposers or despisers
Night page torn word missing

The family silence
gave up the ghost (*Nonconformist's Memorial* 74)

As we have observed, for Howe an antinomian is an enthusiast, and a true poet must be something of both. Peter Nicholls interprets Howe's trope of enthusiasm as "the force of desire which unsettled the 'wilderness' of language, ungrounding legalism and its eschatology" (591–92), and that is certainly what takes place here. Stepping well beyond the ghostly controversy surrounding the execution of King Charles, Howe gives us a highly elliptical myth of the poet's origin, a psychic "autobiography," the inscription of a life she both witnesses (reads) and personally experiences (writes).

From a state of Blakean innocence ("a green meadow"), the poet falls into the violent "stage of history" and beholds the world's "madness." She is "furious," less in the sense of angry than mad, suffering from a divine fury or inspiration. "Fell" functions crucially as both the past participle of "fall" (and "fell / Arriving on the stage of history") but also as an adjective, meaning deadly and, again, furious or mad. In other words, the mad or inspired poet sees and gives voice to the madness of the fallen world. She alone is "Stripped of falsification / and corruption" and hears (or sings) "anthems . . . in Authorem." "Authorem" would appear to be a nonce word, resembling both "author" and "authority," and related in turn to "the Father." The parataxis of these lines resists a determinate interpretation, but it would seem that the poet is asserting her own authority ("by my words will I be justified") against that of patriarchal law. This then is indeed her "autobiography." "Legal righteousness" may have at first made her one of the "servants," but forced servitude also makes "good hearers // Opposers or despisers." Despite the "Night page torn word missing"—the lost or suppressed story of marginalization and resistance—"The family silence / gave up the ghost." Howe, the poet-medium, brings back the ghost, assuming the visionary power necessary to break the "family silence." The silence dies ("[gives] up the ghost") but does so by literally "[giving] up the ghost" to the poet, who makes the history of violence palpable. "I feared the fall of my child" she then declares; "resting quietly with some hopes // as a bird before any" (*Nonconformist's Memorial* 74). Will the family silence be recapitulated, so that the poet's innocent, birdlike "child" will "fall" as she did? This remains an open question. Back reads the last pages of the poem, including its final collage texts, as a further reassertion of the mythic and historical powers of the feminine and the antinomian, including the powers of the poet, in their opposition to patriarchal law. And to be sure, Howe strongly affirms her "Election–Vocation– / Justification–" (*Nonconformist's Memorial* 75). But election and vocation always mean terrible risk, for the poet is never fully in control of the spirits with whom she traffics.

This, I believe, is the significance of the two quotations from *David Copperfield* near the end of Howe's *Bibliography*, which, as a true stroke of genius, serve as a comic satyrs' play after the sublime terror of the sacrificial tragedy. The quotes come from chapter 14 of Dickens's novel, in which David, now living with his aunt Betsy Trotwood, meets Richard Babley, known as Mr. Dick, who also lives with Aunt Betsy. Aunt Betsy has rescued Mr. Dick, who is "a little eccentric," from the insane asylum, when he was about to be confined by his brother. Mr. Dick is obsessed with the beheading of King Charles I. As he says to the young David in the passage Howe quotes, "if it was so long ago, how could the people about him have made that mistake of putting some of the trouble out of *his* head, after it was taken off, into *mine*?" (*Nonconformist's Memorial* 77). The sorrow and injustice that Mr. Dick has faced have driven him insane, and his obsession with King Charles is explained by Aunt Betsy as "his allegorical way of expressing it. He connects his illness with great disturbance and agitation, naturally, and that's the figure, or the simile, or whatever it's called, which he chooses to use. And why shouldn't he, if he thinks proper!" Mr. Dick has made a kite, which he and David eventually spend time flying; the kite "was covered with manuscript, very closely and laboriously written; but so plainly, that as I looked along the lines, I thought I saw some allusion to King Charles the First's head again, in one or two places" (*Nonconformist's Memorial* 81). As Mr. Dick says of his kite, "when it flies high, it takes the facts a long way. That's my manner of diffusing 'em. I don't know where they may come down. It's according to circumstances, and the wind, and so forth; but I take my chance of that" (81).

As Aunt Betsy would say, this is Howe's own "allegorical way of expressing it." Like Mr. Dick, the trouble in King Charles's head has moved into her own, and like Mr. Dick's kite, Howe's poem flies high and takes the facts a long way, for that is her manner of diffusing them. It too is covered with manuscript, layer upon layer, text upon text. And like David Copperfield, the reader of Howe's *Bibliography* is both witness to and participant in this frightening "eccentricity."

:::

The séance or ritual invocation of the dead is the means by which Howe achieves what Spicer would call a poetry of dictation, but at the same time, it also permits a high degree of agency on the part of a poet who remains determined to recuperate lost or repressed historical narratives. In *Thorow* (1990) the poet initially contemplates the flight of "spirits from holy places" while in the town, "or what is left of a town," of Lake George, New York: "two Laundromats, the inevitable McDonald's, a Howard Johnson, assorted discount leather outlets, video arcades, a miniature golf course, two run-down amusement parks, a fake fort where a real one once stood, a Dairy-Mart, a Donut-land, and a four-star Ramada Inn built over an ancient Indian burial ground" (*Singularities* 41). The spirits have fled because the holy place has been repeatedly profaned; indeed, as Howe goes on to observe, in the seventeenth century "pathfinding believers in God and grammar spelled the lake into *place*. They have renamed it several times since." Standing "on the shores of a history of the world where forms of wildness brought up by memory become desire and multiply," Howe enters "unknown regions of indifferentiation. The Adirondacks *occupied* me" (41). As the spirits of the place, bearing lost names and lost desires, occupy the poet—invade her, colonize her, possess her—her own spirit is given over to their voices, their wills. As

in her quote from Thoreau, she gets "the Indian names straightened out—
which means made more crooked" (42). And, contrary to Sir Humphrey
Gilbert in his *A New Passage to Cataia*, who would "proove that the Indians
aforenamed came not by the Northeast, and that there is no thorow pas-
sage navigable that way," Howe and her poem *become* that "thorow passage,"
just as they "make more crooked" the Indian names (42). The spirits move
through her; hence the title of the poem.

One of the most important issues in the interpretation of *Thorow* has to
do with the author's complicity in the history of violence and exploitation
that the poem presents. This issue is usually discussed in terms of colonial,
patriarchal, and textual politics: even the most astute critics of the poem do
not seem to take Howe's concern with the sacred as anything more than an
aspect of the conflicted historical ideologies under investigation. For these
critics, the idea that the poem may be a vehicle for sacred experience is not
taken seriously. In other words, experience of the sacred *through* the poem is
subordinated to a secular understanding of religious beliefs as represented
in the poem. Howe contributes to this situation due to the multiple roles
she plays in her work: committed scholar-activist, guilty historical witness,
postmodern linguistic skeptic, she is also antinomian prophet, visionary
elegist, possessed medium. In short, Howe's multiple subject positions in a
poem like *Thorow* are a matter of "Complicity battling redemption" (*Singu-
larities* 55).

Commenting on this line, Paul Naylor argues that "*Thorow* investigates
the 'complicity' between normative discourse and the 'progress' of his-
tory generating the conditions [Howe] confronted during her stay at Lake
George" (58). Similarly, Jenny L. White claims that "The wanderings of the
poet and speaker of this poem are complicit with and in opposition to the
European exploration and settlement of this place. The poem considers the
'place' of the author/poet, not only by opening with an explanation of her
relationship to this place but also by considering the poem's position vis-à-
vis the American authors she invokes, its 'complicity' in the European cul-
ture and ideology that destroyed the Native Americans, and the possibility
for the poem to reconstitute or redeem this history" (257). And Will Mont-
gomery states that Howe's poem "could not help but embody some of the
problems it wishes to expose. . . . *Thorow* laments the impossibility of such
redemptive return even as it desires it" (744). Thus, "*Thorow* situates itself

on the borders of coherence, striving pessimistically for an experience of enchantment that it knows to be inaccessible" (752).

Among these critics, Montgomery in particular understands that the "experience of enchantment" is crucial to our understanding of what is desired, what is achieved, and what is thwarted in *Thorow*. As a séance, the poem's representation of competing belief systems is in itself a kind of enchantment. The self-consciousness of the authorial subject and the self-reflexivity of the poem's form are products of Howe's "Elegiac western Imagination," leading in turn to a text that is a "Mysterious confined enigma / a possible field of work" (*Singularities* 55). *Thorow* is the celebration of a mystery as well as the historical examination of that mystery; like *A Bibliography of the King's Book*, it reenacts the scene of sacrificial violence, analyzes it, and memorializes it, thus becoming a "Spiritual typography of elegy" (*Singularities* 55). Drawing on Freud's concept of the "daemonic" power of the repetition compulsion in *Beyond the Pleasure Principle*, Montgomery insightfully observes that "Howe is enacting—again and again—a return to barely articulable but traumatic repressed material. This material arrives in the poetry with the force of 'outsideness'—it unsettles syntactical coherence and demonstrates the 'daemonic' qualities of which Freud writes" (749). Montgomery goes on to consider one of the most compelling lyrics in *Thorow*:

Fence blown down in a winter storm

darkened by outstripped possession
Field stretching out of the world

this book is as old as the people

There are traces of blood in a fairy tale (*Singularities* 44)

Montgomery contrasts Freud's positive view of the fence as analogous to the "acculturated ego" to Thoreau's distaste for fences in favor of the wild. Thoreau would presumably find the "Fence blown down in a winter storm" to be a good sign; not so Freud, who would regard the image of the blown down fence as a sign of a "dæmonic" assault upon the boundaries of the ego. As Montgomery notes, "The 'daemon'—let us say a principle of externality compelling speech—lives on both sides of the fence in *Thorow*, and is implicated in the voicing of both paradise and apocalypse. The poem embarks on an attempt which it knows must fail to reimagine an Edenic wilderness and encounters instead a landscape marked by territorial strife" (750). If such is the case, then "darkened by outstripped possession" means that the ego of the poet who is channeling this strife is subject to a dæmonic force that darkens consciousness, stripping and possessing her, so that a history of territorial struggle, of "outstripped possession," may be revealed. Open to this force, she enters a "Field stretching out of the world" and is compelled to read from a book "as old as the people." Which people? The answer must be all people, Native Americans and Europeans both, throughout the long history of violence. This is why there are "traces of blood in a fairy tale," for in effect, *Thorow* itself is that fairy tale. The spell that the poet casts in her possessed state exposes her readers to her dæmon, which we discover to be our own. This is indeed "The literature of savagism / under a spell of savagism" (*Singularities* 49).

This couplet needs to be put in its proper context, which is the first lyric in part 2 of *Thorow*, one of the most important and stirring passages in all of Howe's work:

Walked on Mount Vision

New life after the Fall
So many true things

which are not truth itself
We are too finite

Barefooted and bareheaded
extended in space

sure of reaching support (*Singularities* 49)

Walking on Mount Vision would surely seem tantamount to what Howe elsewhere calls "writing as a physical event of immediate revelation" (*Birthmark* 1). Despite our finitude, we may witness "So many true things // which are not truth itself." Yet how can we in our vulnerability, "Barefooted and bareheaded / extended in space," be so "sure of reaching support"? For the visionary poet, language and history, despite their mysteries and opacities, can apparently provide that support, as we see in the remainder of the lyric:

Knowledge and foresight
Noah's landing at Ararat

Mind itself or life

quicker than thought

slipping back to primordial
We go through the word Forest

Trance of an encampment
not a foot of land cleared

The literature of savagism
under a spell of savagism

Nature isolates the Adirondacks

In the machinery of injustice
my whole being is Vision (*Singularities* 49)

There is a high degree of indeterminacy in these lines, and they work effectively to convey both a feeling of dæmonic or ghostly otherness and of a more historical materialist investigation.[14] Here, "quicker than thought," in the "Trance of an encampment" (one wants to read "Trace" for "Trance"), we are granted both "Knowledge and foresight," enmeshed by Howe's extraordinarily self-reflexive discourse in a "literature of savagism / under a spell of savagism"—part magic, part rational analysis. Opposed to "the machinery of injustice" that is revealed by historical research, we find ourselves "slipping back to primordial." Thus "We go through the word Forest"—lost in the wilderness of an endlessly dictated, pathless language (the "Word Forest") and relentless tracking a comprehensible sociolinguistic event (the word "Forest"). As a result, "my whole being is Vision," an experience comparable to Emily Dickinson's "White Election" (#528) or her recognition of "The rest of Life to *see!*" (#174).

But what is the nature of this primordial vision that Howe opposes to the machinery of injustice? After the Flood, the Ark settled on Mount Ararat, which became a sort of "Mount Vision" for Noah. It was from there that he sent forth the raven and the dove, from there that he and his family and the animals left the Ark. Presumably, it was on Mount Ararat that Noah built the altar, made a sacrifice "of every clean beast, and of every clean fowl" (Genesis 8:20) and received God's promise that "I will not again curse the ground any more for man's sake; for the imagination of man's heart is evil from his youth; neither will I smite any more every thing living, as I have done" (Genesis 8:21). Is Howe ironically comparing the Adirondacks, with its history of violence, to Ararat, where the proper sacrifice elicited God's everlasting covenant? Or is she holding out the possibility that the Adirondacks can be redeemed, that the failing American myth of regenerative violence can still lead to understanding or even, as she names it a little later in the poem, to "Expectation of Epiphany" (*Singularities* 50)?

There is no simple answer to this question, as is true of the other questions critics have posed about *Thorow*. Not only does the author's complicity remain at issue throughout the poem, not only are we led to wonder whether the spirits will return to the holy places, but from beginning to end, the very form of the poem calls itself into question. What does it really mean to walk on Mount Vision? Perhaps it means

Not to look off from it
but to look at it

Original of the Otherside
understory of anotherworld (*Singularities* 50)

As is so often the case with Howe, we find ourselves inside and outside, subject and object, looking off from the mountain but also looking at it. The poem seeks to return to the "Original of the Otherside," only to discover there is no Original. As one discovers when one communes with the "Otherside," any "understory" the spirits choose to tell will be matched by a counter-story. "I have imagined a center" declares a voice in the poem (is it Howe's?), "Wilder than this region / The figment of a book" (*Singularities* 54). To create a form, however open to the uncertainties of history and language, one must do just that. Near the end of her "figment of a book," before it falls into fragments and word roots, Howe (and I believe it *is* Howe) cries "You are of me & I of you, I cannot tell // Where you leave off and I begin" (58). This loss of self is the price the poet pays when she becomes a medium. Nor are the spirits happy to have been called forth. What do they think of the poet? The last "word" of *Thorow* is "Thiefth" (59).

:::

"The shadow of history / is the ground of faith" (*Nonconformist's Memorial* 13) declares Howe in *The Nonconformist's Memorial*, her poem on the Resurrection scene in the Gospel of John, one of the most controversial in all of New Testament scholarship (see Back 162–63). PIt is, she then writes, "A question of overthrowing." As recounted in chapter 20 of John, the empty tomb visited by the Beloved Disciple, Simon Peter, and Mary Magdalene; the two angels appearing before the weeping Mary; and the sudden reappearance of the risen Jesus ("Touch me not; for I am not yet ascended to my Father")—all have the spooky, portentous theatricality of a séance, a spiritual manifestation engineered by God Himself. For Howe, this most problematic of the Gospels (due in part to Mary Magdalene's importance in the story) is the "shadow of history"; despite this (or because of it), it is "the ground of faith." Faith is grounded in the shadow of history, not history itself; it is insubstantial, and yet its often violent material effects are felt from generation to generation. When the tomb is found to be empty, we must faithfully account for a miracle, and when we can no longer bear the burden of that miracle, it must be overthrown. Another miracle takes its place, another ritual, another "Narrative of Finding." The climax of the poem—and for me, one of Howe's most remarkable lyrics—reads as follows:

> I wander about as an exile
> as a body does a shadow
> A notion of split reference
> if in silence hidden by darkness
> there must be a Ghost
> Iconic theory of metaphor
> a sound and perfect voice
> Its hiding is understanding
> Reader I do not wish to hide
> in you to hide from you
> It is the Word to whom she turns
> True submission and subjection (*Nonconformist's Memorial* 30)

In Howe's "Iconic theory of metaphor," one of the most important aspects of her poetics, "there must be a Ghost." As I observed in my discussion of *A Bibliography of the King's Book*, Howe understands a poem to be an icon, a sacred image. As an icon, the poem is itself a metaphor, a verbal equivalent of something that was once held sacred, but which now can only be perceived or comprehended as a ghost. A ghost is a shadow, wandering in exile from its lost body. Hence, to read a poem is to encounter the ghost of the sacred, to experience words as "split reference," part spirit, part body. The poet, likewise in exile, longs to submit and subject herself to the Word, for as she knows from the beginning of the Gospel, "In the beginning was the Word, and the Word was with God, and the Word was God" (John 1:1). To give oneself to this "sound and perfect voice" would perhaps transform *her* voice too, making it likewise sound and perfect. But in a fallen world, in a world of exile, it is not to be. As in the case of Jack Spicer, we have gone from Logos to lowghost. In a world in which language is a matter of split reference, in a world of "silence hidden by darkness," speech is always impeded, fragmented, scattered, and at risk. A medium or necromancer rather than an evangelist, the poet is abashed: "Reader I do not wish to hide / in you to hide from you." Yet given the nature of her work, she cannot avoid it. She hides herself from us, and we lose her in these most readerly of texts. "If I could go back / Recollectedly into biblical / fierce grace" (*Nonconformist's Memorial* 32) laments the antinomian poet, knowing that the possibility of such a direct, unmediated experience of the Word has been lost forever. Instead, she presents a different scenario:

I am not afraid to confess it
and make you my confessor
Steal to a place in the dark
least coherent utterance
and Redactor's treasured proof
Love for the work's sake (23)

Out of "Love for the work's sake," the poet and her readers "Steal to a place in the dark," attending to this "least coherent utterance." There, as we observe her performance and seek to interpret it, Howe makes us her confessors and redactors, willing or not. And yet, as we have discovered in reading Howe,

As though beside herself
I want to accuse myself
would say to her confessor
Confessions implode into otherness (25)

In the dark, what remain after the implosions are poems.

5

Michael Palmer

Operating necessarily from the inside, borrowing all the strategic and economic resources of subversion from the old structure, borrowing them structurally, that is to say without being able to isolate their elements and atoms, the enterprise of deconstruction always in a certain way falls prey to its own work. (Derrida, *Of Grammatology* 24)

Susan Howe's fascination with transgression, blasphemy, and antinomian forms of belief is directly related to the formal experimentation so prominent in her poetry. Michael Palmer, equally well-known for his experimentalism, would appear to be a very different case. Indeed, a discussion of Palmer's work in a religious context of any sort might appear odd to some readers, for whom this poetry represents a highly refined instance of radical linguistic and epistemological skepticism, and a complex play of signification usually associated with the most sophisticated forms of postmodernism. Yet there is another dimension to Palmer's poetry that sometimes complements and sometimes counteracts such a characterization. In an interview with Peter Gizzi (1994), for instance, Palmer cites the philosopher E. M. Cioran,

> who talks about the heresies of Meister Eckhardt in relation to his belief in form, and he says . . . "Like every heretic, he sinned on the side of form, an enemy of language. All orthodoxy, whether religious or political, postulates the usual expression. In the name of a sclerotic word, the stakes, the pyres were erected."
> . . . So heretics are utterly significant figures in a poetic sense. There's a poetics to heresy like Meister Eckhardt, and he points to the fact that it's not the ideas really, it's the form these ideas take. Likewise among certain mystics. I think it equally applies to poetry. ("Interview" 163)

If there is a poetics to heresy, could there also be a heretical poetics? If there is, it looms large in Palmer's conception of the poem, and might even be one of the driving forces of his imagination. Palmer's thinking about heresy and poetics involves *form*, which, as he conceives it, stands in opposition to linguistic orthodoxy, "the usual expression," the "sclerotic word." In a certain respect, this notion is related to the modernist concept of defamiliarization, the application of literary techniques that lead readers to rethink the role that language plays in regard to reference, meaning, and so forth. Part of the writer's task is to challenge received ideas about signification, to undermine authoritative modes of discourse. But by bringing in the notion of heresy, or what we may more broadly call the politics of belief, Palmer, like Howe, complicates the modernist position, connecting it to much older but equally conflicted religious and philosophical traditions and textual practices. From this perspective, poetic form itself is heretical, and the imaginations of the poet and the heretic have a great deal in common. Form charges ordinary language with powers beyond itself; language, in effect, is turned against itself through the act of *poesis*. The passion of form bringing itself into being is a heretical act, for it challenges all types of orthodox discourse. In the imaginative tradition I am seeking to define in this book, the valences of religion and poetry are continually shifting, the power of belief moves continually through various registers of discourse, but the concept of form, its making and unmaking, remains constant.

Palmer's connection of poetry to heresy takes us back to Duncan's words in *The Truth and Life of Myth*: "what I speak of here in the terms of a theology is a poetics. Back of each poet's concept of the poem is his concept of the meaning of form itself; and his concept of form in turn where it is serious at all arises from his concept of the nature of the universe, its lifetime or form, or even, for some, its lifelessness or formlessness" (*Fictive Certainties* 16). As we have seen, the dissolution of form in Duncan's *grand collage* is directly related to a realignment in his thinking in regard to the beliefs that held sway in his imagination. Although Palmer's opus does not constitute a *grand collage* in quite the same manner as Duncan's, he honors this conception of poetic form, not only as an endlessly reconstellated set of countertraditions, but as a pointedly heretical scripture, a writing that continually unsettles any normative belief system or conventional understanding of linguistic meaning. In regard to form, Palmer is not nearly the romantic enthusiast that Duncan is. Rather, Palmer maintains a cool, controlled, almost classically balanced tone, a deceptively elegant surface (often deliberately disfigured), and a highly self-conscious sense of order and arrangement from one volume to the next, with seriality almost always determining the trajectory of the work. The aesthetic as a category maintains itself despite whatever upheavals one may encounter on the surface of the text. Even Palmer's most overtly engaged political poems, bitter and witheringly ironic as they can be, attempt to withhold themselves in ways that indicate the poet's resistance to instrumentality or recuperation.

But despite these differences, Palmer, to borrow Peter O'Leary's key term, has surely inherited Duncan's (and Spicer's) "gnostic contagion" as much as Nathaniel Mackey, whom O'Leary reads as another of Duncan's heirs in this regard.[1] This is not a matter of apostolic succession, canonic status or anxiety of influence. On one level, it is a matter of poetic calling: how do poets imagine themselves as agents of psychic and historical powers that transcend their singular personal identities? On another level, it is a matter of belief: how do poets negotiate the religious, philosophical, and cultural traditions that constitute what they understand to be "the truth and life of myth"? And finally, it is, again, a matter of form, or of what Duncan calls the Form of Forms: how do poets shape their poems so as to challenge received truth and defamiliarize conventional expression? Another passage from Duncan's *Truth and Life of Myth* comes to mind, for it encompasses all three of these matters, and is as relevant to Palmer as it is to Duncan himself: "In the world of saying and telling in which I first came into words, there is a primary trouble, a panic that can still come upon me where the word no longer protects, transforming the threat of an overwhelming knowledge into the power of an imagined reality, or abstracting from a shaking experience terms for rationalization, but exposes me the more" (*Fictive Certainties* 7). As with Duncan, Palmer's work is riddled with a primary trouble, which manifests itself in a shuttling movement between exposure and protection, between imagined reality and its rationalization, between form as threat and form as stabilization.

Recalling the debates among the New American poets at the Vancouver Poetry Conference (1963), which he attended as "an engaged, twenty-year old student of modernist principles," Palmer notes that "even among sympathetic peers . . . Duncan felt the need to assert the force of heretical opinion, which in turn for him was grounded in the authority of timeless heretical *gnosis*" ("Robert Duncan and Romantic Synthesis"). Duncan's insistence on Romantic models of inspiration and composition, his devotion, against what he perceived to be modernist and postmodernist orthodoxies, to what Palmer names "the dimension of Spirit, with that troublesome, rebarbative capital letter," at first shocked the younger poet but eventually proved a major influence on his thinking. Palmer never gives himself over to that dimension very readily, and as often as not, resists it. He frequently proposes an *agnostic* countertruth through his linguistic skepticism or the materialism of the signifier. Like many other poets of his generation, including the somewhat younger Language poets, Palmer has always been fascinated by the "meaning of meaning," and has made it one of his great themes. Investigating the social, ethical, and political dimensions of signifying processes remains of the utmost importance to him. But there is another side to Palmer, and it is the confluence and conflict of these tendencies, and his astonishing skill in their negotiations, that mark him as a poet of the highest cultural ambitions.

In my essay "The Case of Michael Palmer" (1988), which focuses on *Notes for Echo Lake* (1981) and *First Figure* (1984), I characterize Palmer's situation as "the confluence of two poetic tendencies, both of which affect but also transcend matters of style and school: on the one hand, the desire to transform poetry into a quasi-religious secret doctrine or language of mystery, complete with reader-initiates; on the other hand, the desire to level all possible modes of poetic discourse, so that a synthetic language of otherness supplants and disperses the human subject altogether" (532–33). Yet of late there may be less Stein and more Stevens in Palmer: the highly inventive semiological play that characterizes his work through the late eighties (and which aligns that work to some extent with that of the Language poets) has given way in recent years to an equally inventive, equally philosophical engagement with agencies of desire, meaning, truth, and yes, "Spirit, with that troublesome, rebarbative capital letter." In poetry as complex and intellectually restless as Palmer's, it is difficult to identify turning points and decisive changes, but *Sun* (1988) is certainly a crucial volume in this regard. The major works in *Sun*, the Baudelaire Series poems and the two-part title poem, bring certain radically skeptical—and radically secular—tendencies in Palmer's poetry to their highest pitch, producing, in effect, a crisis in the work that simultaneously clears a space for a new kind of poetic investigation that continues into the present. It is no accident that after publishing the three brilliant volumes in the eighties that culminate in *Sun*, it would take Palmer seven years to bring out his next book, *At Passages* (1995).[2]

Why does *Sun* represent a crisis in Palmer's work? What sort of crisis? As we have seen, changes in both Duncan's and Spicer's poetry are related to an intellectual crisis or even a crisis of belief, though it could be argued that in Spicer's case, his entire career constitutes one long, sustained upheaval of this sort. This is not so with Palmer, who, in his public statements and eloquent interviews, has never alluded to such matters, either in his thought or in his personal life.[3] In his formidably intelligent interviews, Palmer emerges as a steady and consistent thinker who does not convey any sense of an abrupt change of mind or heart as his poetry evolves. On the contrary, in an interview from 1984, Palmer notes that "one learns to listen to the poem as it unfolds" ("A Conversation" 77). This listening relates in turn to "an interior discipline of attention to get beyond a certain level in which I would simply write more Michael Palmer poems of a particular order. . . . For me, a lot of this has been learning that I have to be quite private in my life, that I have to read and think in certain degree of solitariness a lot of the time" (79). Palmer's emphasis on the discipline of attention, on privacy and solitariness, on a kind of reticence in regard to the making of poems within the motion of a life lived, causes his practice to resemble that of a mystic seeking a similar condition of inwardness. But rather than listening for God, Palmer listens for the poem, to be present at its unfolding.

My use of the term "crisis," then, relates paradoxically to this seemingly gradual unfolding, to the internal trajectory of the work, what has been attempted over the course of the poet's career and how that attempt has *taken form*. Up until *Sun*, Palmer's work is, on the one hand, hermetic, dreamlike, portentous, ritualistic, and *mysterious*, a kind of postmodern kabbalism based on a withdrawal or distantiation of meaning, as in the Lurianic notion of *tzimtzum*. On the other hand, it is obsessed with codes, signification, the connections and disruptions between words and things in the contemporary world of the simulacrum, an endless play of signs through which all modes of discourse and experience are leveled, and, as it were, *profaned*. These two dimensions are made to coincide through the extraordinary resonance and musicality of Palmer's writing: rhythm, stanza structure, diction, voicing, and tone all contribute to a well-defined style. Indeed, however much he may have been grouped with other experimentalists, by the mid-eighties there is no mistaking a Michael Palmer poem.

Such is the case stylistically, or, as it were, on the micro level of the work. On the macro level, the work unfolds largely through seriality and the highly overdetermined idea of the Book. Palmer tells us that "I tend to like very much the idea of a book which has a particular shape, just as a sentence has, and a poem within that has a particular shape. All these units of enclosure are levels of identity. So when a book fails to have a level of identity, when it's simply a gathering, it's the loss of one possible area of resonance. I think a lot of my earlier work in series, for example, proceeded from that same idea of defining things beyond their particular events as poems" ("A Conversation" 85). This notion of the book as an entity that is more than a gathering of poems reminds us of the importance of Jack Spicer to Palmer's poetic. In his second Vancouver lecture, which is devoted to the subject of seriality and the book, Spicer argues that "a serial poem, in the first place, has the book as its unit—as an individual poem . . . has a poem as its unit, the actual poem you write at the actual time, the single poem. And there is a dictation, the actual poem you write at the actual time, the single poem. And there is a dictation of form [that is, the larger form of the book] as well as a dictation of the individual form of the individual poem" (*House That Jack Built* 52). In addition to Spicer, Palmer may well have in mind Derrida's analysis of the book in *Of Grammatology*, which we considered in regard to Duncan's work in chapter 1. According to Derrida, "the idea of the book is the idea of a totality, finite or infinite, of the signifier; this totality of the signifier cannot be a totality, unless a totality constituted by the signified preexists it, supervises its inscriptions and its signs, and is independent of it in its ideality. The idea of the book, which always refers to a natural totality, is profoundly alien to the sense of writing. It is the encyclopedic protection of theology and of logocentrism against the disruption of writing, against its aphoristic energy" (18). It would appear then that Derrida provides a conception of the book that both Spicer and Palmer violate, since both poets, in their application of dictation and seriality (that is, "writing") to the book, undermine the book's traditional relation to totality, theology, and logocentrism. Spicer, of course, could not have read Derrida, though he would have been familiar with Mallarmé's idea that if man's connection to divinity "is to be made clear, it can be expressed only by the pages of the open book in front of him" (*Selected Prose* 25). In working out his own notion of the book, Spicer, given his antinomian gnosticism, would certainly seek to undermine that connection. Palmer likewise seeks to disrupt the book's heritage; his use of the concept, the form, and the term as it frequently appears as a title or within the text of his poems, may therefore be viewed as a manifestation of his heretical *écriture*.

Considering Palmer's serial work through *Notes for Echo Lake*, Joseph Conte notes that Palmer "pursues an 'interstitial' method whereby an ongoing, open series of poems is interspersed with other poems not counted as part of the series itself." This method, which is similar to Duncan's in writing *Passages*, simultaneously affirms and negates the concept of the book; as Conte notes, it works so as "to point out that each section is not locked into a series (as a sequential presentation would imply), thus losing some degree of its particularity." Thus "the series is the ideal form to assert both the interconnectedness and the uniqueness of things" (279), confirming Palmer's view of book and poem: that "these units of enclosure are levels of identity" ("A Conversation" 85).

But what happens when things begin to lose their uniqueness and identity, when interconnectedness becomes totalizing, leaving less space for difference? How does the poet respond when the interstices begin to close, particularity is lost, and what appear to be various levels of identity are revealed to be homogenous and monological? This is what occurs under the historical conditions of modernity and then postmodernity, conditions Palmer addresses with increasing seriousness on the political level, on the cultural level, and the level of the individual psyche. "The concept of progress," writes Walter Benjamin in *The Arcades Project*, "must be grounded in the idea of catastrophe. That things are 'status quo' *is* the catastrophe" (473). It is this catastrophe, or crisis, I would hypothesize, that is both represented and addressed in *Sun*. The poetry in this volume both enacts a catastrophic loss of "Spirit" and criticizes those forces of progress that lead to its destruction, making the book a crisis point in Palmer's own progress as well. Not only is this specifically thematized, it is also manifested formally. The Baudelaire Series poems, as indicated by the title, form a single series with no other poems interspersed, while the two closely related title poems in *Sun* are wholly sustained, individual texts, the first of the two being the longest single poem of Palmer's career. Unlike Duncan, whose gnosticism leads to the diffusion of seriality and the ultimate disintegration of the work, Palmer's writing actually solidifies here, in response to the closing of interior space, the systematic undoing of cultural alternatives, and the pervasive destruction of what Benjamin (who looms large throughout *Sun*) calls "aura."[4] Palmer describes the Baudelaire Series poems as "an investigation of lyric form since its 19th-century origins in Hölderlin and others" ("Dear Lexicon" 12). At the risk of being overly schematic, I would argue that the poems in the Baudelaire Series constitute a critical review of modernism, while *Sun* extends Palmer's analysis to the contemporary, postmodern world. Ironically, the more fragmented (yet paradoxically, homogeneous) culture becomes, the more vacuous the interior life, the more coherent becomes the poet's response. The contradictory impulses in the earlier work are subordinated to an increasingly determined mode of utterance, and although Palmer largely maintains his cool tone, his vision of cultural disintegration in this extraordinarily ambitious volume grows increasingly focused and his sense of disaster is sustained throughout.

:::

Baudelaire, according to Benjamin, is the first poet fully to face the problem of lyricism under the conditions of modernity; thus, he is the natural choice to play the tutelary spirit or *daemon* of Palmer's serial poem. "Baudelaire patterned his image of the artist after an image of the hero" (*Charles Baudelaire* 67), Benjamin observes, because "it takes a heroic constitution to live modernism" (74). Yet as Benjamin demonstrates repeatedly, the posture of the heroic lyricist is continually undermined by modernity; or as Spicer will say years later, "Heros eat soup like anyone else" (*My Vocabulary* 376). The decay of the lyric aura since *Les Fleurs du Mal* is, in effect, Palmer's subterranean theme in the Baudelaire Series poems; hence the ghostly appearances in the text of other major lyric figures of the century, including Rilke, Celan, Vallejo, Creeley, and Duncan. Seriality, in this instance, sustains the resonance that the "progressive" forces of modernization threaten to undermine: as in *Les Fleurs du Mal* itself, poems in the Baudelaire Series speak to each other, both interconnected and individualized. The individual poem stands forth against the backdrop of the entire sequence; yet we are simultaneously aware of the latter's comprehensive intellectual motivation and purpose as we move from one lyric utterance to the next. But unlike *Les Fleurs du Mal*, which addresses the debased conditions of the anti-heroical lyric poet in what Benjamin calls the "Era of High Capitalism," the Baudelaire series really is something of a historical survey, almost a tour of the ruins of modernism and modernity, covering at least one hundred years. Thus, in the proem of the series, in which Palmer channels or is possessed by Baudelaire (as Spicer is similarly possessed by Lorca in *After Lorca*) we read that

> A hundred years ago I made a book
> and in that book I left a spot
> and on that spot I placed a seme
>
> with the mechanism of the larynx
> around an inky center
> leading forward-backward
>
> into snow-sun
> then to frozen sun itself
> Threads and nerves have brought us to a house
>
> and clouds called crescent birds are a lifting song
> No need to sail further
> protesting here and there against some measures
>
> across the years of codes and names
> always immortal as long as you remain a man
> eating the parts of him indicated by the prophets
>
> stomach skull and gullet
> bringing back the lost state
> Yes I dreamed another dream and nobody was in it (*Codes Appearing* 163)

Baudelaire's (and Palmer's) book contains a spot, a place that is also a seme or sign, which in turn corresponds to "the mechanism of the larynx," the voice or phonocentric utterance of the subject enunciating itself. But this spot/seme/voice is to be found around an "inky" or written center that is really no center at all: writing decenters the self and challenges the myth of presence, contradictorily "leading backward-forward // into sun-snow."

Baudelaire's notorious spleen ("nerves"), the condition of lyricism frustrated into boredom and melancholy by a hostile modern environment, in addition to his theory of symbolic correspondences ("threads" or relations between words and things) lead to "a lifting song" of Romantic transcendence. Yet for Palmer, like Baudelaire himself, the worth of such transcendence is questionable: there is "No need to sail further"; "the years of codes and names" that constitute the history of poetry promise immortality for the individual poet, but only at the price of heroic self-sacrifice, the martyrdom of self-expression and the ritual cannibalization or consumption by generations of readers who "immortalize" the life and canonize the poems.[5] This, it would appear, is the only means through which the poet, intent upon "bringing back the lost state," the lyric harmony of self, word, and world, can achieve anything near his goal. But as the poem ends, another possibility opens: "Yes I just dreamed another dream and nobody was in it." Suddenly the heroic stance of Romanticism and modernism gives way to postmodernism: the dream of the text continues, but it is a dream of absence; no self at all is to be found.

Baudelaire is a heretic to the faith of Romantic poetry: his modernist vision of heroic self-sacrifice through the willing loss of the aura violates the creed of the transcendent poet-prophet.[6] And analogously, Palmer is a heretic to the faith of modernist poetry: in renouncing the self-sacrifice of the poet-hero, he carries Baudelaire's vision one step further, to a postmodern deconstruction of any modernist heroism.[7] Visionary transcendence modulates into self-sacrifice, which in turn modulates into absence: first, the poet's aura is lost without his minding it; next, the poet attempts to abscond with himself entirely. Yet his disappearance is marked by verbal traces, for in a certain respect, he disappears into language, and the poems are the traces he leaves behind. Thus,

Words say, Misspell and misspell your name
Words say, Leave this life

From the singer streams of color
but from you

a room within a smaller room
habits of opposite and alcove (164)

From visionary singer to *poète maudit*: consigned to "a room within a smaller room," the poet is called upon to "misspell" or unname himself and leave a life that has less and less use for him and his poems. Indeed, a later poem in the series reads, in its entirety,

> ... by the name of Ceran
> or Anlschel
>
> "blooming field of weeds"
> what letters displaced (174)

After two years in Nazi labor camps, with both parents murdered, Paul *Antschel*, a young German-speaking Jew from Bukovina, displaced the letters of his name and misspelled himself, becoming Paul *Celan*, the greatest poetic witness to the disaster of modern European culture. From *poète maudit* to the poet exterminated: like a "blooming field of weeds," the poet's words spring up, marking a kind of life-in-death or afterlife, the only kind of life possible for such a figure after the Shoah.[8]

In the Baudelaire Series poems, the poet who mediates, in effect, between Baudelaire and Celan, between the traumatic inauguration of modernism and its even more catastrophic collapse, is Rainer Maria Rilke.[9] Like Yeats, Rilke is both one of the "last Romantics" and a trailblazing modernist. Influenced by French symbolists such as Baudelaire, and in turn, an important precursor of Celan, Rilke is present in at least two crucial poems in Palmer's sequence. In the first, Palmer is virtually possessed by Rilke, as he was previously possessed by Baudelaire; the result is an uncanny conflation, a double-voiced discourse that employs an epistolary form of address, one of Palmer's most effective techniques:

> Dear Lexicon, I died in you
> as a dragonfly might
> or a dragon in a bottle might
>
> Dear Lexia, There is no mind
>
> Dear Book, You were never a book
> Panther, You are nothing but a page
> torn from a book
>
> Stupid Lake, You were the ruin of a book

Dear Merline, Dearest Lou, Here the streets
have their fullness and their flow
like a blind man on a carousel (166)

Once again, the poet loses his mind, dies or departs life through language, his "Lexicon" transformed into "Lexia," a deadly muse or femme fatale. He writes to her even as Rilke wrote to his lovers, including Merline (Rilke's pet name for Baladine Klossowska) and Lou Andreas-Salomé. Rilke's ambivalence toward women is well known; throughout his life he would develop intimate relations only to withdraw into what he regarded as the necessary loneliness of his art. But in this poem, Palmer transfers erotic ambivalence to the poet's relation to the work itself, both his own, referring to *Notes for Echo Lake* ("Stupid Lake, You were the ruin of a book") and Rilke's, referring to the *Neue Gedichte* (*New Poems*, 1907–1908). This two-volume work, surely one of the most important in international modernist poetry, represented a major breakthrough for Rilke and made him one of the most famous European poets of his generation. The *Dinggedichte* ("thing-poems") of this collection decisively turn from Romantic expressivity to embrace a new sense of objectivity, a melding of the lyric subject with the "thing" before it, whether a natural entity or a human artifact. Rilke wrote "The Panther," one of the earliest and best known of these poems, after being sent by Rodin to observe the animals in the Jardin des Plantes of Paris. With no sign of the poetic ego, the poem is given over entirely to the baffled pacing of the panther in its confining cage, "like a dance of strength around a center / in which a great will stands numbed" (*New Poems* 63). The same objective presentation and withdrawal of the ego applies to the animal figures of "The Carousel" and to "The Blind Man" ("And as on an empty page // the reflections things make are painted / on him" [223]).

Palmer's references to these poems, and to the movement from lyrical expressivity to objective presentation that they represent, extend his heretical critique of modernism. The panther is conflated with the description of the blind man and becomes "nothing but a page / torn from a book": neither the Romantic symbol nor the modernist *ding*, but a disposable signifier. The blind man himself is positioned on the whirling carousel, a fit simile for the "fullness and flow" of Paris, a city which Rilke, as he writes to Lou Andreas-Salomé, found "terrible," or as Palmer puts it, "hateful": "Hateful City, in the

dream the tree was first a word / then became a column in a dark arcade"
(*Codas Appearing* 166). The word "arcade" returns us to Benjamin's great
analysis of Baudelaire's Paris, the *locus classicus* of social and technological
transformation that Rilke, Baudelaire's poetic heir, despises for the very
modernity it represents. In the poet's dream (both Rilke's and Palmer's),
the tree, a natural entity, becomes its verbal signifier before becoming part
of the supporting structure of the arcade, that feature which for Benjamin
is most representative of the city's modernity. The sense of loss and regret
is palpable: the romantic object of nature, with all its organic implications,
becomes merely a word, a counter in endless verbal exchange, before it is
transformed into a part of the "Hateful City."[10] This verbal slippage or dis-
semination threatens identity itself. The poem ends with these lines:

> Dear George, So long
> Will you now have memory again
>
> Who's one and who's nothing
> in the game she asked
> I couldn't understand the rest (166)

Here we have another instance of a poet changing his name. As a young
man, after attending the Vancouver Poetry Conference, that famous gather-
ing of the New American poets, George Michael Palmer changed his name
to Michael Palmer. As he explains, "I think '65–'66 was when I sort of said
now I'm out of, I'm free from college, I've done my duty and I'll be somebody
else entirely—not that one ever is, of course. That self I carry with me is
part of the problem and maybe part of the solution" ("Interview" 168). The
dutiful Italian American son, having attended Harvard, transforms himself
into the rebellious, heretical avant-garde poet: "Dear George, So long." In
the game of identity that the poet plays with his reader, selfhood dissolves
in dubious memory, goes from one to nothing and ultimately becomes
incomprehensible.

The second poem in the Baudelaire Series based on Rilke's work is a re-
writing of the earlier poet's "Orpheus. Eurydike. Hermes," also from the
Neue Gedichte. Here, the intertextuality between Palmer and Rilke takes
us even deeper into the spiritual crisis posed by the passage from roman-
ticism to modernism to postmodernism. The "logic" of this crisis, which,

however necessarily historicized, may also be regarded as an ongoing condition of *poesis*, is analyzed in Allen Grossman's magisterial essay "Orpheus/Philomela: Subjection and Mastery in the Founding Stories of Poetic Production." According to Grossman, "all speaking about Orpheus is speaking about the origin and logic of speaking in the poetic way. . . . [I]t is the story that is always enacted when poetry becomes the action of the person" (*Long Schoolroom* 19–20). This person, the poetic maker, "is always present in the making of civilization. . . . 'Orpheus' signifies the person who is set the task of constructing a human world by singing, *because* the givenness of the world (the inevitability of any relationship of persons or terms) is lost" (20).

In "Orpheus. Eurydike. Hermes," Rilke (who is a touchstone for Grossman in his understanding of the modern orphic condition) presents what amounts to the primal scene of poetic loss: the moment when Orpheus, having won permission from the gods of the underworld to bring Eurydice back from death, turns back in doubt, only to see his beloved slip back into Hades forever. Along the "single path" through the fantastic underworld landscape, Rilke depicts Orpheus, "the slender man in the blue mantle, / who mutely and impatiently stared straight ahead" (*New Poems* 141). Behind him come Eurydice hand in hand with Hermes, the "god of faring and of distant messages." Orpheus is both desperate and determined: "he told himself they *were* coming, / said it aloud and heard the words fade away. / They *were* coming, it was only that they walked with fearful softness" (143). In contrast, Eurydice "was within herself, like a woman close to birth . . . / And her having-died / filled her like abundance," though death has also given her "a new virginity." Having already forgotten her husband and her life on earth, she does not recognize Orpheus, and is hardly affected when Hermes "stopped her and with pain in his voice / spoke the words: *he has turned around*—, / she was puzzled, and answered softly: *Who?*" (145). "By the bitter logic of the poetic principle," Grossman tells us, "Eurydice must be lost" (*Long Schoolroom* 29). As for Orpheus, his myth as it is inherited by Rilke and other modern poets "becomes increasingly an inquiry into the impotence of the master—his subjection to the violent logic of a story in which he redeems the world, but not himself." Rather, Orpheus "sacrifices as the cost to himself of his vicarious powers for others the destination of his own desire" (28). This sacrifice releases him into song, takes him to the greatest heights of his lyric power, or as Rilke declares, "that from lament a world arose, in which / everything had life again" (143).

The cult of the self-sacrificing artist, which modernism inherits from romanticism, is certainly affirmed in Rilke's engagement with the Orpheus narrative, this "founding story of poetic production." Overreaching desire undoes the poet and frees the lyric impulse; language is no longer limited to the expressivity of the individual subject but opens to the pathos of human life in general; as Grossman puts it, "Orpheus has become the true poetic voice who arouses feeling but cannot reciprocate the feeling he arouses" (36). Rilke's representation of Eurydice's loss is therefore the simultaneous representation of Orpheus's (and poetry's) redemptive power at the moment of its becoming.

This leads us to Palmer's untitled poem, which is written "after Rilke, 'Orpheus. Eurydike. Hermes.'" *After* literally means *following*, in the way Palmer follows Rilke, but also in the way Eurydice follows—and then fails to follow—Orpheus out of the underworld. Rilke's poem both celebrates and deconstructs the orphic myth: Orpheus means nothing to Eurydice, who has already forgotten him by giving herself to death, and it is precisely out of that loss and neglect that Orpheus achieves the pinnacle of his lyric powers. Palmer furthers the deconstructive aspect of Rilke's poem by emphasizing the radical negativity that Orpheus must endure through his loss, thereby taking to the limit what we have seen Grossman identify as modern poetry's typical treatment of the myth, which is "increasingly an inquiry into the impotence of the master." Here are the first three stanzas:

> She says, Into the dark—
> almost a question—
> She says, Don't see things—
> this bridge—don't listen
>
> She says, Turn away
> Don't turn and return
> Count no more lines into the poem
> (Or how could you possibly not have known
>
> how song broke apart while all the rest watched—
> that was years ago)

Don't say things
(You can't say things) (*Codes Appearing* 177)

These lines undoubtedly present "the impotence of the master," as sadis-
tically imposed by the beloved muse and masochistically reported by the
poet himself (Orpheus/Rilke/Palmer). As she passes "Into the dark," the
void of death and unbeing, she unmakes the poet's power to perceive the
world and to sing its being. The "bridges spanning voids" mentioned at the
beginning of Rilke's poem cannot be seen. The song, which unbeknownst
to the poet had already broken apart "years ago," now leaves him unable to
"say things," to perform the sacred orphic task of world-making. "I'm not
the same anymore // I'm not here where I walk" (177), declares Eurydice,
as the muse absents herself. As for Hermes, "the messenger confused," Eu-
rydice merely notes in parentheses "(He's forgotten his name)," indicating a
further breakdown in the cosmic movement between the worlds and in the
hermeneutic transformation that must occur between objects and language
if the poet is to sing. "Some stories unthread what there was," she concludes
in the last stanza of the poem; "Take nothing as yours" (178). In effect, the
poet participates in an act of de-creation, of desacralization, narrating an
antimyth that leaves both him and his audience with "nothing," in a condi-
tion of radical worldlessness.

Yet the poem is there, a trace, a sign of an absent presence, a ruin. It is what
remains in the wake of unmaking, and its condition as that which remains,
as an uncanny text that is both alive and dead, is one of the most hereti-
cal aspects of Palmer's poetics. Throughout *Sun*, he ruthlessly exploits the
way in which signification unfolds in the ontological space between pres-
ence and absence; the book's self-reflexive and deconstructive procedures
move restlessly through varied levels of discourse, sometimes enacting high
pathos, sometimes absurdist comedy. "Ideas aren't worth anything" goes
the refrain in one of the most outrageous poems in the Baudelaire Series, a
phrase that in true deconstructive (or perhaps simply sophistical) fashion is
itself an idea, and therefore affirms what it simultaneously claims to negate.
"Let's unmake something" declares the impish voice of the poem, and glee-
fully proceeds to do so, producing "a trace / to dry in tomorrow's sun" (167)
"Imitate me says the elm / Give me an azure sky huge and round / Give me
something in words for a change" (167). How, one may ask the elm, can a

poem be in anything but words, and how can some process of reference or imitation not take place in the context of linguistic utterance? But given the tone of the piece, we find a marked devaluation of referential language, an impatience with the process that ludicrously appears to originate with the object world, but actually stems from the poet himself.

This makes perfect sense: because there is no secure relation between objects and language (or as the poststructuralists tell us, the relation between referent and sign is indeterminate), then the poet's faith in words, his faith in himself and in his orphic calling, is bound to collapse as well. "If we're really mirrors in a poem / what will we call this song" (168): because the song no longer engages in the act of naming, it can no longer be named as such, and the singer, likewise nameless, finds himself trapped in the hall of mirrors that constitutes this process of (de)signification.[11] Palmer's antipathy to the representation of a stable self in his poetry has long been a matter of record,[12] but my particular concern here is for the way the poet, like his poem, becomes figured in terms of presence and absence, or to put it more urgently, life and death. As we hear in another poem in the Baudelaire Series,

> Said the Speaker:
> It is a great pleasure
>
> to be not-dead
> here again
>
> and to be speaking to you
> from this notebook or
>
> journal or Book of the Dead (194)

If poetry, as Eric L. Santner argues, has the power to free our psyches from what he calls the "undeadness that keeps us from opening in the midst of life" (23), then here Palmer takes a great risk: the figure of the "not-dead" Speaker, with his hypertrophied voice of authority coming from a "Book of the Dead," simultaneously reifies and criticizes the invasive totalitarianism of undeadness. Appropriately, Santner's other term for this condition is "Egyptomania," an egomaniacal condition produced by a surplus of authoritative social energy, which he relates in turn to Freud's death drive. As part of the work of *psychotheology*, poetry can transform our undead social relations by reviving "the sparks or blessings of 'more life' *within* those relations, which can be liberated from their undeadness by the intervention of the right word" (142). But for Palmer, the great question that the poet must answer in the wake of modern history—in the wake, to put it reductionistically, of the Holocaust and of poetry such as Celan's—is precisely how to find the "right word." On the one hand, this has always been the question that history and social life pose to the poet: after all, poetry has always been a matter of finding the "right word." But on the other hand, when confronted by the unspeakable as historical fact, and by the overwhelming undeadness of contemporary social relations (and the contemporary abuses of language), the poet's task has become well nigh impossible, since all significant utterance now may be either completely appropriated or completely ignored—in either case, utterly silenced.

The political and ethical dimensions of this dilemma are illustrated in what Palmer calls "the Adorno poem" ("Dear Lexicon" 31), perhaps the most frequently considered section of the Baudelaire Series. Robert Kaufman describes this fourteen-line poem as "an experimental modern sonnet" in which "the whole formal poetic tradition weirdly yet rightly works a path into the poem's content, so that the way history itself converges back upon the age-old problematics of the sonnet is writ large" (211–12).[13] In other words, at this crucial point in the Baudelaire Series poems, Palmer's reworking of the sonnet, a formal mainstay of the lyric tradition, coincides with his consideration of the historical crisis of lyric expressivity (that of poetry, but also that of music) that comes to a head as an aftermath of the Holocaust. Adorno's notorious statement that "to write a poem after Auschwitz is barbaric" (*Prisms* 34) is wholly inadequate for Palmer; he notes in a discussion of Celan that "Celan was for me, first of all, someone who spoke to the fact that political significance can manifest itself in the most deeply privatized—apparently—work. It's interesting that for me Celan stands as a kind of—first of all—*rebuke* to Adorno—obviously, for his remark about the impossibility of a poetry after the Holocaust, which I would answer with the impossibility of *not* having a poetry after the Holocaust" ("Dear Lexicon" 14). Palmer's "Adorno poem" is that point in his work at which Adorno's challenge is met and answered, the point, as it were, at which the sacralizing pronouncement of the great Marxist philosopher, critic, and musicologist is heretically countered by a poem in which both form and content destabilize any such portentous historical declarations:

> A man undergoes pain sitting at a piano
> knowing thousands will die while he is playing
>
> He has two thoughts about this
> If he should stop they would be free of pain
>
> If he could get the notes right he would be free of pain
> In the second case the first thought would be erased
>
> causing pain
>
> It is this instance of playing
>
> he would say to himself
> my eyes have grown hollow like yours
>
> my head is enlarged
> though empty of thought
>
> Such thoughts destroy music
> and this at least is good (*Codes Appearing* 172)

Kaufman ably summarizes the operation of the poem: "The poem's formal casting—its dissonant sound-and-rhythm off-rhyming of *pain* and *playing*, its strange, wavering between numb recitative and charged ghost song, its overall architectural shaping and pitiless grammatical machinery—is so acute, simultaneously so elegant and so rigorously logical, so invitingly asphyxiating, that each new level of grim joke unfolds precisely as any ability to experience even dark humor is pulled from beneath us" (209). I would add that this terrifying operation takes place, in effect, on the level of *ritual*. The sacrificial nature of the man's pain as he sits at the piano (Kaufman cunningly notes that the poem's turn, or *volta*, "leaves it entirely unclear whether the man has been playing and thinking or only thinking about playing" [212]) is related to the sacrificial nature of poetry in general, or at least poetry in the orphic/Romantic tradition, which Palmer, like his precursors (Duncan, Spicer, Rilke, Celan and others) both endorses and deconstructs. But unlike the orphic poet, whose personal loss or sacrifice of desire results in cosmic song, the sacrifice of the man at the piano (who is both the modern lyric poet and the modern *critic* of lyric poetry) results from a conflict between playing and thinking, between free lyric expression and self-conscious reflection. This conflict is inevitable given the historical circumstances in which he finds himself ("thousands will die while he is playing"), circumstances that produce his contradictory, no-win situation.

Traditionally, lyricism is both an expression of pain and a liberation from pain, both the height of self-consciousness and an escape from self-consciousness. As Adorno himself declares, the poem's "detachment from naked existence becomes the measure of the world's falsity and meanness. Protesting against these conditions, the poem proclaims the dream of a world in which things would be different" ("Lyric Poetry" 215). Palmer's poem indicates that modern poetry has passed beyond such a paradigm. The promise of freedom from pain and loss that poetic sacrifice previously held out to the poet ("If he could get the notes right he would be free of pain") is no longer valid; poetry itself must be sacrificed if the thousands are to be "free of pain"—though it is worth noting that this in no way means they will necessarily be saved from death. Rather, to think about lyric expression leads one to eliminate lyric expression, to "destroy music," though it would also seem that to think such thoughts leaves one's head "empty of thought" as well. The enduring irony, of course, is that, as in the earlier poem that states the idea that "Ideas aren't worth anything," the notion here that "Such thoughts destroy music / and this at least is good" is also an utterance in a poem, in a work of "music." In these poems, the utterance encompasses the contradictions of their statement-language; what they *are*—and how the reader experiences them—both contradicts and transcends what they *say*. And as the Adorno poem makes painfully clear, the ritualistic making and unmaking one observes in the poems of the Baudelaire Series are not merely language games, philosophical conundrums, or even interventions in the increasingly vexed tradition of the lyric. They are all of these, but they are also the enactment of a spiritual and sociopolitical crisis that extends outward from modernism to postmodernism, from the Baudelaire Series to the two other texts that together constitute *Sun*.

:::

As I indicated earlier, the cultural contradictions represented by the rhetoric and allusions in the Baudelaire Series poems are subordinated to an increasingly determined and single-minded mode of utterance in *Sun*. This utterance sometimes borders on hysteria, yet it is never out of control: on the contrary, if anything, it is overly controlled, miming, in all its terror, the Egyptomania that Santner sees as "a trauma generated by a *too much of an address*, by an excess immanent to an address that resists metabolization, that is symbolically 'indigestible'" (32). This "too much of an address," for both Santner's psychotheology and Palmer's poem, is directly related to the increasingly centralized, authoritarian social forces that interpellate the individual subject and insinuate themselves into the psyche, constituting themselves as an array of voices that supplant any "genuine" sense of inwardness and concomitant power of expression. The result is a schizoid vision of a world that makes altogether too much sense.

This all-consuming sense of rigor is reflected in the first part of *Sun* by its relentless march of unrhymed couplets, and in the second by its brief, almost memolike prose paragraphs. The language of both parts moves insistently, even violently, toward the nominative and the imperative, as if to capture and stabilize reality and to take command of the subject: "Let's call this The Quiet City / where screams are felt as waves" (*Codes Appearing* 213). Yet it is also in a state of constant flux, bombarding the reader with a surplus of imagery, as if one were locked in front of a television, endlessly channel surfing. Like so much of Palmer's work, the poem's discourse engages the problematic nature of verbal representation under the cultural conditions of postmodernity, and the impact that the crisis of signification has upon subjective experience. Thus the question of the self and of lyric expressivity is passed on from the Baudelaire Series poems to *Sun*. Yet unlike the poems in the Baudelaire Series—and for that matter, the many elliptical shorter pieces and serial texts in most of Palmer's earlier volumes—*Sun* is a sustained and insistent poem that gradually rises out of the detritus of language with mournful, bitter urgency, until it becomes an outcry against "The World As It Is / tango converted to a fugue // black milk, golden hair / cliffs, bridges, grey lake // and a grave in the air" (228). The references are to Celan's "Todesfuge," probably the most famous poem written in response to the Holocaust. Celan's earlier title for the poem was indeed "Todestango," referring to the tangos and other dance tunes played by musician prisoners at the command of the authorities in Auschwitz and other death camps.[14] But perhaps even more important than the allusion itself is the fact that as the poem became more famous, anthologized in postwar German high school textbooks, Celan came to believe that it had become appropriated by a society seeking an ungrantable "forgiveness" for past crimes. The original terrifying vision and radically defamiliarized locutions ("Black milk of daybreak we drink it at evening"; "we shovel a grave in the air") had become too easy, too accessible, leading Celan to write even more difficult and elliptical poems.[15]

What this means for Palmer in *Sun* is that the disasters of modern history cannot be understood apart from daily life, from "The World As It Is." Its governing powers respond to works of art that choose to engage this history by appropriating them and neutralizing their oppositional force. Thus the centralizing vision of *Sun* is of a wholly administered world of capitalist consumption, where "We, the center, offer narratives" in which competing ideologies fluidly transform themselves into their opposites, since "Symbolism died for your sins" (214). This vision is both reified and contested by the poem's relentlessly intelligent, self-referential language games and (despite the obvious pain of its discourse) its cool, distanced tone. The jarring discontinuities, disturbing imagery, and densely clustered allusions that impede one's progress through the text, are part of "the zero code / system of assemblage and separation" (216) that reveals the poet's dark irony and ineluctable skepticism. As the poet inquires of both himself and his readers, "Can you decode the birth of the sign // from the miniskirt, the unconscious, TV, the / mirage // of the referent, the equation / of A with A" (212–13). The philosophers, semioticians, and cultural theorists who haunt the pages of *Sun* (and who can be counted as part of the poem's implied readership) may well be able to negotiate these complex hermeneutical transactions—but to what end? For Palmer, "All these stories are the same / There is only one story— / but not really—" (215–16). The tautological and self-contradictory assertions of the poem induce not a visionary but a "versionary state" (220), a state in which "A body disappears into itself / its mirror self or sister self" (213), in which "This I is the I who speaks" (214), implying the radical fragmentation of the self into a series of disjointed utterances.

"Place yourself here as if on a surface" (212) orders one such utterance early in the poem. In *Sun*, the surface on which one places oneself is an un-

canny site that is both all too familiar and weirdly defamiliarizing, trivial-
ized and dreadfully serious:

> Through the glass box words
> pass unrecognised, thinking us
>
> now dead to you, reader,
> now an ammonite curve
>
> incomplete, now tablet
> of faint scratches, now redness
>
> in margins, now past
> and pastness. Now a filament of light
>
> penetrates the image-base
> where first glyphs are stored,
>
> Lucy and Ethel, the Kingfish,
> Beaver and Pinky Lee
>
> are spoken, die and undie
> for you
>
> like a war viewed from poolside
> by philosophers and sheiks
>
> senators and dialectician-priests (224)

Here, instead of the scratched clay tablets of antiquity, TV shows from the
1950s provide "the image-base / where first glyphs are stored." The ephem-
erality of the postmodern simulacrum is represented by the words passing
unrecognized through the television's "glass box," and the inane images
that "die and undie / for you." The power brokers of contemporary society
viewing the war from poolside are frighteningly prophetic of the television
coverage of the Gulf War, against which Palmer will protest in *Seven Poems
within a Matrix for War*, from his subsequent volume, *At Passages* (1995). Yet
a strongly self-critical tendency also can be observed at this point in the
poem: it is not only sheiks and senators relaxing around the TV, but philos-
ophers and "dialectician-priests" as well: an elite class of intellectuals that
includes avant-garde artists and poets such as Palmer himself. "Throughout
the city," declares Palmer, "there's the sound of broken glass // We have for-

gotten it / slipped between the pages" (*Codes Appearing* 223)—though what rises from the text into which "we" disappear is a "Song to End a World" (224).

This self-critical quality becomes even more explicit in the second part of the poem, in which a recurrent imperative phrase from the first part, "Call it . . . ," (or more politely and inclusively, "Let's call it . . .") modulates into the terse command "Write this." The move from calling to writing indicates a higher degree of technicality, a further distance from the referent. The result is horrific: "Write this. We have burned all their villages // Write this. We have burned all the villages and the people in them // Write this. We have adopted their customs and their manner of dress" (233). Imperialist violence results in new styles for the metropole, as native cultures are expropriated and transformed into commodities. Yet the process of commodification also turns back upon those who would criticize it: "Let go of me for I have died and am in a novel and was a lyric poet, certainly, who attracted crowds to mountaintops. For a nickel I will appear from this box. For a dollar I will have text with you and answer three questions" (233). The death of the poet (now entombed in an increasingly old-fashioned narrative form) seems to have made little difference to the individual in question: jack-in-the-box or whore, the corpse of the poet seems perfectly willing to accept his status as a mere entertainer, when once he was a prophetic figure "who attracted crowds to mountaintops." The lyric tradition reaches the ultimate danger point: "Pages torn from their spines and added to the pyre, so that they will resemble thought / Pages which accept no ink" (234). The poem, in effect, resists its own composition; it will not permit itself to be inscribed. As *Sun* comes to an end, real thought can be conveyed in poetry—in language—only in spite of itself, for language is confirmed once more to be a frighteningly neutral instrument of expression. "G for Gramsci or Goebbels" we read in one of the last lines, one single letter standing for the martyred Italian Communist whose insights into the workings of cultural hegemony bear directly on the poem, or for the heinous Nazi Minister of Propaganda, who fostered the worst forms of totalitarian art. Poised between the two, we learn that "The villages are known as These Letters—humid, sunless. The writing occurs on their walls" (235). If Palmer's poem is among these "sunless," *unilluminated* sites of writing, then it has lost its aura and has been stripped of all relation to the sacred. What we are reading then is only an appropriated, commodified version of the original, through which we adopt its mode of utterance as we adopt the villagers' "customs and their manner of dress" once the original "villages"—letters, poems—have been burned.

Or was there an original to begin with? What, in the end, are we to make of "The Letters" that constitute this poem? "Letters," after all, is a term meaning both the components of an alphabet, out of which we make words, and written communications sent from an author to a reader. As Roland Barthes might say, *Sun* offers an immense surplus of second-order signifiers that together constitute a myth of the postmodern. But it is also a desperate, self-incriminating missive, an epistle mailed off from the present to some unknown future recipient, telling of what we have become, explaining why this "future" may be the same as the present, why it is always already here. "We have entered an arena," writes Paul Mann, "where meaning can no longer be defined intrinsically—as a matter of either form or content—nor in terms of the customary extrinsic formations of sociopolitical analyses (the work as a repository of ideological formations). Meaning must now be defined as circulation within the discursive economy. It is this economy that finally writes the meaning, and discourse will always find a meaning to write. The meaning is the exchange" (30). This is a paradigm that Palmer both confirms and attempts to resist. What is represented in *Sun* is the act of "circulation within the discursive economy" itself: the poem lays bare the endless process of discursive exchange that would constitute the bad infinity of empty meaning but cannot, since the idea of "the work as repository of ideological formations" no longer obtains. For Mann, whose *Theory-Death of the Avant-Garde* was written nearly at the same time as *Sun* and sometimes reads like a ghostly commentary on it, virtually all artistic resistance through avant-garde strategies like Palmer's leads not merely to appropriation or recuperation, but to an uncanny situation in which "what dies is not the need or desire to produce new, advanced, adversarial work but the discursive space in which that impulse is permitted and permits itself to operate. . . . Hence the strange failure of failure, the curious double triumph and stalemate of recuperation, the way its arms clamp shut and are broken open even as they close, because they close, as a condition of their closure" (41).

To call *Sun* both a triumph and a stalemate is to name the book, as I did at the beginning of my reading, the representation of a crisis in literary culture that coincides with the overall trajectory of Palmer's work—an indication of its importance for poetry in our time. The evacuation of spirit and the loss of aura are experienced in every discursive register in the text, which yields to endless circulation, meaning as (empty) exchange. Again, I defer to Mann's analysis: "One might call it a crisis were it not for the fact that it announces an end of crisis theories of art.... Crisis is normative, hence there is no more crisis; only its exhaustion is critical.... A situation in which difference can be reproduced but can no longer be different. A situation characterized by the acceleration of the rate of recuperation past the rate of differentiation ... the entropic leveling of points of exchange within the discursive econo- my; the supersaturation of the dialectic; the whiting out of cultural maps" (115). But perhaps the whiting out of cultural maps can open up new spac- es: after all, despite the pessimism of the situation, we can acknowledge, as Mann does rather grudgingly, that "the need or desire to produce new, advanced, adversarial work" does not actually die. This is not to say that the cultural conditions with which we are dealing are simply left behind, which is an historical impossibility in any case. Rather, from the "supersatu- ration of the dialectic" emerges—dialectically—a mode of lyric expression that assumes the risk of discursive entropy through endless recuperation but nevertheless insists on the possibility that poetry may still be of service to such apparently lost and inescapably problematic notions as inwardness, aura, and spirit. This refunctioning of lyric is the task Palmer takes up in *At Passages*, while still following the serial procedures and deconstructive rhetoric that characterize his masterful style.

 :::

At Passages begins with *Letters to Zanzotto*, a sequence of eight poems ad- dressed to the Italian poet Andrea Zanzotto. Zanzotto was born in Treviso in 1921 and published his first book of poems in 1951; by the late sixties he was recognized as one of Italy's leading experimentalists. When Palmer be- gan reading Zanzotto's work in 1983, at the suggestion of Edmond Jabès, he felt an immediate kinship:

> It's one of those moments when, just as you think you are working, in some awful sense, alone, you realize that the conversation goes on—maybe even behind the speakers' backs. Naturally, his audacity with syntax, with the lexicon, delighted me. So I felt an affinity. I had been thinking backward, as you know, about the century, its voices, its wreckage, its monstrous events, all that cannot be spoken,

and all that is darkly carnivalesque. So I thought, Well, I'll write these "letters," direct these questions, to Zanzotto, or maybe "Zanzotto." Impossible questions about the century, borrowing language from his kit in homage to him." (e-mail)

Note the idea of conversation, of dialogue, that Palmer stresses here, as well as the sense of poetic comradeship, of being brought to Zanzotto's work through Jabès, the friend and fellow poet. The result is a different sort of "letter": rather than the corrosive self-reflexivity and the relentlessly desacralizing semiotic play of *Sun*, we find a strangely intimate mode of address, somehow both personal and public, which investigates the wreckage of modern history while offering, as Palmer indicates in "Letter 3," "The sign // we make for 'same as' / before whatever steps and walls" (*At Passages* 5). Then again, despite the distinct similarities between the poets and the sense that the conversation may continue unbeknownst to the interlocutors, it may well be "Zanzotto" and not Zanzotto to whom Palmer writes—an imagined version of the actual Italian poet, part of a utopian community in earnest but still playful communication in the face of the century's monstrous events. "Zanzotto" is not necessarily, or not only, the man himself, but another lyric subject confronting the same radically ironized conditions for poetic utterance; his absent presence provides Palmer with what Duncan would call the "permission" to enter a contested, dangerous zone of writing.[16]

In the foreword to the English edition of Zanzotto's *Selected Poetry*, Glauco Cambon compares Zanzotto to Wallace Stevens in that "the two poetical phenomenologists appear similarly engaged in staking rhetorical artifice against the elusive essence of things" (xx). This remark also points to the way Zanzotto's work resonates with that of Palmer, who may be regarded one of the boldest of Stevens's current descendents. The key term for both poets is "rhetorical artifice": it is only in the formulation of an ironized, highly self-conscious rhetoric, a stance that simultaneously acknowledges the necessity for and the impossibility of a contract with the reader, that the "essence of things" can be approached. This approach, however, also calls the very idea of essence into question. As the Italian critic Gino Rizzo says of Zanzotto in the afterword of the *Selected Poetry*, "freeing the sign from any link to a pre-existing 'meaning', the linguistic speculation of the poet becomes the mirror for an heteronomous intelligence of socially conditioned linguistic codes: his verbal fabrication presents itself as a program for an alternative social fabric" (309–10). This observation could as easily apply to Palmer, whose poetry seeks to free the sign from preexisting meaning in order to interrogate the ways in which linguistic codes are socially determined.

Yet as we have observed of such works as *Sun*, this interrogation, however it might present itself "as a program for an alternative social fabric," inevitably produces both criticism and self-criticism, accusation and self-accusation. Can the poet recover the lost essence of things—broken aura, abandoned spirit—or, because of the procedures to which he is devoted, does he only guarantee the impossibility of its recovery? The lyric subject's implication in the historical conditions it would seek to resist and undermine remains inescapable. Yet it is out of this very knowledge that the magnificent "Letter 1" emerges:

> Wasn't it done then undone, by
> us and to us, enveloped, sid-
> erated in a starship, listing
> with liquids, helpless letters—
> what else—pouring from that box,
> little gaps, rattles and slants
>
> Like mountains, pretty much worn down
> Another sigh of breakage, wintering
> lights, towers and a century of hair,
> cloth in heaps or mounds, and limbs,
> real and artificial, to sift among
>
> Did they really run out of things
> or was it only the names for things
> in the radial sublimity, that
> daubed whiteness, final
> cleansing and kindness, perfect
> snow or perfection of snow (*At Passages* 3)

These opening stanzas demonstrate the mastery of grammar and of tone that have always been at the center of Palmer's art. Here, ellipsis, condensation of imagery and reference, and the almost casual note of inquiry and observation all work together to ironically produce a sense of terrible pathos. "Wasn't it done then undone, by / us and to us": the question of agency, of responsibility, of subject and object, is urgently posed by these "helpless letters," and then nearly lost in the rush of observation. The distraught or unbalanced condition of the speaker is reflected in the enjambment of the lines, the "listing" that means both a compiling of things in order to name and know them, as well as an uncontrolled leaning to the side as the starship poem is "siderated," thunderstruck, blasted by malign sidereal forces. We are moving through space-time at a tremendous speed; like an impossibly fast-forwarded film of mountains in nature, we are worn down and experience a kind of psycholinguistic erosion or breakage. But what is happening to us is not a matter of nature but of history at its most monstrous, given the elliptical imagery of genocidal atrocities: "towers and a century of hair, / cloth in heaps or mounds, and limbs, / real and artificial, to sift among." For Palmer, however, this sifting through the horror of history is never a matter of unmediated experience, but of semiotics; thus we face a shortage not of things but of "the names for things." And indeed, what names can be applied to this terrible absence, this "daubed whiteness" (as if reality were a blank canvas, or Malevich's painting *White on White*), this "final / cleansing and kindness"? One thinks of the "final solution," of "ethnic cleansing." But given the multivalence of Palmer's discourse, the "cleansing"—not of people, but of language—may also prove to be "kindness," a search for a degree zero of discourse reflecting a "radial sublimity," "perfect / snow or perfection of snow."

Many of the phrases in "Letter 1" refer to Zanzotto's "The Perfection of the Snow," a poem from his revolutionary volume *La Beltà* (*Beauty*, 1968). As the title indicates, the poem engages the "perfection" of particular natural objects, or what Zanzotto calls "totalities," in their relation to the always unfinished human processes of understanding and *poesis*, which in comparison to the snow are "abstractions astrifications astral formulations / star-chill, across sidera and coelos." In the presence of the snow, the poet declares that "I involved myself in the middle of this radial movement-faintness / alas the first shiver of ascending, of understanding, / they fall into marching-order, they challenge: that's all" (211). The challenge Zanzotto faces complicates Palmer's situation in "Letter 1" as well; the former writes of "radial movement-faintness," the latter of "radial sublimity." Radial refers to rays moving from or toward a center point, creating a symmetry, a perfected roundness. In the presence of such perfection, the poet experiences a faintness that is also "the first shiver of ascending, of understanding," which in turn relates to the sublime, a kind of transcendent terror we experience in the presence of nature's inexpressible beauty—or in the presence of the numinous, the divine.

Thus in Palmer's poem, drawing partly from Zanzotto, three ideas come into play: the sublime perfection of the natural creation, the disaster of human history, and the dubious, unreliable, but necessary power of language, through which we attempt to articulate both perfection and failure. Triangulating those ideas, the poem is an inquiry into *"Whoever has not choked on a word,"* a phrase printed in italics and set off as a stanza unto itself. The phrase is ambiguous: we cannot tell if it is a rhetorical question or an adjectival phrase. On the one hand, what thoughtful individual, sensitive to the degradations of language in the media, in politics, in marketing and so on, has not "choked on a word" at one time or another? On the other hand, could it not be said that it is the poet, "calling in counter-talk" as Palmer puts it, who remains most responsible for maintaining the viability of utterance in modern society, so that we do not continually choke on words? The risk that Palmer's poetry must take is based on its engagement with those social forces and formations that would negate the possibility of poetry altogether. It must risk the destruction of its aura in order to preserve its auratic condition; it must expose its hermetic inwardness in order to continue to voice that inwardness. The last lines of "Letter 1" invoke

> Torches, cobbles and red flags?
> The calcined walls facing whenness
> meant as witness. The few
> trans things smelling of sex and pine
>
> said what to them
> and to us as them   (*At Passages* 3)

The poem returns to the ambiguities of agency and responsibility proposed at its beginning. Who stood against the "calcined walls" at some moment of crisis, even atrocity, the historical moment of "whenness / meant as witness"? Who did what to whom? And what of those "trans things"? Are they commodities in a perpetual state of flux, "smelling of sex and pine" to appeal to a "them" who is also an "us"? These are the unanswerable questions posed by these "helpless letters," which, given the correspondence between poet and poet, may not be as helpless as they first appear. For it is in the act of poetic correspondence that Palmer is able to continue his investigation into what, in "Letter 2," he calls, "Belowabove: hum of the possible-to-say" (4).

And what, for Palmer, as he communes with Zanzotto, exactly *is* the possible-to-say—and what, conversely, is the *impossible*-to-say? The "Below-above," like Zanzotto's "first shiver of ascending," reminds us that these letters are concerned with the (im)possibility of *transcendence*. "Letter 5" begins "Desired, the snow falls upward, / the perfect future, a text / of wheels" (7). Like the siderated starship that is "Letter 1," this poem too is fueled by desire and hurtles towards the perfect future, only to be impeded by the vicissitudes of modern history. Thus "Days were called the speed book / then the scream book, rail / book then the book of rust": history accelerates, becomes horrible in its efficiency (again, consider the Nazi deportation of Jews to the camps by rail) or simply rusts into obsolescence. It becomes a matter of old photographs, "the images negated in ornate frames, / firebricks, funnels and trucks, / figment and testament as one" (7). The poem presents itself as both figment and testament, arbitrary fabrication and truthful declaration, a covenant that calls itself into doubt.

Such is the instability of poetic language, or language in general, as Palmer reminds us in "Letter 6." Here is the poem in its entirety:

Dear Z,
So we accused mimesis, accused

anemone
and the plasma of mud

accused pleasure, sun
and the circle of shadow (8)

"So we accused mimesis" refers to Zanzotto's "The Elegy in Petèl," also from *La Beltà*, in which the poet declares "I break nothing not already broken but quickly mended, / I break very little and—though they're unplaceable— accuse / mimesis irony compassion" (*Selected Poetry* 241). To accuse mimesis is to accuse the language of representation, to gesture toward the impossible condition of a purely poetic "thing language" (as Spicer would say) that is broken by utterance but always capable of self-repair. "Petèl," according to Zanzotto's translators, "is Veneto dialect for the caressing baby-talk mothers and nurses address to small children, with which they try to approximate the children's own talk.... Petèl is a pre-language and at the same time suggests the end of language and of poetry.... Petèl remains an undefined field of expression that could no longer exist. It is as though it had no beginning and were reluctant to come to a formal poetic conclusion" (336). Thus Zanzotto and Palmer share, on the one hand, a pervasive skepticism of mimetic language as it functions in the grownup world, the Lacanian symbolic order; and on the other hand, a somewhat abashed desire for an impossible, utopian return to the pre-Oedipal imaginary, the order of the undifferentiated subject and object, where all language is poetry and yet poetry is beside the point. I say "abashed" because these poets understand the impossibility of such a return, which is why Zanzotto accuses irony *and* compassion, why Palmer accuses both mimesis *and* pleasure, both sun *and* the circle of shadow.

Yet as we see in "Letter 7," the desire for a language that is commensurate with ecstatic or transcendent experience remains, despite the poet's continued ambivalence toward his medium of expression:

> But the buried walls and our mouths of fragments,
> *no us but the snow staring at us ...*
>
> And you Mr. Ground-of-What, Mr. Text, Mr. Is-Was
> can you calculate the ratio between wire and window
>
> between tone and row, copula and carnival
> and can you reassemble light from the future-past
>
> in its parabolic nest
> or recite an entire winter's words,
>
> its liberties and pseudo-elegies,
> the shell of a street-car in mid-turn
>
> or scattered fires in the great hall
> I would say not-I here I'd say *The Book of Knots* (*At Passages* 9)

The italicized second line comes from Zanzotto's "Yes, the Snow Again," also from *La Beltà*. In Zanzotto's poem, as in "The Elegy in Petèl," the perplexity of the lyric subject facing even the most basic and objective of natural phenomena leads to an investigation of the child's experience of language. "Yes, the Snow Again" reflects Zanzotto's bitterness toward what "the avant-garde found" in that investigation, as well as toward the "con-consuming of the consumers": both social groupings, usually seen at odds with each other, have lost "the enthusiasm the rising to the Empyrean the ecstasy" (219) that traditional lyricism could at least promise, if not always provide. Palmer follows suit, turning directly to "Mr. Ground-of-What, Mr. Text, Mr. Is-Was," figures whose names are suggestive of both characters from a children's book or TV show, and of mimetic writing practices that reify even the most fundamental categories of space and time. Once again his tone is accusatory: can these mere figures of speech "reassemble light from the future-past," that is, change the disasters of history that we know have occurred in the past, and worse, are bound to occur again in the future? Like Zanzotto, Palmer refuses to offer any "pseudo-elegies" by way of consolation; he rejects the blandishments of poetic self-expression, writing instead a "*Book of Knots*," a poem of the "not-I," a lyric stutter addressed to a lost twin:

> Dear Z, I'd say it's time, it's nearly time, it's almost, it's just about, it's long past time now time now for the vex- for the vox- for the voices of shadows
>
> time for the prism letters, trinkets and shrouds,
> for a whirl in gauzy scarves around the wrecked piazza (*At Passages* 9)

As is so often the case in Palmer's work, the strange list is weirdly suggestive. Given the course of history, it's time, it's nearly time for the vexing vox or voices of shadows—repressed, heretical voices—to speak. These voices are not quite like that of Antonio Gramsci's *Prison Letters*, written while the great Italian Marxist languished in Mussolini's jail. Rather, they are "prism letters," endlessly refracted speech acts that deceptively present themselves as "trinkets and shrouds" suitable "for a whirl in gauzy scarves around the wrecked piazza," as if the poem has become a scene from some postwar Italian film, filled with stylish gestures and an ineluctable sense of mortality.

And indeed, things get more crazily cinematic as the poem modulates into the voice of a flight attendant or tour guide who is simultaneously a visionary or prophet:

> Messieurs-Dames, Meine Herren und Damen, our word-balloon, you will note,
>   is slowly

rising over the parched city,

its catacombs, hospitals and experimental gardens,
its toll-gates, ghettos and ring-roads,

narcoleptics and therapists and stray cats
Ladies and Gentlemen, our menu for this flight

due to temporary shortages,
will be alpha-omega soup, Bactrian hump, and nun's farts

As we enter the seventh sphere, you will discover a thin
layer of ice just beginning

to form on your limbs
Do not be alarmed, this is normal

You will experience difficulty breathing, this is normal
The breathing you experience is difficulty, this is normal (9–10)

In a moment of severe but unnamed crisis, the "parched city" experiences "temporary shortages," yet business appears to be going on as usual. Palmer alludes in these lines to the siege of Paris during the Franco-Prussian War in 1870, when slaughtered zoo animals appeared on the menus of fashionable restaurants and Léon Gambetta, the French minister of the interior, escaped from the capital by balloon. The disasters of that war, of course, led to the even greater tragedy of the Paris Commune, toward which Palmer, in the main, would be quite sympathetic. Thus in "Letter 7," the sophisticated, multilingual poet/guide treats the bourgeois dignitaries—or vacationing tourists—to "alpha-omega soup" (both the jumbled letters of alphabet soup and a sign of the apocalypse), "Bactrian hump" (exotic, but perhaps filled with nothing but ordinary water) and "nun's farts" (the divine afflatus turned grossly profane). Or are they only being served words? A "word-balloon," after all, gestures toward an old-fashioned means of transport but also refers to the rounded spaces above the heads of talking comic strip characters. Somehow the contract between poet and reader (tour guide and tourist) has gone terribly awry, reduced to a cartoon, and as the word balloon floats above the sphere of conventional readerly expectations, the poet appears to express a certain deadpan but nonetheless sadistic glee as ice forms on the limbs of the passengers and their breathing becomes difficult. Or rather,

"The breathing you experience is difficulty": if poetry at its most primal level is a matter of drawing in the divine breath, of "inspiration," then the "normal" condition in a poem of this sort is a difficulty that is never found in more easily consumable literature. In other words, the poet as prophet, as one who leads his readers to a higher sphere through vision and testimony, must acknowledge that his calling has become totally self-ironizing, though the yearning for transcendence remains.

In the Ptolemaic system of the heavens on which Dante bases his *Paradiso*, the seventh sphere, the sphere of Saturn, is the crystal sphere of ice. In Dante's allegory, it is the sphere of temperance, where may be found the souls of monks who have lived lives of contemplation and restraint. It would appear that poets may continue to breathe in this rarefied atmosphere, while passengers or readers, used to more earthly indulgences, are bound to have more trouble. Returning to earth, the end of "Letter 7"—this letter from the seventh sphere—becomes even more ominous:

> Dear Z, Should I say space
> constructed of echoes, rifts, mirrors, a strange
>
> year for touring the interior
> Should I say *double dance, Horn, axis* and *wheel*
>
> Dear A, Scuttled ships are clogging the harbors
> and their cargoes lie rotting on the piers
>
> Prepare executions and transfusions
> Put on your latest gear (10)

As Palmer indicates, the two poets have together produced a space "constructed of echoes, rifts, mirrors." And with what seems to be yet another political crisis on the horizon, it is indeed a strange year for touring such an interior space—though perhaps the crisis makes such a tour all the more important. Are the temporary shortages mentioned earlier in the poem due to those rotting cargoes, cargoes of words from scuttled poems? As A dons the latest gear, whose executions are being prepared? One thinks of the slaughter of the Communards, at the dawn of an age of both political horrors and trendy consumption. Faced with such conditions, what can the ironic poet-prophet do?

In "Letter 8," the last poem in the sequence, Palmer offers at least a pro-
visional answer, both an affirmation of his calling and its heretical refusal.
"A" appears again: "So A's finally, alephs and arcades" (11). The poem begins
by acknowledging that it is the last of the letters to Zanzotto, though it has
also returned to the first letter of the Hebrew alphabet, the ancient, mysti-
cal source of unutterable truth. The mention of "arcades" also reminds us
of Walter Benjamin's *Arcades Project* and of the modernist phenomena that
he examines with virtually kabbalistic intensities. Balanced, therefore, be-
tween ancient and modern truths, Palmer asks

> But what does the whir- the wer- what does the word
>
> need—world need to be gone—to perform—what
> does the world
>
> before you need
> to become perfect (11)

The stuttered shift from "whir" to "wer" to "word" to "world" indicates that
the utopian search for a language commensurate with both desire and real-
ity must continue: the world must be gone, must disappear, must perform
its own unmaking, but only because the desire for perfection continually
remakes it. Can the poet even begin to articulate the desire for such tran-
scendence? Can he speak, as Palmer puts it,

> . . . aloud, unearthed
> as a language of nets
>
> Actual blue and citron
> Actual grey underleaf—so
>
> many bundles to burn—take them to the woods
> and burn them in heaps
>
> A's before B's
> Take the versions in your mouth
>
> Take inside into your mouth
> unearthed, all smoke, blue
>
> and citron, actual word
> for that earth and that smoke. (11–12)

As is sometimes the case in Palmer's work, the poem adumbrates some obscure, private ritual. Following the poem's instructions, the poet speaks aloud an unearthed (that is, uncovered or revealed) language of nets (and all language is a language of nets) that seems to capture the actual qualities of reality. The words that represent the actual are then bundled up, taken into the woods and burned. It is as if all the words that represent all the things are being sacrificed in alphabetical order, so that, like the smoke rising from an altar, or the fumes before a sybil, they may be inhaled by the poet. In this way, the poet's contract with language and reality, the covenant he makes with the orders of the cosmos, is renewed. He will know again the "actual word / for that earth and that smoke." But Palmer also knows (and the lessons of Duncan, Spicer, and earlier precursors loom large for him) how inherently, persistently volatile such a covenant is—and how, paradoxically, especially under contemporary historical conditions, the poet keeps faith with it by the violation of the lyric aura, the heretical renunciation or betrayal of his traditional role.

:::

Having read the *Letters to Zanzotto* in some detail, I would like to step back and review the most important points I have been trying to make in regard to the problem of Spirit in Palmer's work. I will then proceed to a consideration of a few more poems in *At Passages* and indicate how this volume may be understood as an opening to Palmer's more recent, twenty-first-century poetry.

First, Palmer's understanding of the poet is analogous to that of the heretic, and in his work the sacred and the profane are often indistinguishable. Although he acknowledges the romantic idea of the poet as prophet, he honors it more through its violation, through dispelling the lyric aura and questioning unself-conscious expressions of transcendence. Not only does poetry undermine and challenge all systems of belief, often promiscuously appropriating various philosophical and theological formulations, but poetry, according to Palmer, must continually and rigorously undermine itself, calling the premises of its own utterance into question and opposing its orthodoxies and conventions even as they come into being.

Second, this attitude is directly related to matters of form, structure, and genre. Language is fundamentally unstable, indeterminate, and polysemous. Poetic form entails both a making and an unmaking, a binding and an unbinding, because *poesis* is, to borrow Jerome Rothenberg's definition, "an inherently impure activity of individuals creating reality from all conditions & influences at hand" (9). Palmer's poems are meticulously crafted, making use of innovative, unsettling rhetoric and subtle technique, yet they also insist on their discursive "impurity" and appear, as often as not, to be the work of a conjuror engaged in a sort of syntactic sleight of hand. Images are distorted; words are repeated, rhymed, punned, excised. Principles of seriality and contiguity shape but also deform sequences of poems and even whole books; sustained, broken off, and resumed, Palmer's sets (and I am thinking here of a set as in a jazz performance) are structured around gaps, interstices, discontinuities, and silence.

Third, History is in crisis and therefore Spirit is in crisis—or vice versa. Yet this crisis enters into Palmer's work at at least one remove, through constant observation of the simulacrum and the endless play of signification. Under the conditions of postmodernity, therefore, Spirit may be "troublesome and rebarbative," but as a category of being, as a way of experiencing and understanding the contemporary world, it is in no way privileged, and surely no more so than the political or the ethical dimensions of Palmer's work. "And the name once again to be the old one" writes Palmer in "H," one of the *Seven Poems within a Matrix for War*; "Saint Something, Saint Gesture, Saint Entirely the Same / as if nothing or no one had been nameless in the interim / or as if *still* could be placed beside *storm*" (*At Passages* 21). Written at the time of the first Gulf War, of Operation Desert Storm, these lines indicate that the perpetual crisis may be understood in terms of the exhaustion and depletion of religious categories, and that, conversely, the political status quo has been elevated to a level of sainthood; that is, has taken on the aura of the sacred. Though Palmer's poems always risk the reification of these conditions, ultimately they challenge them, defamiliarizing the signifying practices to which we have become inured and manifesting themselves "like tongue-tied and transparent angels" (20), difficult to understand but still full of light.

This situation becomes more apparent in "Untitled (September '92)," which provides the title for *At Passages*.[17] I have already referred to this crucial poem in the introduction; now I wish to unpack it in detail. Here are the first five stanzas:

Or maybe this
is the sacred, the vaulted and arched, the
nameless, many-gated
zero where children

where invisible children
where the cries
of invisible children rise
between the Cimitière M

and the Peep Show Sex Paradise
Gate of Sound and Gate of Sand—
Choirs or Mirrors—
Choir like a bundle of tongues

Mirror like a ribbon of tongues
(such that image will remain
once the objects are gone)
Gate of the Body and Gate of the Law

Gate of Public Words, or Passages,
of Suddenness and Cells, Compelling Logic, Gate
of the Hat Filled with Honey
and Coins Bathed in Honey (73)

"The vaulted and arched" leads one to think of a cathedral, or, given the indeterminate "this," the poem as cathedral. In either case, it is a traditional site of the sacred, yet here it is a "nameless, many-gated zero." Its power is gone, which means it cannot perform the transactions between human and divine orders that we associate with religious rituals, and, in its origins, with poetry as well. It amounts to nothing, and without a name, it will be lost to memory. But again, in a typical move, Palmer goes on to name the many gates or points of interaction of this non-edifice, some of which at least (Gate of the Law, Gate of Public Words) connote modes of discourse we traditionally associate with authoritative religious, state, or cultural institutions.[18] The choir of this degree zero cathedral (compare Shakespeare's "Bare ruined choirs where late the sweet birds sang") is "like a bundle of tongues": it does not sing in one harmonious voice, and if anything, it is like a mirror, narcissistically reflecting the viewer or retaining only images "once the objects are gone." Perhaps this choir is made up of the ghostly "invisible children" whose cries "rise / between the Cimitière M // and the Peep Show Sex Paradise," and if such is the case, then Palmer may be suggesting that the poem/cathedral itself is uncannily situated between the two.

The Cimitière M refers to Paul Valéry's "Le Cimitière Marin" (1920), a late symbolist masterpiece in which the poet contemplates the virtues of the Absolute in relation to the spiritual and intellectual limits of mortality. "Chanterez-vous quand serez vaporeuse?" (150) asks the poet of the soul (Will you sing when you are vapor?). Despite the lure of transcendence and the inevitability of death, Valéry recognizes that pure, unchanging spirit is an impossible goal for humanity, especially for the poet, who longs to sing. Though the poem may be born "Entre le vide et l'évenement pure" (149) (Between emptiness and the pure event), the poet concludes, "Il faut tenter de vivre!" (151) (It is necessary to try to live!), not only as an existential imperative in general, but as a poetic one in particular.

But how is one to live, how is one to sing, and where does one locate one's song? Apparently somewhere between Valéry's sublime spiritual meditation on transcendence and death, and "the Peep Show Sex Paradise." One of the most rarefied of modern poetic utterances is counterpoised to the most vulgar form of "artistic" (that is, pornographic) gratification, the peep show. But note that the operative term is "Paradise": the peep show is wholly profane, but still bound to a founding cultural myth in which the desire of soul and body are satisfied as one. Thus the poem is indeed "The Gate of the Body," a place of "Passages / of Suddenness and Cells, Compelling Logic." It is a site of sudden incursions, of reason and desire, of discrete discursive units or cells that are nevertheless held together through Palmer's uncanny powers of tone and measure. "At Passages," Palmer declares later in the text, "we peer out / over a tracery of bridges," as the poem, like Duncan's precursor work, becomes an interminable weave of intertextual connections. Yet Palmer's attitude toward such open work does not entirely coincide with his mentor's exuberance:

> And at Lateness we say
> *This will be the last*
> *letter you'll receive*
> *final word you'll hear*

from me for now
Is it that a fire
once thought long extinguished
continues to burn

deep within the ground,
a fire finally acknowledged
as impossible to put out,
and that plumes of flames and smoke

will surface at random
enlacing the perfect symmetries
of the Museum of the People
and the Palace of the Book (*At Passages* 74)

Palmer is undoubtedly familiar with "The Fire, Passages 13," one of the most important of the poems in Duncan's series, a poem that juxtaposes Duncan's mythic and religious notions to his prophetic understanding of political history and current events. Peter O'Leary observes that "'The Fire' is a compelling illustration of the joining of personal myth with political conflict into a master gnostic narrative" (*Gnostic Contagion* 83). The complex and ambiguous image of the fire itself may be linked to what O'Leary calls "Duncan's creative power . . . a combative contemplation of the fraught genesis of the cosmos, both his personal cosmos and the warring world at large" (84). "Do you know the language of the old belief?" (*Bending the Bow* 41) asks Duncan near the start of the poem, and what follows may be read as an attempt, if not to actually regain knowledge of this lost language, then at least to establish that the old belief still endures and that its power is still to be felt.

Along the same lines, Palmer's fire, "once thought long extinguished" is now "finally acknowledged / as impossible to put out." Utterly transformative, it is both threatening and creative, "enlacing"—but not destroying—the "perfect symmetries" of the established social order in the form of its basic modern repositories, the museum and the archive. In "Untitled (September '92)," we move, then, from an apparently desacralized holy place or verbal gesture emptied of ritual force, to "the Museum of the People / and the Palace of the Book" that are both threatened and enhanced by an ancient but irrepressible fire that "will surface at random," a destabilizing spirit that "speaks / in a language unfamiliar / unlike any known, / yet one clear enough" (*At Passages* 74). Is it the language of the old belief? Yes and no: the poem, like the "houses of blue paper" with which it ends, seems "built over fault lines / as if by intent" (75). What does it mean for a poem to be built by intent over the fault line of belief? The instability of the sacred that is thematized in "Untitled (September '92)" is an old story, but one that takes on an increased urgency under the conditions of postmodernity through which and against which Palmer writes.

"Even as it passes / we can't make out its name" (79) begins another crucial poem in Untitled, called "Under the Perseids." The Perseids are a great meteor shower occurring every summer. The "it" may be a meteor flashing by, but as in the case of "Untitled (September '92), the pronoun may also refer to the poem itself, a meteoric moment of light in the dark. Palmer's rethinking of the poem as sacred site now leads him to question whether "the b—the buzz—of blessing / might have been all knowledge." This is surely an instance of what Duncan calls "primary trouble," the feeling of panic occurring when "the word no longer protects, transforming the threat of an overwhelming knowledge into the power of an imagined reality" (*Fictive Certainties* 7). The hesitance of the stuttered "b" moving to "buzz" and then "blessing" reveals a great deal: in the buzz of endless discourse to which we are continually exposed, might we also hear a blessing? Does that buzz constitute a blessing in itself—or does it interfere with the reception of the blessing? Does that blessing constitute in turn the entirety of "knowledge"? Secular knowledge, the mastery of *techné* or science? Or knowledge as *gnosis*, Duncan's "overwhelming knowledge" that entails the imaginative leap of spiritual transformation?

There are, of course, no definite answers to such questions, which is precisely the point that Palmer's enigmatic poems make again and again. But the importance of the poems in the Untitled sequence lies in the way they explicitly present themselves as sites wherein the sacred and the secular, blessing and buzz, may be contested. These poems are haunted, uncanny places to which the ghosts of belief and of the cultural traditions that have mediated belief in the past may return, only to be rearticulated through the poet's heretical sensibility. Thus in "Under the Perseids," blessing and knowledge are found

> swimming in a blank book
> a stone book opened flat

or maybe just a phrase book
where bread translates as bread

felt opposite of itself (*At Passages* 79)

In reading Palmer's work, we can never take the status of "the book" for granted. The question we must always ask of "the book"—the scripture, the *écriture* that presents itself as a book but also opposes the book ("a blank book / a stone book")—is whether a word is to be taken to mean itself or to be translated, by way of a hermeneutic, into something else again. Does bread translate as bread or the "opposite of itself"? Are we still caught in what Derrida calls the book's "encyclopedic protection of theology and of logocentrism," or are we outside of the book, projected beyond it through the endless play (or buzz) of signification? Under these conditions, what still constitutes the act of blessing? Reading the book becomes "An encounter, it says // as if such were as simple / as tossing dust in the air." "Under the Perseids" becomes the site of this encounter, a contest between the nominal and the real, the sacred and the profane, and an inquiry into whether spirit can still reside in the house of language. The poem is the place where "this question, the angle of a gaze // the paradise it describes / and the one it denies" may be posed. Posed in this way, language may or may not describe paradise, depending on how one looks at it. But rather than speak in generalities (because, after all, this is neither philosophy nor theology, but poetry), Palmer, in the rest of the poem, offers a particular scenario:

A few friends are seated on a verandah
in the impossibly heavy air

The music floating up
seems some combination

of theramin and washboard
fiddle and mandolin

We do not believe it
Do we believe instead

in the blue of history,
the flare of a spirit lamp

bridging two bodies,

how the surface of the hand

will imitate a map
Whatever it is

mirror to mirror
that suddenness of crows

tremor as the body opens
always perishing (80)

A theramin (usually spelled theremin) is an electronic instrument invent-
ed by a Russian, Leon Theremin, in 1919. It is played by waving one's hands
near the instrument's two antennae, one controlling pitch, the other volume,
producing an otherworldly sound. It has been used in soundtracks of science
fiction films and by rock bands, including the Beach Boys in their hit "Good
Vibrations." To pair such an instrument with washboard, fiddle, and mando-
lin, all traditionally used in country jug band music, would be strange indeed,
so it makes sense that the friends on the verandah "do not believe it." What
they do believe is more difficult to determine, but there is something very
poignant about "the blue of history" and the intimacy of the bodily imagery
that follows. Perhaps for the poet and his friends, love and history face each
other as *"mirror to mirror"*: the body opens to love despite the certain knowl-
edge of its perishing. In the brief, enigmatic lyric just prior to "Under the
Perseids" called "From the Anthology (W's Dream)," Eros takes on (or reas-
serts) a primal, mythic power that links it to the moment of creation itself,
however caught up in the endless regress of textuality and representation:

A book full of dark pictures
or was it a poem
discovered in a book
whose first line read

"A book full of dark pictures"
dark as the river of Eros
or Creation's mists
Who will even notice

among such images
if we should exchange breath

for breath, enter
each other

with pain and pleasure mixed
as in a book full of dark pictures
dark as a dream of translation
or Creation's mists (78)

There is something both simple and deeply mysterious about this poem; for me, it achieves the grace and inevitability that I associate with poetry of a very high order. The erotic encounter at the heart of the poem, the exchange of breath for breath, the entrance into the desired other "with pain and pleasure mixed," is connected through the repetition and play of representation (is it a book of pictures? a poem about a book of pictures? a poem about a poem about a book of pictures?) to "the river of Eros / or Creation's mists." In many mythic accounts, Eros is the divine power that brings Creation into being; the force of desire flows through all things like a river and out of misty nothingness the created world arises. This "dream of translation" brings the lovers together, but it is also the dream that draws the poem and its reader together, making a comprehensible whole. Divine Eros, in other words, accounts for the continuity of poetry, whatever the difficulties of "translation."

It is risky to generalize about a project as complex as Palmer's, but I would venture to say that some of the most important work in his recent volumes, *The Promises of Glass* (2000) and *Company of Moths* (2005) takes as its inspiration the idea that moving through the heterogeneity of creation—and the heterogeneity of discourse—is a spirit of desire that seeks to ritualize the poem while at the same time continually desacralizing it, demystifying it. "We share the invisible nature of these / things, our bodies and theirs" (*Company of Moths* 4), declares the poet at the end of "And," the first poem in his most recent volume. Or as the opening line of the title poem goes, "We thought it could all be found in The Book of Poor Text" (15). The ensuing poem casts this possibility into doubt, but the poet is still urging "Faith in the Poor Text" (16) as it draws to a close. Does he heed his own words, and should we? It remains difficult to decide. Such is problem of spirit in Michael Palmer's poems.

6

Nathaniel Mackey

SHAMANISM AND THE UNITY OF ALL RITES

Shamanism is like a theatrical performance in which one actor plays all the roles at once. (Girard, *Violence* 286)

Tricks played with letters,
                              little
  else...
(Mackey, *Whatsaid Serif* 68)

If Michael Palmer's poetry represents an evacuation of the sacred under the aegis of a heretical secularism (or a secular heresy), then by contrast, Nathaniel Mackey's poetry represents a proliferation, a surplus of spirit, a comprehensive process of sacralization that may be observed throughout his career. This pervasive tendency to sacralize and mythologize poetic utterance does not, however, produce a "religious" or "devotional" poetry in any normative sense. Mackey is every bit as agonistic (or as he would put it, "discrepant") as Palmer, or, to invoke their precursors, as Duncan and Spicer. But whereas Palmer's poetry offers only lingering traces of its spiritual agon, presenting instead a kaleidoscopic vision of modernity through its continued emphasis on verbal play, Mackey's work teems with spirit—and spirits. Few poets today approach Mackey's status as a "technician of the sacred" (Mircea Eliade's term, popularized by Jerome Rothenberg), and few volumes of contemporary poetry seem quite so much like gatherings of rituals, catalogues of sacred acts, and books of spells as do *Eroding Witness* (1985), *School of Udhra* (1993), *Whatsaid Serif* (1998), and *Splay Anthem* (2006).

Mackey has been unusually fortunate in regard to his closest readers: with attention bordering on religious devotion, critics, scholars, and (most revealingly) fellow poets have researched and interpreted the immense range of cross-cultural myths, texts, historical events, and schools of thought and belief that rhythmically pulse through and punctuate the open, recursive, and frequently obsessive turns of his work. Mackey himself has led the way in this enterprise: a brilliant critic in his own right, his essays, gathered in *Discrepant Engagement* (1993) and *Paracritical Hinge* (2005), provide a clear path through the often recondite and unfamiliar cultural materials that so inspire him. His lengthy interviews further indicate the degree to which he wishes his work to be illuminated through explanation and conversation with reader-initiates. Yet Mackey's academic training and scholarly concerns take on a certain uncanny quality in light of his poetry and fiction. With his degrees from Princeton and Stanford and his longtime position as a professor of literature at the University of California, Santa Cruz, Mackey may appear rather remote from the adepts and magi, the gnostic initiates, wandering mystics, tribal elders, and cultic devotees who appear in his work. Even the careers of many of the modern poets and musicians he regards as his immediate precursors have an unsettled, nomadic, "bedouin" quality compared to Mackey's steady development, his remarkably focused attention to just a few projects over many years.

Be that as it may, Mackey is still a latter-day shaman whose textual practices both wound and heal, unsettling the linguistic and psychosocial expectations of his readers, taking possession of them and carrying them beyond themselves. Reading Mackey deeply and becoming his commentator means being possessed by the poetry, recapitulating the possession that first led to the composition of the work. Mackey is the spokesperson for what he names, in the preface to *Splay Anthem*, "the flight and fugitivity the poems point to and report. The poems' we, a lost tribe of sorts, a band of nervous travelers, know nothing if not locality's discontent, ground gone under. Sonic semblance's age-old promise, rhyme's reason, the consolation they seek in song, accents and further aggravates movement. The songs are increasingly songs of transit" (x). Reading Mackey, we join him as members of this band; our inchoate, previously unrealized sense of existential and cosmic exile is gradually revealed to us as we experience "the flight and fugitivity" of his haunted song.

Then again, a phrase such as "flight and fugitivity" is bound to remind many readers more specifically of the plight of escaped slaves in the years before the Civil War. One thinks, for instance, of the Fugitive Slave Act of 1850, which heightened the tensions between North and South and increased the determination of the abolitionists. But note that in Mackey's discourse, such a phrase serves as a ghostly historical reference; it is not fully and specifically unpacked and certainly does not become the subject per se of a poem. Rather, it is woven into the textual fabric of "rhyme's reason." In this way, the conditions of diaspora, both historical (the African diaspora) and spiritual (gnosticism's view of a general spiritual exile) come to define Mackey's poetry. Under these conditions, which he so elegantly, so urgently describes, we become strangers to ourselves; in wandering with him, we meet ghostly versions of ourselves in whom we recognize long-suppressed truths, grounded in a history of oppression and loss but that also point to gnosis, knowledge of the exile that defines our spiritual being. Mackey uses a quote referring to the followers of Simon Magus from one of his favorite books, Jacques Lacarrière's *The Gnostics*, as a revealing epigraph to "Song of the Andoumboulou: 17": "to remove the very categories of I, Thou, He, *and to become We*, such must be the meaning of the so-called 'mysteries of the Simonians'" (*Whatsaid Serif* 9).[1] Removing pronominal categories to form a collectivity grounded in both history and myth is fundamental to Mackey's poetic. Toward this end, as René Girard would have it, the poet/shaman plays all the roles at once.

But this is not necessarily an open invitation. In Mackey's case, as is true of gnosticism in general, both reading and writing are *esoteric* activities; hence my use of the term "reader-initiate." Esoterism as a textual practice is fundamentally disruptive of normative religious belief, and I believe a parallel can be drawn in regard to the reading of "secular" poetry and the equally "secular" practice of literary criticism. To read Mackey seriously is not only to be possessed, but to be initiated, to enact *ta'wil*, or spiritual exegesis, a term that Mackey has appropriated for his poetry and which he originally learned in his reading of Henry Corbin, the great scholar of Islamic mysticism. Corbin refers to the "Event" of *ta'wil*

> as the mainspring of every spirituality, in the measure to which it pre-eminently furnishes the means of going beyond all conformisms, all servitudes to the letter, all opinions ready made.... [T]he *truth* of *ta'wil* rests on the simultaneous *reality*

of the mental operation in which it consists and of the psychic Event that gives rise to it. The *ta'wil* of texts supposes the *ta'wil* of the soul. . . . Reciprocally, the soul takes its departure, accomplishes the *ta'wil* of its true being, by basing itself on a text—the text of a book or cosmic text—which its efforts will carry to a transmutation, raise to the rank of a real, but inner and psychic, Event. (*Avicenna* 28, 31)

Mackey's understanding of poetry is a "going beyond all conformisms, all servitudes to the letter." The constant references to "books" in his poetry indicate a soul taking its ecstatic departure through the transmutative Event of writing, which is recapitulated by his reader through the process of commentary.

"The *ta'wil*," observes Corbin, "presupposes a flowering of symbols and hence the active Imagination, the organ which at once produces symbols and apprehends them. . . . By its very essence the *ta'wil* cannot inhabit the realm of everyday fact; it postulates an esoterism" (*Creative Imagination* 14–15). Historically, such esoterism, requiring initiation upon a path toward gnosis, has met with resistance, whether in Islam, Christianity, or Judaism, none of which regards itself, normatively, as an initiatory religion. Analogously, we do not ordinarily think of reading poetry as requiring initiation, though it could be argued that exposing students to the deep reading of poetry is precisely that—an initiatory test that most students resist, and therefore fail. In its cross-culturality, Mackey's poetry seems remarkably democratic, and it surely serves as an explicit rebuke to any form of identity politics. His imagination knows no borders: one has only to consider the tables of content of his two collections of essays to see the diversity of his interests. But to go as far as Mackey wants us to go in our reading of him is a different matter. What holds his diverse interests together and produces, as it were, the unity of all rites? To answer that question requires, as Corbin puts it, "the active Imagination," and a willingness to endure the trials that the poems both witness and become. Shamanism in tribal, oral culture; exegetical mysticism in religious, literate culture; poetry in modern, secular culture: all call equally for initiation leading to gnosis.

:::

"The Unity of All Rites" is a phrase I have borrowed from René Girard, who uses it as the title of the penultimate chapter of *Violence and the Sacred*. Girard's sweeping anthropological theory of myth, ritual, generative violence, and sacrifice leads him to assert that all rites and their cultural derivatives in the arts and literature may be traced back to the efforts of primitive societies throughout the world to contain the plague of violence that continually threatens the communal order. For Girard, violence and the sacred are one and the same; what distinguishes them are the patterns of worship, ritual, and belief in various societies, all of which are intended to propitiate the powers of uncontained violence and set ordered forms of sacrificial violence in their place. According to Girard, "'Conservative' is a word too weak to describe the rigidity of spirit and terror of change that characterizes those societies in which the sacred holds sway. The imposition of a socio-religious order appears as an enormous boon, an unhoped for act of grace that could at any moment be withdrawn" (282). Girard's theory seeks to account for the immense variety of religious rituals and experiences in both primitive and modern cultures, shamanism included. In Girard's view, shamanic initiation, with its visions of dismemberment and rebirth, recapitulates rituals of sacrificial violence; the reborn shaman, at first a victim, becomes a visionary healer, "commander in chief of the forces of Good, which finally rout the forces of Evil" (286). Shamanic healing, which often involves the magical extraction of threatening objects from a sick person's body, is a drawing forth of a symbolic or materialized threat of violence: "The patient is induced to give birth to his own cure, just as the entire community at one time gave birth, in the midst of collective violence, to a new order" (287).

Violence is rarely depicted in an explicit fashion in Mackey's poetry, but the signs of violence are pervasive. The slave trade, the middle passage, racial discrimination, religious and ethnic conflict over the centuries all serve as background, or rather, as a ground bass for a lamenting music of loss. The "Sigh of the Moor," which serves as the title for one of the *"Mu"* poems in *Splay Anthem*, names that place where Boabdil, last Moorish king of Granada, looked back at his lost kingdom before fleeing the Spanish and sighed. The sound of that sigh echoes throughout Mackey's poems. History is the record of a gnostic catastrophe, the violent cosmic upheaval that has led to our current fallen condition. The human community, like the cosmos itself, longs to be ordered and made whole, and I read Mackey's poetry as a shamanic attempt to bring about that order, that cure, despite a nearly irredeemable sense of despair.

Mackey comes to us like the "Gnostic stranger" in "Song of the Andoumboulou: 18," even as we commune with him in the *altjeringa*, the mystical dreamtime of the "Long / Night Lounge" (*Whatsaid Serif* 14). This stranger is both self and other; he knows what we know but cannot bring ourselves to say: "Plopped / himself down beside me and / said, 'So.' Over and over / again said / only 'So'" (*Whatsaid Serif* 14). As Corbin puts it, "It is by awakening to the feeling of being a Stranger that the gnostic's soul discovers *where* it is and at the same time forebodes *whence* it comes and *whither* it returns" (*Avicenna* 19). As a double or twin, this gnostic stranger is an *uncanny* figure; the cosmic distance he signifies is also a psychic distance within the self. Freud observes in "The Uncanny" that the relation to the double involves "transferring mental processes from the one person to the other—what we should call telepathy—so that the one possesses knowledge, feeling and experience in common with the other, identifies himself with another person, so that his self becomes confounded, or the foreign self is substituted for his own—in other words, by doubling, dividing and interchanging the self" (234). Freud speculates that the uncanny feeling produced by the double is due to its formation as a psychic defense at a very early period of mental development, when "it wore a more friendly aspect. The 'double' has become vision of terror, just as after the fall of their religion the gods took on daemonic shapes" (236).[2]

In "Song of the Andoumboulou: 18," the poet wakes (or does he?) from this dream encounter to the sound of *"flamenco's gnostic / moan,"* an "Ethiopian moan. Monophysite / lament." The song further blurs the sense of self, producing a multiplicity and dispersal of pronouns, the paradoxically disparate collectivity that recurs frequently in Mackey's work: "He to him, she to her, they to them, / opaque / pronouns, 'persons' whether or not we / knew who they were" (14). It is a psycholinguistic condition that the poet seems to both embrace and resist. Unpacking this episode, Peter O'Leary notes that Monophysite Christianity (condemned as a heresy except in a few Churches in Syria, Egypt, and Ethiopia) holds "that the union of God the Logos with the flesh of the Incarnation was so complete that even to consider Christ's human nature as separate from his divine nature is to suggest a division where such an act is impossible. Etymologically, *monophysite* means 'one nature'; we might paraphrase that to be 'one union', an idea compatible with Mackey's integration of a phantom realm with the elusive world of the poem" (*Gnostic Contagion* 213). For O'Leary, this "phantom realm" of poetry, with its figurations of ghosts, specters, doubles, and of the half-created Andoumboulou, the mythic Dogon "rough drafts" of humanity, is a sign of Mackey's skepticism, his doubtful, conflicted attitude toward the cross-cultural world-poem he has been drawn into writing. Poetry, given its spectral nature, itself becomes the psyche's gnostic twin.

Even more deeply gnostic than his mentor Duncan, Mackey is haunted by the Monophysite lament, the Ethiopian moan that echoes throughout the Middle East and in the flamenco of Andalusia. It is a song of loss and redemption that resonates in the blues, jazz, and other musical traditions that are heard on the omnipresent jukebox located somewhere in all his poems. He cannot accept the myth of unity that his musical experiences proposes for his poetry, yet in turn he laments his inability to accept the "one nature" of the poem.[3] Like the flamenco musicians of Andalusia with their "cante moro" (Moorish song), and like Federico García Lorca, who meditates so profoundly on the cultural conditions that bring forth these "black sounds," Mackey is possessed by *duende*, the deep, raspy, disruptive spirit that rises up through the earth and into the body. Felt in the stamp of the dancer's foot and in the hoarse cry from the depths of the singer's throat, *duende*, for Mackey as for Lorca (and for Spicer, who came into his own through "translating"—or channeling—the Spanish poet), is "a taking over of one's voice by another voice" (*Paracritical Hinge* 186).[4]

In effect, it is through such possession that Mackey is transformed into a "What-sayer" who continually breaks into and deranges the narrative—even when the narrative is of his own making. In regard to the figure of the what-sayer, Mackey quotes Ellen B. Basso's study of Kalapalo myth and ritual performance, *A Musical View of the Universe*, as an epigraph to *Whatsaid Serif*: "in order for the story to be told at all, it must be received by a responder or 'what-sayer', who is a crucial actor in the situation. The what-sayer may be someone who asked to be given the narrative or the recipient of a story that exemplifies explanatory principles needing clarification during the course of some other discussion; the person serving as what-sayer can change during the course of a telling" (Basso 15). Thus the stranger in "Andoumboulou: 18" simply repeats the word "So" as he confronts the poet, whereas later, in "Andoumboulou: 20," the two change places: "I was the whatsayer. / Whatever he said I would / say so what" (*Whatsaid Serif* 22).[5] In Mackey's work,

this aesthetic and spiritual rupture, often experienced through a displace-
ment and doubling of the self, also implies resistance to dominant histori-
cal narratives, and therefore has a political dimension as well. Memories of
historical disaster are submerged but insistently resurface: "To the outer /
principalities of Onem we were / brought," declares the what-saying speaker
in "Andoumboulou: 20," "bought, / sold / on blocks, auctioned / off." Out
of such experience comes an overdetermined language, "words meaning /
more / than the world they / pointed at" (22). On all levels, then, the result
is a gnostic catastrophe, an act of cosmic and verbal fragmentation, lost full-
ness that has fallen away.

Paradoxically, it is just this gnostic myth of primal loss and fragmentation
that goads Mackey further into the Book, goads him to further the Book, to
recursively continue his writing. Readers of the Song of the Andoumbou-
lou series know that the poet and his companions are sometimes on a boat,
sometimes on a train, sometimes on a bus. But in "Song of the Andoumbou-
lou: 42,"

> What we rode was a book. We
> fell out of it, scattered.
>   The book fell out of my
> hand while I slept. Page
>   upon page upon page
>   nodded
> out on . . . (*Splay Anthem* 29)

The image of the book on which the poet rides, the book of scattered pages
falling through dreamtime, is an image of ineluctable loss and attempted
reclamation, as later in the poem, the poet and his companions "come to
where, if / at all, / we'd live again" (30). That Book, that transgressive Text,
obsessive in its harmonies and dissonances, its uncanny meetings and di-
sastrous impediments, its luscious sensuality and grating severity, extends
beyond and doubles back through all of Mackey's work in poetry, fiction,
and criticism. "Recursiveness, incantatory insistence," asserts the poet, " is
liturgy and libation, repeated ritual sip, a form of sonic observance aiming
to undo the obstruction it reports. It plies memory, compensatory posses-
sion, reminiscent regard and regret" (*Splay Anthem* xiv).

Given the literary, musical, and religious traditions out of which Mackey works, and the violence of history against which he works, the notion of doubleness variously expressed as "compensatory possession," "regard and regret" or "sonic observance aiming to undo the obstruction it reports" is particularly provocative. "In some sects," explains René Girard, "possession is regarded as beneficial, in others as harmful. And there are still others that consider possession beneficial or harmful, depending on the circumstances. . . . The phenomenon of possession, therefore, can appear as sickness, cure, or both at once" (*Violence* 166). Possessed by the spirits and cast repeatedly into a trance (though for the poet in a literate culture, as opposed to the shaman in an oral culture, it is a *trance of writing*), Mackey experiences a simultaneous sickness and cure that ultimately compensates for the cosmic and historical disjointedness, the original catastrophe, which, as a gnostic, he understands to be the defining condition of being. In his possessed state, Mackey bears the "alien spore" of his sickness "into a land of ghosts, a realm simultaneous with the sunlight world in which he dwells. In this world, invisible vampiric beings suck out the life Mackey offers them, even as he starves his own malady of words. Rather than fading, the gnostic contagion thrives in a netherworld of partial, fragmented creation" (O'Leary, *Gnostic Contagion* 205). The shaman's way involves suffering and restoration, travail and ecstasy. But what makes Mackey's experience of possession specifically compensatory is the way in which it opens him not only to the ghostly netherworld, the "andoumboulousness" of the half-created rough draft that is human being, but also to the redemptive, utopian vision arising at the far horizon of his gnostic myth. Writing of the relationship of redemptive dreamtime to catastrophic history, Mackey observes that "Even the gnostic indictment of history as nightmare and delusion carries a prescribed awakening which, if gnosis is to be gnostic enough, would have to allow it might itself be only a dream." The redemptive or utopian promise held out by Mackey's poetry involves, therefore, "awakening to rather than from the dream" (*Splay Anthem* xiii).

The catastrophic and redemptive tendencies in Mackey's gnostic vision correspond, to a certain extent, to the two ongoing serial poems, the Song of the Andoumboulou and *"Mu,"* which made their first appearance in *Eroding Witness* and take up most, if not all, of the subsequent volumes of Mackey's poetry. In the preface to *Splay Anthem* (as important to Mackey's trajectory as the preface to *Bending the Bow* is to Duncan's), Mackey tells us that the poems are "now understood as two and the same, each the other's under-study. Each is the other, each is both, announcedly so in this book, by way of number, in earlier books not so announcedly so. By turns visibly and invisibly present, each is the other's twin or contagion, each entwines the other's crabbed advance" (ix). One recalls the interplay of the Structure of Rime poems and the Passages poems in Duncan's later work, a movement that eventuates in a totalizing gnostic scripture that launches itself into the void. But in Mackey's case, the serial poem as counterpart/counterpoint is found to be "repeatedly circling or cycling back, doing so with such adamance as to call forward and back into question and suggest an eccentric step to the side—as though, driven to distraction by shortcircuiting options, it can only be itself beside itself. So it is that 'Mu' is also *Song of the Andoumbou-lou, Song of the Andoumboulou* also 'Mu.' . . . One finds oneself circling, the susceptibility of previous moments in the work to revisitation and variation conducing to a theme of articulation's non-ultimacy, a theme too of mortality and new life" (xii).

These qualities of Mackey's serial poems—their oneness in twoness and the "non-ultimacy" of their continual backtracking—make it difficult to generalize about the more specific "themes" and "content" of the work. In Mackey's poetry, content is almost always coming into being through form, and despite (or perhaps because of) his devotion to what we can broadly call "New Americanist" principles of composition, he manages to turn the Olson/Creeley dictum that "form is never more than an extension of content" on its head. The pressure of composition-as-process, much as in jazz improvisation, moves the two serial poems both toward and away from any stated theme. Mackey tells us, however, that in relation to each other, "'Mu' carries a theme of utopic reverie and elegiac allure recalling the Atlantis-like continent Mu. . . . The places named in the song of the Andoumboulou, set foot on by the deceased while alive but lost or taken away by death, could be called 'Mu'. Any longingly imagined, mourned or remembered place, time, state or condition can be called 'Mu'" (x). The musical inspirations for both series, Don Cherry's *"Mu"* albums, Cherry's work with John Coltrane, and François Di Dio's recording *Les Dogon*, likewise serve increasingly as counterpoint: "The [Dogon] antelope-horn trumpet's blast and bleat, Cherry's ludic warble and Trane's recursive quandary are variations on music as gnostic announcement, ancient rhyme, that of end and beginning, gnostic accent or note that cuts both ways" (ix–x) And always, at all points, the two series offer a productive tension, a movement between shamanic dreamtime (*altjeringa*) and what Mackey calls historical "rendition." The result is "a way of challenging reality, a sense in which to dream is not to dream but to replace waking with realization, an ongoing process of testing or contesting reality, subjecting it to change or a demand for change" (xiii). In this regard, the diasporic travels that regularly punctuate Song of the Andoumboulou poems always lead us both toward and away from the Atlantean/Utopian domain that is "*Mu.*" "Seriality's mix of utopic ongoingness and recursive constraint is blutopic," declares Mackey, borrowing Duke Ellington's neologism. It produces "an idealism shaped or shaded by blue, in-between foreboding, blue, dystopic apprehension of the way the world is" (xiv). The result is a continuous, recursive, sideways movement as the two poems veer between the extremes of catastrophic fall and ecstatic redemption, traveling through landscapes and dream spaces variously shaded by idealism and foreboding.

::::

Movement or travel in Mackey's serial poems is both a compositional principle and an open set of thematized situations or scenarios. Travel is dangerous in the poems of Song of the Andoumboulou where the "we" are constantly in a state of jeopardy, however determined they are to reach the utopian spaces variously signified by and in "*Mu.*" As in the case of the whatsayer, Basso's work on Kalapalo narrative performance may help us understand the strange sense of movement, the disruptions in space and time that we experience in reading Mackey's poems (though in this case, Mackey does not explicitly mention it). According to Basso,

> Kalapalo notions of time are closely connected to ideas about space, and spatial imagery in Kalapalo myths is complementary to that of time. It is constructed by means of the ubiquitous device of traveling that lends a sense of contrast between qualitatively different experiences while distinguishing between different places or sites as, on the one hand, social, predictable, and ordinary, and on the other, antisocial, magical, dangerous, and liminal. The distinction emerges from the language describing the journey, which is a way of establishing boundaries that are both geographic and psychological and that are treated less as visual objects than as spatial relations experienced through human temporal sensitivity. Traveling modes, involving active experiences of time and the contrasts experienced in different places, thus serve as symbols for different consciousnesses. (31)

In regard to Mackey's poetry, two ideas in this passage are particularly striking: (1) that travel leads to the distinction between the "social, predictable, and ordinary" and the "antisocial, magical, dangerous, and liminal"; and (2) that travel or movement through space/time, is experienced as "both geographic and psychological" and produces "symbols for different consciousnesses." In the Song of the Andoumboulou and the *"Mu"* poems, both places and the modes of travel between them (train, bus, boat, and so forth) are experienced, to coin a word, as "psychogeographic" phenomena; likewise, the situation of the travelers at any given instant can shift dramatically from safe and ordinary to dangerous and magical. Of course, it is arguable that everything that *takes place* in these poems is magical, that all movement *from place to place* is magical. Psychically speaking, the goal of such movement is ultimately ecstatic, however much it may be blocked or impeded by foreboding, depressive, even demonic forces. As Mircea Eliade observes of the shamans' cosmic travels, "only they transform a cosmotheological concept into a *concrete mystical experience*. . . . In other words, what for the rest of the community remains a cosmological ideogram, for the shamans (and the heroes, etc.) becomes a mystical itinerary" (265). Taken together, Mackey's two serial poems constitute such a mystical itinerary, an elaborate, endless logbook of spiritual travels.

These travels, insofar as they constitute a "book" (recall that "What we rode was a book"), occur not only on the geographical and psychological levels, but on the tropological level as well. Mackey's "lost tribe," his "band of nervous travelers" moves from one place to another, from one psychic state to another, and from one set of tropes to another, in an endless web or network of language. Indeed, at a crucial moment of "Song of the Andoumboulou: 56," the poet distinguishes between *being caught in a web* and *being a web*:

> It wasn't we were
> prey,
> buzzing fly, flying fish,   wasn't we
> were inside Ananse's web, Anuncia's
> net. Web it was we were, it wasn't
> we were caught. It wasn't we
> were web's, we were web . . . (*Splay Anthem* 95)

Ananse is the West African spider god, son of the sky god Nyame, a trickster figure but also a culture hero who brings various forms of wisdom to humanity. In the Song of the Andoumboulou series, according to Megan Simpson, the trickster figure, like the what-sayer, functions as "a kind of deconstructive angel, the one who continually challenges, thwarts assertion, perceives the gaps and artifice, present in any description or expression" (40).[6] Anuncia (in Spanish, related to "announcement," "advertisement," or "omen") and Nunca (Spanish for "never") are the alternate names of the desired female figure who haunts *Splay Anthem*, as *Whatsaid Serif* is haunted by a related figure called Sophia, gnostic goddess of wisdom. In the preface to *Splay Anthem*, Mackey associates her, in a similarly deconstructive fashion, with "poetry's perennial boon . . . the increment or enablement language affords, promise and impossibility rolled into one (Anuncia / Nunca)" (x). In the lines quoted above, the deities related to the elusive wisdom of language (Ananse, Anuncia) do not capture and have power over the travelers through their discursive webs. Rather, "we were web": collectively, the travelers themselves take power over their language, enter into the being of their language, in order to utter and enact the spells that are, in effect, the vehicles of their journey.

As weaver of this web, Mackey draws on a number of techniques to produce what Charles Olson calls "the *kinetics* of the thing" (240). A sort of hybrid of narrative and lyric, of telling and singing, Mackey's poetry is premised on a complex notion he variously calls buzz, rasp, burr, or rub. He discusses this quality at length in his essay "Cante Moro," relating it to Lorca's notion of *duende*, and finding numerous instances of it in both music and poetry. Poems "buzz with meanings, implications, and insinuations that complicate, contaminate, 'dirty' one another" (*Paracritical Hinge* 197).[7] Likewise, in the *Splay Anthem* preface, Mackey itemizes some related poetic procedures and gestures: "Rub a kind of erasure, statement backtracks or breaks off, ellipses abound, assertion and retraction volley, assertion and supplementation: addition, subtraction, revision, conundrum, nuance, amendment, tweak" (xi). The play of call-and-response, the anagrams, the multilinguistic (or sometimes, *pseudo*-multilinguistic) puns, the repetitions, reversals, and sliding transformations of phrases, words, syllables, even single vowels and consonants that one finds increasingly in Mackey's recent books—all are further manifestations of this principle, signs of the *duende* at work.

Psychic travels, the dangerous but ecstatic journeys of the soul that constitute Mackey's poetry, are also experienced *musically*, and music as both method and metaphor is crucial to Mackey's verbal art. Given that words and music are both fundamental to the shamanic rituals and séances that are the archaic antecedents to Mackey's poetry, this makes perfect sense. Mackey's knowledge of world music, particularly of the music of Africa and the African diaspora, is encyclopedic; he draws on it constantly throughout his poetry, fiction, and essays.[8] For Mackey, as he explains in his magisterial "Sound and Sentiment, Sound and Symbol," music is both "orphic" and "orphaned." It stands as "prod and precedent for a recognition that the linguistic realm is also the realm of the orphan," and that poetic language in particular "is language owning up to being an orphan, to its tenuous kinship with the thing it ostensibly refers to" (*Discrepant Engagement* 233–34). Mackey thus invokes a vexed tradition, one that is both ancient in its orphic lineage and modern in its orphaned view of referentiality. According to Gerald Bruns, the orphic poet's "sphere of activity is governed by a mythical or ideal unity of word and being, and whose power extends therefore beyond the formation of a work toward the creation of the world" (1). But for Mackey, the problematic relationship of music and poetry calls the orphic vision of unity into question, reminding us of the gap between word and being, or in structuralist terms, between sign and referent. The orphic experience is actually the orphaned experience; unity is really separation, or, to use one of the poet's favorite terms, it is a discrepant engagement. And if, as Mackey declares, "music is wounded kinship's last resort" (*Discrepant Engagement* 232), this is true for poetry as well. The "bedouin" quality of Mackey's poetry is thus orphic and orphaned, connoting spiritual loss but also spiritual seeking, as the myth of Orpheus, with its probable shamanic origins, itself connotes.[9]

At one point in "Sound and Sentiment, Sound and Symbol," Mackey, in the midst of an analysis of William Carlos Williams's relation to jazz, asserts, apropos of the "Satyrs dance" passage in book 5 of *Paterson*, that "this would also be a way of talking about the 'variable foot', less an aid to scansion than a trope—the travestied, fractured foot" (243). He notes that earlier in *Paterson*, Williams quotes John Addington Symonds on the "limping iambics" of the ancient Greek poet Hipponax, which Mackey in turn relates to the limping trickster god Legba, "the Fon-Yoruba orisha of the crossroads," who is also worshiped in New World religions of the African diaspora, such as *voudon* and *santería*. This is a crucial, or, if you will, a crossroads moment in Mackey's analysis: under the aegis of Legba, the limping dancer, a number of paths in Mackey's thought cross. The ancient Western poetic tradition crosses with African culture, since Hermes, the Greek messenger god is in some respects a parallel figure to Legba. Likewise, the poetics of Williams, the white modernist (who, as his friend Ezra Pound liked to point out, was never truly "American," given his mixed English, Hispanic, and Jewish ethnic background), encounters the black modernism of a jazz aesthetic. Additionally, a technical matter of scansion—Williams's controversial "variable foot," which Mackey aligns with the syncopations of jazz—melds with "trope," a symbolic pointing to a transcendent or metaphysical condition we recognize in the limp. Mackey goes on to interpret the limp ontologically as "a 'defective' capacity in a homogeneous order given over to uniform rule. Legba's limp is an emblem of heterogeneous wholeness, the image and outcome of a peculiar remediation . . . as though the syncopated accent were an unsuspecting blessing offering anomalous, unpredictable support" (244).

So for Mackey, as we see in regard to the syncopated rhythms of black music, method is metaphor. In his essay on Amiri Baraka, he notes that black music serves a "dual role of impulse (life-style or ethos as well as technique) and subject matter" (24). How poets and musicians approach their work on a formal level has everything to do with their vision of reality and of the cosmos, their sense of the art as a revelation of the unfolding of being, which Mackey sees as a "heterogeneous wholeness" that opposes any "homogeneous order given over to uniform rule." Taken together, Mackey's two serial poems constitute such heterogeneous wholeness: their doubling or twinness, their extravagant verbal procedures, their harrowing, ecstatic departures and their uncanny, visionary arrivals are all expressions (however thwarted or impeded) of the "syncretist wish to be beyond schism" (*School of Udhra* 68), a sustained attempt to recover the "City of the spirit we lost / our way towards. Utopia / lost in the mind" (59).

:::

At this point, a close look at a single passage in Mackey's work seems appropriate, given its broken and dispersed surfaces, its relentless allusiveness, its dizzying verbal pyrotechnics, and its strangely private mythologizing.

All of these intertextual, weblike characteristics work against a sustained analysis, and yet if we are to understand the nature of Mackey's practice as a technician of the sacred, the particular kinds of magic he seeks to effect, then we need to examine at least one of his spells line by line. In referring to the often fragmentary passages of Mackey's poems as spells, and in thinking of them generally as *spellbinding*, I am highlighting the lyrical quality of Mackey's art in relation to its psychic power as it manifests itself in the physical world. In his discussion of lyric as a genre in *Anatomy of Criticism*, Northrop Frye identifies *melos* as the musical essence of lyric, relating it to what he calls, somewhat apologetically, "babble," in which "rhyme, assonance, alliteration and puns develop out of sound-associations. The thing that gives shape to the associating is what we have been calling the rhythmical initiative" (275). Furthermore, "The radical of *melos* is *charm*: the hypnotic incantation that, through its pulsing dance rhythm, appeals to involuntary physical response, and is hence not far from the sense of magic, or physically compelling power" (278).

But as I mentioned above, Mackey's poetry is a hybrid of narrative and lyric (a perspective that I believe is just as useful in reading Mackey's prose fiction). The overriding notion of movement and travel in the two serial poems indicates that on a fundamental level, these poems are telling an open-ended, episodic story that, for both thematic and structural reasons, cannot cease in its recitation. Because they are always approaching a utopian horizon that is forever receding before them, the serial poems *"Mu"* and Song of the Andoumboulou simply cannot end. And inasmuch as the temporal movement forward toward a utopian space is also a movement backward toward an originary space (hence the shamanic concern with ancestral spirits, ascent of the dead and so on), any given place where the poetic utterance is heard is not only an unimaginable "no-where" (*u-topia*) but also a sacred place, a place where, before the fall, humanity could communicate freely with cosmic powers. The fact that in the present, we can envision neither a utopian future nor an unfallen past, makes the recitation of the narrative, the chanting of the spell, all the more urgent.

One of the terms Mackey uses in relation to these concepts is "Nonsonance," and it is to Nonsonance we go for our close reading, in a passage that concludes "Song of the Andoumboulou: 29." "Nonsonance" is itself, as the sound implies, a nonce word, that is, a coinage. On the one hand, it is related to the word "nonsense," which connotes verbal irrationality and linguistic play; on the other hand, it is akin to "resonance," the intensifying and prolonging of sound when articulated by the voice or produced by a musical instrument. Resonance is a quality naturally associated with music, but we may speak of highly charged verbal artifacts, such as poems, as resonant as well. Nonsonance, therefore, may be regarded as a metonym for Mackey's poetry in and of itself.

The arrival at "Nonsonance" (for in the text it is presented as much as a place as a condition) comes at the end of a poem that is itself virtually metonymic for the whole of Mackey's poetry. "Song of the Andoumboulou: 29" presents itself as a ritualized speaking in tongues, a shamanic séance "Spoke in / tongues until tongues' lipped / itch exhausted us" (*Whatsaid Serif* 69). This ventriloquized act of utterance contains within it a number of signature tropes from the series as a whole: the "loquacious" lovemaking of the initiate with Sophia, seen as "his gnostic / twin" (72); the travels by "B'Us" (a coded term suggesting "bus," "be us," and "buzz"); and the doubling, through the inspired music of the Spanish *saeta*, of a "ghost of his / whatsaid self, dead already, called himself 'so-called me'" (71).[10] The "somewhere" that is Nonsonance therefore appears as an amalgam of some of the most important of the esoteric rites that Mackey's recursive recitation embraces. It is the place toward which the text is always going, to which it always arrives.

Places, therefore, are almost always way stations in the text, but are also language events; thus "voiceless / the word whose adumbration / bound our book,   booked / blood wood's admonition, / trickling / wood played on by mallets, / balafonic bridge we crossed over / on" (74). It's hard to say why the word is "voiceless"; perhaps it is because "Nonsonance" resists normative, conventional articulation or utterance. Nevertheless, its "adumbration" (a sketchy outline or prefigurement) binds "our book," which is simultaneously the poem, the place, the journey, and perhaps even the body of the poet. Note how "book" and "booked," through assonance, slide over to "blood" and "wood," while "adumbration," through rhyme, is transformed to "admonition," a gentle but still serious warning or cautionary advice. We can thus interpret this to mean that Nonsonance is both prefigurement and warning, a foretold or destined place or experience felt in the body, the blood, to which the poet and his company crosses, toward which we go.

This crossing takes place through music, across a "balafonic bridge," the balafon being a large West African xylophone with hollow gourds used as resonators. Mackey likens the bars of the balafon to railroad ties, so the musical instrument becomes a railroad bridge crossing "Ribbed water," appropriate to the journey taking place in the poem, which is conducted alternately (or perhaps simultaneously) by boat, bus, and train, among other modes of transport. In jazz, a bridge is a transitional passage between the head or theme of the piece and the solos, or vice versa. (Thelonius Monk once remarked that the function of the bridge is "to make the outside sound good" [Botman].) In all these instances (music, poem, journey) there is forward movement through time and/or space, while the water beneath the bridge "made 'were' / to itself," a punning sound that connotes pastness or time left behind.

Crossing a bridge is also suggestive of one of the most significant roles played by the shaman. In his analysis of the bridge and the "difficult passage," Eliade identifies the belief held by many tribal cultures that "*in illo tempore,* in the paradisal time of humanity, a bridge connected earth and heaven and people passed from one to the other without encountering any obstacles, because there was not yet *death*" (483). Because that time has passed and we dwell, in effect, in a fallen or ruptured cosmos, it becomes the task of the shaman, through ecstatic techniques, to cross in spirit what is now a bridge fraught with danger (in this case, perhaps, represented by the mallets falling on the "blood wood" keys of the balafon). As Eliade tells us,

> By crossing, in ecstasy, the "dangerous" bridge that connects the two worlds and that only the dead can attempt, the shaman proves that he is spirit, is no longer a human being, and at the same time attempts to restore the "communicability" that existed *in illo tempore* between this world and heaven. For what the shaman can do today *in ecstasy* could, at the dawn of time, be done by all human beings *in concreto*; they went up to heaven and came down again without recourse to trance. Temporarily and for a limited number of persons—the shamans—ecstasy re-establishes the primordial condition of all mankind. (486)

In Mackey's text, the shamanic "we," having crossed the bridge, find themselves "On the edge of an 'it' otherwise / out of reach." If the somewhere to which they've come is Nonsonance, it is a place of the spirits that is both reachable and unreachable, nameable and unnamable, signified by a "rim of no well we'd ever / drink from,   asymptotic / water,   hyperbolic thirst." The well cannot be drunk from for it is the well that waters Paradise. I take "asymptotic" to mean unreachable, as it is rhymed with and transformed into "hyperbolic," exaggerated, overly expressed. The "er" in "water" slides into the "ir" of thirst, the object of spiritual desire and the desire itself, the latter unreachable, the former unsatisfiable, even for the shaman, who temporarily travels through this heavenly realm. In the next lines, the shamanic trance comes to an end, as the poet gradually returns to himself and discovers "Where we were slowly lulled us / to sleep." "Music from the year I was / born leapt off the box," the omnipresent jukebox of the Song of the Andoumboulou series indicating a return to the fallen world, the world of the body's birth, which in Mackey's case is 1947. "Bird's / Benzedrine reed woke us up. / Too late / for that, nonsonant wood announced, said without sound" (*Whatsaid Serif* 74): Charlie Parker's sax on the jukebox, like a shot of speed, jolts him awake, and the soundless spirit music of the balafon, made of "nonsonant wood," fades away. One is reminded of Keats, entranced before the ecstatic scene depicted on the Grecian Urn: "Heard melodies are sweet, but those unheard / Are sweeter; therefore, ye soft pipes, play on; / Not to the sensual ear, but, more endear'd, / Pipe to the spirit ditties of no tone" (372).

As for Mackey & Co., at this impossible place of frustrated desire, where sound and silence, sense and non-sense, earth and heaven are poised forever at odds, "Lacktone said it best. / Layered / 'say' so mute, so nonsonant we / winced, thick skin thinner / the farther we went, thin skin / rubbed / away" (*Whatsaid Serif* 74). With these final lines ("away" floating free, bumping against the right-hand margin), the passage and the poem end. The layered complexity of sound, whether musical or verbal, is both present and absent: nonsonant indeed. The journey continues, but its saying is temporarily muted, said (or unsaid) by "Lacktone"—perhaps a member of the band, perhaps some sort of a blocking agent, analogous to the demons who attempt to block a shamanic ascent, since in both music and poetry, nothing is worse than a lack of tone. No longer thick skinned, Mackey's band of initiates is, rather, increasingly thin skinned, painfully sensitized to the power of sound and increasingly mindful of the spell producing the ecstatic movement into the realm of the spirits.

:::

One of the most explicitly shamanic passages in all of Mackey's poetry is the
beginning of "Song of the Andoumboulou: 52":

> Never not another bridge to
> cross, not before then so
>   stark. We were beginning to be
>   dead it seemed. Sought
>   silence's
>   counsel, wise in that way,
>   leaning toward light,
> off-balance . . . (*Splay Anthem* 81)

Here, the stark image of the bridge that must be crossed, which is central to
the shaman's vocation, is combined with the growing sense that the travel-
ers are "dead." As we have observed, the shaman can cross the bridge only
because he has become a "dead man"; thus he is "able to contribute decisive-
ly to the *knowledge of death*," and hence his importance to what Eliade calls
"the psychic integrity of the community" (509). The shaman's commerce
with the dead, especially the tribal ancestors and deceased shamans, is fre-
quently part of his initiation: "Having contact with the souls of the dead
signifies *being dead oneself*. . . . [T]he shaman must so die that he may meet
the souls of the dead and receive their teaching; for the dead know every-
thing" (84). Mackey's concern for the dead in Song of the Andoumboulou
is foundational and extends throughout the series: the original song on the
album that inspired Mackey is a part of the Dogon funeral rites, and the very
first lines of the series are

> The song says the
>   dead will not
> ascend without song.
>
>   That because if
> we lure them their names get
>   our throats, the
>   word sticks. (*Eroding Witness* 33)

One of the shaman's most important roles is that of psychopomp; he escorts
dead souls to the afterlife and shows the way to those who are reluctant
to leave the precincts of the living. As we can see from juxtaposing these

two passages, one from the beginning of Mackey's series and one more re-
cent, the "we" of the poem are both responsible for the ancestral dead, as-
sisting them in their ascent, and are also schooled by the dead. The names
and words of the dead "get / our throats," meaning that to some extent, the
dead *possess* the poet and his band. Then again, we see that they "Sought /
silence's counsel / wise in that way," so that if we understand "silence" as the
condition of the dead, it becomes the poet's task to make the dead speak, to
give up their wisdom from the silent realm to which they have gone. Once
more from Eliade: "It certainly seems that the chief function of the dead in
the granting of shamanic powers is less a matter of taking 'possession' of the
subject himself than of helping him to become a 'dead man'—in short, of
helping him to become a 'spirit' too" (85).

"It wasn't riskless we imagined / we'd be but not defenseless. A / feather
broke our fall" (*Splay Anthem* 81): the shaman's way is fraught with danger,
and in his cosmic flights, the animals with which he is most often associated
are various types of birds. The beginning of "Song of the Andoumboulou:
52" includes nearly all of the most significant aspects of shamanic experi-
ence, despite the initiates' insistence that "It wasn't ecstasy as yet / but we
kept hoping." But in effect, it *is* ecstasy, and the shaman's ecstatic trance, in
which his body remains present but his soul traverses the celestial regions, is
a séance or performance with the tribe as audience and, at crucial moments,
participants as well. Hence, "A feast / had been set we'd been told . . . / A
token rope let down from the / sky / hung out of reach and began to / un-
ravel, / wind what we took to be . . ." (81). The rope, more often a post or
ladder (and the image of a ladder appears frequently in the Song of the An-
doumboulou series), is symbolic of the *axis mundi*, the archetypal tree that
structures the cosmos, often depicted with a snake at its root and a bird in its
branches. Ascent of the tree is culturally ubiquitous to shamanic (and more
broadly, mystical) rites; indeed, the shaman is that figure who may ascend
and descend the tree to enact the psychic unity necessary for the good of all
being. In this passage, however, the rope unravels and the ascent appears to
fail. "The bridge we began with vanished," the poet declares a few lines later;
"No way could we have walked / it. We wanted it even so. A bed / of hot /
coals it would've been, carpet of / scars . . . / Bridge being what it was, we
turned / away" (81–82). Walking across a bed of hot coals is a demonstration
of the shaman's power to cross the bridge; the fear and failure expressed here

indicates that Mackey's travelers are just as often thwarted in their journey outward and upward, since they are "turned away not / knowing where we'd go next." The passage ends with the loss of communion; the dead, apparently, fail to speak: "No such whisper of soul tugged / our / feet" (82).

Mackey's poetry enacts a search for gnosis and magical power that emerges from, but also produces, what he calls "*ythm* (clipped rhythm, anagrammatic myth)" (xiii). This impulse is present in both form and theme, or as Mackey would put it, "sound and sentience." *Ythm* makes itself felt in the shaman's cosmic struggle, the mystic's erotic longing for knowledge (Sophia), and it is most palpable, for the poet himself, in the alternations and intersections of his two serial poems: "The song of the Andoumboulou is one of burial and rebirth, *mu* momentary utterance extended into ongoing myth, an impulse toward signature, self-elaboration, finding and losing itself" (xiii). And sure enough, if we follow out this impulse beyond the boundary of any single poem, we see what *ythm* is all about. In *Splay Anthem*, "Song of the Andoumboulou: 52" is followed immediately by "Sound and Sentience (—*"mu" thirty-second part*—)," which begins with a more successful shamanic flight:

> Scales what would once have been
> skin . . . Feathers what would once
>   have been cloth . . . There that
>   claiming heaven raised hell, fraught
>   sublimity, exits ever more to
>   come . . .
>   A drum's head it was we walked on,
>   beats parsed out by ghost feet,
>   protoghost feet our feet had
>   become. It was a dream of beaten
>   earth,
> beaten air, beaked extravagance,
>   birds we'd eventually be. Albeit
> feeling took flight's place, flight
>   familiarity's run, movement found our
>   feet, what once had been wood . . . (86)

Shamanic experience is "fraught sublimity," an experience of heights and depths, ascent and descent, heaven and hell. Playing on his drum, dancing on the beaten earth, the shaman enters his trance, becomes a "protoghost"; his spirit becomes a bird and takes flight. Approaching Mu (though never arriving), the poet and his band recognize themselves as "ythmically / elect but loosed even so, earth a / dream / of drums come / true" (87). As the poem draws to a close—not really an end, since in the mythic dreamtime of origin that is also the utopian horizon of futurity, there can be no end—it becomes clear that the shamanic status of the band has been secured:

> Comings and goings not gotten over.
> Death not gotten over, goings away
> glimpsed again had us gone without
> going,   on to the heard-about
>   City,
> sounded
> out (87)

In relation to death, the shaman in his trance is preeminently that figure who is "gone without / going"; that is how he contributes to the community's knowledge of death and helps maintain its psychic integrity. The glimpses he provides of the other world are immensely beneficial, therapeutic on the most fundamental psychosocial level. As Eliade puts it, "it is consoling and comforting to know that a member of the community is able to *see* what is hidden and invisible to the rest and to bring back direct and reliable information from the supernatural worlds" (509). But what can this mean in a modern, secular context, especially today, where religious debates become violently polarized even as religious belief and discourse have become fully intertwined with our political processes? Mackey's restoration of Mu, his "heard-about / City / sounded / out," is an ancient myth with remarkably modern resonances. We may or may not desire knowledge of the "supernatural worlds" per se—indeed, we may claim to reject religious or transcendental thinking entirely—but we still long for a vision of community and respond powerfully to an art that may provide it. The disturbing but revealing paradox of Mackey's poetry, a paradox of which he is quite aware, is that this utopian vision, this vision of cosmic wholeness, can only be realized through an arduous process of initiation, a seemingly interminable crossing, a mystical, erotic longing for gnosis that cannot be fulfilled.

:::

In the epilogue to *Shamanism,* Eliade asserts that the shaman's "pre-ecstatic euphoria constituted one of the universal sources of lyric poetry"; that the shaman obtains a "'second state' that provides the impetus for linguistic creation and the rhythms of lyric poetry" (510). As Eliade eloquently puts it, "poetic creation still remains an act of perfect spiritual freedom." For primitive cultures, the spectacle of the shamanic séance offers a great opportunity to see "the world in which *everything seems possible,* where the dead return to life and the living die only to live again, where one can disappear and reappear instantly, where the 'laws of nature' are abolished and a certain superhuman 'freedom' is exemplified and made dazzlingly *present*" (511). This is certainly a contrast to Girard's interpretation of the shaman's theatrical spectacle, for in his vision of sacred violence, it is not freedom and possibility that shamanic ritual offers but order and protection. In Eliade's view, the community is brought closer to the supernatural realm, while for Girard, the supernatural is kept at a secure distance. In both views, the shaman remains a "technician of the sacred," whose power has passed to the poet to a greater extent than to any other cultural arbiter in modern society. Yet that power, in the end, is not the same, and no poet writing today understands this more acutely than Nathaniel Mackey. For if Mackey's work represents the great lyric potential of esoteric mysticism and shamanic ritual, it self-consciously represents their poetic limits as well.

The last group of poems in *Splay Anthem* is called Nub, a term Mackey variously interprets in his preface, including among the possibilities "the dreariness of recent events as well as ontology, the imperial, flailing republic of Nub the United States has become, the shrunken place the earth has become, planet Nub" (xv). These poems present a dreadful vision of war and corruption, a Girardian "sacrificial crisis" of universal proportions, a collapse of the social order into violent chaos that ritual cannot contain. As in Duncan's Vietnam War sequence in the Passages poems (about which Mackey has written brilliantly), Mackey brings together a gnostic vision of irredeemable catastrophe with the imperial violence of recent American history: "Multiple the / names it went by, legion, wars / over / which one fit broke out, nation of / none though we were . . ." (112). In the face of such a demonic onslaught, the poet declares that "all the old attunements gave / way, late but soon come even so . . ."; the travelers on their journey appear to be on a "political trek" as much as a "mystic march" (125). "[P]olitics kept us at bay,   nothing / wasn't / politics"; nevertheless "all the old stories / echoed / yet again, old but even so soon come . . ." (125). The last vision Mackey offers is of an "Abducted future," of "Death / Lake . . . Where we rubbed / earth in our faces, a feeling we had / for debris." Still, "we ran thru it, / earth-sway swaddling / our / feet" (126). It is an image of death, flight, and—given the use of the term "swaddling"—perhaps of rebirth. Since *Splay Anthem*, Mackey has published a good deal more of both serial poems. He and his band of initiates are still on the move.

Armand Schwerner

God is in every thing as the place in which every thing is, or rather as the deter-
mination and the "topia" of every entity. The transcendent, therefore, is not a
supreme entity above all things; rather, *the pure transcendent is the taking-place of
every thing*.

God or the good or the place does not take place, but is the taking-place of the
entities, their innermost exteriority. The being-worm of the worm, the being-
stone of the stone, is divine. That the world is, that something can appear and
have a face, that there is exteriority and non-latency as the determination and the
limit of every thing: this is the good. (Agamben 13–14)

The deep and abiding interest in such fields as anthropology, ethnomusi-
cology, and comparative religions that shapes Nathaniel Mackey's work is
not, of course, a recent poetic phenomenon, as Mackey's own literary criti-
cism, and his editing of the journal *Hambone* reveal. In one respect, Mackey
can be regarded as a younger participant in ethnopoetics, a movement that
emerges in the previous generation of avant-garde poets. "PRIMITIVE
MEANS COMPLEX" (xviii) declares Jerome Rothenberg in *Technicians of
the Sacred*. In "primitive" poetry, he goes on to observe, "an object is whatev-
er it becomes under the impulse of the situation. Forms are often open. Cau-
sality is often set aside. The poet (who may also be dancer, singer, magician,
whatever the event demands of him) masters a series of techniques that can
fuse the most seemingly contradictory propositions" (xxi–xxii). The resem-
blance of this shamanic figure to the modernist poet's avant-garde practices
is unmistakable.

To a greater extent than any other member of the ethnopoetics move-
ment, Armand Schwerner (1927–1999) understood that the modern attempt

to reconnect with the spirituality of the archaic and the "primitive" had to be accompanied by a deep—and deeply ironic—self-consciousness. Along with his colleagues, such as Rothenberg and Nathaniel Tarn, Schwerner (re)discovered both the poetic and the religious potential in anthropology's study of native cultures and languages. Likewise, the fields of archaeology and paleography inspired in the poet an enduring awareness of the synchronicity of the archaic and the modern, especially in regard to matters of textuality. Schwerner embraced the universalizing spirit of ethnopoetics— the dream of total translation, total performance, total ritual—while at the same time implicitly acknowledging its impossibility. The uncanny pathos that informs Schwerner's work, especially in *The Tablets*, has its origin in a romantic primitivism that is continually undercut by modernist skepticism—and vice versa.

The child of Jewish immigrants from Belgium, Schwerner's first language was French, and it could be argued that an understanding of cultural displacement and the consequent need for continuous translation lie at the heart of his work. This sensibility and background may well account for his attraction to ethnopoetics, while his training in music, comparative literature, and anthropology fully prepared him for participation in both the literary and performative dimensions of that movement. Steeped in European and American modernism, Schwerner's stance toward his art was rigorously avant-garde; he published mainly in little magazines and small presses, and performed his work in alternative venues and with experimental theater companies (including the famous Living Theater), especially in New York City, which was his home nearly all his life. Yet like Rothenberg, and like such older poets as Charles Olson and Robert Duncan, Schwerner's literary experiments result from an awareness of and participation in a broad and generous continuum of cultural and artistic practices that, in effect, deconstruct the boundaries between primitive and modern. In Schwerner's case, however, the connection between the primitive or archaic poet/shaman and the experimental modernist is thoroughly ironized by the problematic introduction of what Brian McHale ingeniously calls "the 'primal scene' of modernist archaeologism: the moment when a consciousness enters into some relation with the past through an encounter of its artifacts, extracted from underground" ("Archaeologies of Knowledge" 242–43). Not the modernist poet, but the modern *scholar* is the parallel to the archaic figure, who, in *The Tablets*, is just as often a scribe as a prophet, shaman, or seer. Further-more, as McHale points out, this "primal scene" is never fully witnessed: "Nowhere in *The Tablets* are we *shown* the translator confronting the arti-facts (the clay tablets or cylinder seals, or a photo of them); at most we hear him discoursing *about* them. Rather, it is *we readers* who enact that primal scene every time we look into *The Tablets*, every time we turn its pages, for the translated tablets are themselves the artifacts, or as close as anyone ever comes to them. No need to represent the encounter with an artifact when the text itself *is* that artifact" (247). *The Tablets*, therefore, confronts its read-ers with an endless (and endlessly distanced) *staging* of the act of transla-tion: the labors of the modern paleographer take on the same burden of ritualized inscription as do the magical and sacred texts (if that is what they really are) that he and the reader encounter on the clay tablets supposedly before them.

During the thirty or more years that he works on this poem, Schwerner writes in a spirit of prophetic urgency that he deliberately frustrates by the mock-pedantry that is *The Tablets*'s modus operandi. Late in the writing, Schwerner notes that "the genre of the archaeological's undone by the sense that whatever could be findable will not be findable—the meaning of the digs progressively wafting into common air—not without the appearances of the epic, the psychodramatic, the irredeemable word-pain. The self-un-doing genre crowded with doing" (*Tablets* 142). At first glance a literary hoax, the twenty-seven sections of this "self-undoing" work are presented by the mediating figure of the "Scholar/Translator" as translations of Akka-dian/Sumerian tablets dating back thousands of years. The Scholar/Trans-lator's accompanying notes, sometimes outrageously anachronistic and hilariously out of sync with the translations themselves, reach an almost Talmudic density in the final sections, taken from his "Laboratory Teaching Memoirs." Schwerner's own "Tablet Journals / Divagations," written over the years of composition, follow the poem, further blurring the distinction between text and commentary.[1] Encompassing numerous poetic registers and a dizzying array of voices, *The Tablets* is actually that rarest of creatures, a religious comedy, indeed, a divine comedy, with the schlemiel-like figure of the Scholar/Translator as both pilgrim and guide.[2]

Schwerner's sense of the modern need for such a poem is made quite ex-plicit in the journal entries appended to *The Tablets*. Consider the following lament: "Poetry, as game, as act of faith, as celebration, as commemoration, as epic praise, as lyric plaint, as delight in pattern and repetition—poetry is in trouble. Not any more trouble than the Earth, concepts of nobility and selflessness, senses of utility. But that's not saying too much" (*Tablets* 135). Schwerner's sense that poetry is in trouble, that it has lost the cultural authority that once allied it closely with religious practices and with mythic forms of knowledge, leads him to a project that is indeed a verbal game that is simultaneously an act of faith. For all its elaborately fake scholarship and outlandish "translations" of the most ancient human utterances, *The Tablets* embodies Schwerner's claim that "the uses of the past, by means of these found archaic objects, are . . . more than ironic and other than nostalgic" (134). Beyond irony and nostalgia, the Scylla and Charybdis of the modern poetic sensibility, *The Tablets* offers "not poetry as obeisance to the sacred, but a creation of it in all its activity; not as an appeal for its survival in spite of a corrosive sense that the sacred is lost, but as a movement which itself might add its own small measure to reality" (130). Thus the poem confirms Schwerner's belief that "poetry must make us live and perceive more intensely, not by the direct use of symbols, but by a religious concern for the present real—the destruction of almost dead categories and nostalgia" (131).

Schwerner's formulations are comparable to Eric L. Santner's idea, based on his reading of Hölderlin and Rosenzweig, that "what poets establish is not some sort of vision or consciousness of the All; rather they introduce into the relational totality of social existence—into the social body divided into parts—the perspective of the 'non-all'" (142). *The Tablets*, written from "the perspective of the 'non-all,'" is a work of what Santner would call *psychotheology*, a work engaged in "the affect-laden process of traversing and dismantling defensive fantasies, the structured undeadness that keeps us from opening in the midst of life and the neighbor/stranger who dwells there with us" (23). In an early article on *The Tablets*, Kathryn Van Spanckeren calls the poem "a self-reflexive or deconstructive exploration of Western consciousness," arguing that "the Tablets revel in the condition of brokenness, illegibility, and loss" (18). The truth of this perspective is undeniable, but as we shall see, Schwerner's "psychotheological" project in the poem takes it beyond a deconstructive celebration of what the text itself calls the "untranslatable," to a point at which the mutual losses of the past and the present, of the ancient scribe and the modern philologist, offer a renewed understanding of what has traditionally been called the sacred. The possibility inherent in Schwerner's poem that this renewal of the sacred still may take place despite—or even because of—the modern disappearance of God, makes *The Tablets* a work of remarkable significance and urgency.

Schwerner's desire to maintain poetry's relation to the sacred is as great as that of any American poet in the last hundred years, and I take the poet at his word when he declares "a *religious* concern for the *present real*" (my italics). Indeed, as we can adduce from his journal entries, Schwerner relates the sacred not, primarily, to myth, ritual, or organized faith, but to *the real*, or *reality*, terms he inherits from various modernist precursors, but perhaps most importantly, from Wallace Stevens. It is Stevens, after all, who writes in his "Adagia" that "after one has abandoned a belief in god, poetry is that essence which takes its place as life's redemption" (*Opus Posthumous* 185).

In "Wallace Stevens: The Movements within the Rock" (1965), based on his Columbia University M.A. thesis, Schwerner emphasizes "Stevens' predilections for the fluid aspects of reality, for the shifting boundaries between imagination and reality, for the freedom found in play, for the dependence of imagination upon reality" ("Movements" II, 47). Schwerner distinguishes Stevens from other poets in the modernist company, such as Yeats, Eliot, and Pound, because his work "explores reality between a desire for finality and a withdrawal from ultimate causes and finalities" ("Movements" II, 55). For Stevens, as Schwerner sees him, "the figure of the poet does not find realization in *making* changes; rather that figure becomes part of the process which itself is change" ("Movements" I, 66). "From the beginning," Schwerner observes, "Stevens would present the quality of the 'vivid' experience of a perception, of man involved in the object perceived, of the merest 'fluttering' as coterminous with change and practically unseizable" ("Movements" I, 73). Equally important, Stevens is a poet who "rejects the implications of the *act of power*" ("Movements" II, 54): though he "shares with Yeats, Eliot, Pound, an investment in some concept of personality; in his case the concept almost appears fortuitous, so skilled is he in creating a fabric of becoming-as-poem in which thing and idea, resemblance and correspondence discover a new reality" ("Movements" I, 71). The radical power of Stevens's work lies in the fact that it "is not the tacit or assertive presentation of a distinct 'self', not a demonstration of concern for the posited 'persona' as it may variously present itself in Browning's monologues, Pound's *Personae*, Eliot's 'Gerontion', Williams' 'Tract.' . . . Characterized by a mode of acceptance, Stevens' work, in its major patterns, inherits little of the rebelliousness of the nineteenth-century romantics, little of the overt committed criticism his great contemporaries directed at contemporary life" ("Movements" I, 69).

These insights, I would argue, constitute an important part of the epistemological and methodological foundations of *The Tablets*, which Schwerner begins around the same time he publishes his essay on Stevens. Schwerner emphasizes that Stevens was virtually alone among the modernists in that "neither history nor myth concerned him significantly as categories of perception. He did not confront the present with the past to demonstrate the fatality of his time; he did not resurrect old mythologies through the filter of a private *Vision*; no ancient civilization presented to him a series of images through which the present might find fulfillment" ("Movements" I, 67). This remark may seem ironic given the poem Schwerner was about to write, but it actually makes a great deal of sense. Schwerner's use of history, myth, and ancient civilizations is relatively remote from the uses put to them by Yeats, Eliot, Pound, Lawrence, or H.D. *The Tablets* stages a confrontation of the past and the present not as an act of judgment or even, primarily, of criticism. It does not seek to replace modern beliefs or ideologies with older, lost, or previously discredited value systems. Rather, the poem, consisting as it does of fragmented "translations," scholarly "commentary," and what Schwerner variously calls in his journals "holes," "silences," or "lacunae," applies Stevens's understanding of poetry as a play of the real to the stuff of myth and history that we usually associate with such poets as Eliot and Pound. The epistemological impulse behind Stevens's lyric explorations of the real meets the debased myths and rituals of *The Waste Land* and the piecemeal documentary material of *The Cantos*. But Schwerner goes back further, to the very beginnings of written culture, circa 5000 B.C.E. In *The Tablets*, the reality of the past struggles to assert itself, even after thousands of years, against the ostensibly authoritative but incomplete knowledge of the present, represented by the technologies of scholarship that the poem continually parodies. Schwerner, therefore, "explores reality between a desire for finality and a withdrawal from ultimate causes and finalities" to at least the same degree as Stevens, but on ground where Stevens chose not to venture.[3]

:::

Before we follow Schwerner onto that ground—ground that is both ar-chaeological dig and sacred space—the poet's concern for "the real," which he inherits from his modernist precursors, might be usefully compared to that of an older contemporary, George Oppen. The two poets had a long and somewhat combative friendship, dating from the early sixties, when Oppen returned from Mexico and moved to Brooklyn, to Oppen's death in 1984. When they first met, Oppen had recently started writing poetry after a twenty-five-year hiatus, and during the next ten years he would produce a body of work that has come to be regarded as one of the crowning achieve-ments of the Objectivist movement, a movement that may be traced back to the poetics of such first-generation modernists as Pound and Williams.[4] Back in New York City, Oppen's writing was reinvigorated through con-tact with a younger generation of poets, and in *Of Being Numerous* (1968), for which he won the Pulitzer Prize, Oppen includes Schwerner among a group of friends who provide "phrases, comments, cadences of speech" that he uses in the text, "in some instances without quotation marks" (*Collected Poems* verso page).[5] He read and responded to Schwerner's poetry both in manuscript and when published, and one of his very few reviews, written for the journal *Stony Brook*, is of Schwerner's *Seaweed* (1969), in which he calls Schwerner "a lyric poet of depth and delicacy and power" (72).

Determining the full extent of Schwerner's relationship to Oppen's work and to Objectivist poetics in general is beyond the scope of this chapter, but the Objectivist project of finding a language that is commensurate with im-mediate perceptions of reality, and, in its more sophisticated mode, of *testing* that language against one's perceptions and beliefs, undoubtedly had a pro-found influence on Schwerner throughout his career.[6] For Schwerner and his colleagues in the ethnopoetics movement, however, perhaps the most important way that the poet could pursue this linguistic search was down the track that led to the archaic and the primitive, to religion and myth, to ritual and magic—the track of the anthropologist and the shaman. Oppen seems to have respected this enterprise while at the same time maintaining a somewhat skeptical distance. References to myth and religion of any sort are relatively rare in his poetry; as he remarks wryly in his interview with L. S. Dembo, "I do believe that consciousness exists and that it is consciousness of something, and that is a fairly complete but not very detailed theology" (Dembo and Pondrom 176). And while he uses the term "primitive" as a poem title and as the title of his last published volume (*New Collected Poems* 133, 263–86), I would agree with Rachel Blau DuPlessis that in Oppen, it has "implications like *basis, basic,* or *first things*" ("Introduction" xx)—in other words, philosophical rather than cultural implications.

Two intertextual episodes will suffice to illustrate the difference between Oppen's stance and that of Schwerner. The first section of Schwerner's poem "Prologue in Six Parts" includes the following lines:

> George Oppen in his clipping voice had said
> "Some of the young men
> Have become aware of the Indian,
> Perhaps because the young men move across the continent
> without wealth, moving one could say
> On the bare ground. There one finds the Indian
> Otherwise not found." (*Seaweed* 53)

The lines that Schwerner quotes come from Oppen's "A Narrative" (*New Collected Poems* 154–55), a poem that, on one level, registers Oppen's responses to various poets with whom he was in contact in the sixties, notably William Bronk. "The young men," therefore, as Schwerner presumes, probably refers to the ethnopoetics group, including Jerome Rothenberg, David Antin, and Schwerner himself. Schwerner's poem is a multicultural mélange, in which references to Wordsworth, the Talmud, African geography and Native American dance are combined with allusions to the poet's daily life to demonstrate that "Poetry / is an act of survival" (53). Schwerner seems to take Oppen's somewhat ironic lines as an endorsement of the "young men's" awareness, though Oppen himself, while praising Schwerner's poem, has a number of reservations. "I am not sure the poem does not lose something in the first movement" writes Oppen to Schwerner, "even justified as prologue—and elsewhere where the tenses and occasions seem to me unclear; where the poem seems to escape into atmosphere and preamble. Amble." (*Selected Letters* 101).[7] The search for the real may "amble" toward other times and cultures, though for Oppen, it may more simply lead to our own society's present need for the "substantial language / Of clarity, and of respect" with which "A Narrative" ends (*New Collected Poems* 156).

Years later, however, Schwerner in his maturity (and probably after Oppen's death) will turn the tables on his old friend, revealing how fully he has considered the strengths—and limitations—of Oppen's Objectivist perspective. "George Oppen, tell me" writes Schwerner in the "Tablets Journals," "if there's no object constancy, what is the shipwreck of the singular? And how is it that a place to start from implies at the very least a potentially identifiable and receiving thereness" (*Tablets* 139). "[T]he shipwreck / Of the singular," the most famous phrase from Oppen's masterpiece "Of Being Numerous," is usually taken to refer to the loss of individual subjectivity associated with "that meditative man" (*New Collected Poems* 166, 168). Oppen's "bright light of shipwreck" (167) signifies not only the loss of individuality in the face of corporate-sponsored mass culture, but the lost possibility of *enlightenment*, the cherished humanistic dream of the poet, philosopher, or rationalistic scholar—just the sort of figure that Schwerner parodies in *The Tablets* as overwhelmed by the loss of "object constancy" in the archaic texts he attempts to decipher. For Schwerner, Oppen does not take his quest for the real far enough; he fails to recognize that in the search for origins, one must recognize "at the very least a potentially identifiable and receiving thereness"—which is one way of conceiving of the divine.

:::

For Schwerner, the poem in the process of uncovering—and making—the real, is simultaneously an act of sanctification and an interrogation of the sacred. The archaeological, linguistic, and paleographical methods of *The Tablets* lead us to reconsider some of our most reified assumptions about religious texts, scriptural canons, prophetic and priestly authority, and most important, the relation of the sacred to the profane. Willard Gingerich captures this aspect of the poem in the opening of his essay "Sacred Forgeries and Translations of Nothing in the *Tablets* of Armand Schwerner." For Gingerich, "Armand Schwerner recalled me again to the paradox of our essential condition: that the inescapable and necessary ground of our being is the voice of the Divine; but the Divine steadfastly refuses to speak. Therefore we find ourselves, age after age, forced to translate an immense silence, a translation whose purpose is to obscure the forgery of its source: the inarticulate Divine" (18).

Extrapolating from this statement, it can be argued that the religious dimension of *The Tablets* becomes increasingly accessible the greater our impediments to the silent voice of the Divine become. The more difficult the task of "translation," the greater the chance of discovering some infinitesimal fragment of sacred Speech out of the conflicted welter of ancient voices—and this is at least as true for the reader of the poem as it is for the Scholar/Translator in the poem. To borrow again from Santner, Schwerner's project may thus be "conceived not as a harmonization of parts within an ordered whole but rather as the representation of an interrupted whole—or better, a *self-interrupting whole*—one animated, as it were, by a 'too much' of pressure from within its midst" (136). Schwerner understands that, beyond a relatively brief lyric, a postmodern religious poem—a poem that seeks to articulate the inarticulate Divine—cannot present itself as inspired utterance, however layered with irony. Nor can it constitute itself as lament, finding in absence what it previously sought in presence. Rather, both of these registers must be folded into a larger and more complicated structure, so that the various verbal and temporal transactions that constitute the real can ultimately produce, in Schwerner's words, "The Space inside the poem [that] is the necessary precondition for a perception of infinity" (*Tablets* 133).

I take this "Space" to which Schwerner refers to be a holy precinct, a place of *sacrifice* or one that has been *made sacred*, though any understanding of these terms in regard to *The Tablets* must be defined largely against their conventional uses in modern, normative religious discourses. Holiness is generally understood to be that category of being related to Divinity, implying a radical separation and difference from all else. According to Allen Grossman, "*holiness* is the abstract term taught man by God to mark God's difference and the nature of everything that comes to be included . . . within his difference" (*The Long Schoolroom* 179). Likewise, "the supreme human work (man's service and creativity) is the voluntary performance of the transactions of holiness," leading in turn to "*a culture of holiness*, a system of transactions by which through the mediation of holiness man and God come to be included within the precinct of the same term" (180).

These transactions have to do ultimately with sacrifice, that is, with ritualized forms of violence, as René Girard explains throughout his work. As we have seen in previous chapters, for Girard, the sacred involves violent transactions of differentiation and containment designed to appease divine powers that threaten the community with greater, comprehensive, "generative" violence. In Girard's view, these sacred powers are to be understood as the violent potential within the community itself, externalized, projected, and distanced: "The complex and delicate nature of the community's dealings with the sacred, the ceaseless effort to arrive at the ordered and uninterrupted accord essential to the well-being of the community, can only be expressed, for want of the naked truth, in terms of optimum *distance*. If the community comes too near the sacred it risks being devoured by it; if, on the other hand, the community drifts too far away, out of range of the sacred's therapeutic threats and warnings, the effects of its fecund presence are lost" (*Violence* 268).

As I see it, these basic religious concepts, as variously understood by theological and anthropological writers, may be observed in their earliest, nascent forms throughout *The Tablets*. In other words, in Schwerner's work we are privy to the formation of the sacred from inchoate utterances within the self and between the self and others—keeping in mind that for this poet, "there is no nuclear self" (*Tablets* 130). This assertion, which points to the congruence of the primitive and the postmodern in Schwerner's audacious project, accounts for the style of the "translations" in *The Tablets*. Violence and the threat of violence loom continually in these texts, not only in physical and social terms, but in terms of psychic integrity as well. Object constancy is problematic throughout the poem. Divinity is both within and without, threatening, awful, and beautiful; holiness as an organized system that distinguishes inside and outside, the human and the divine, has yet to come into being. "Why am I thinking," asks Schwerner in his journal, "of super-subtle Pascal, his raw foundation terror of infinite spaces, when I consider the mindscapes of inhabitants of so many *Tablets*?" (139–40). The result, as he then rather insouciantly remarks, is that "The spiritual inscape of *Tablets* is terror; sometimes it isn't" (141). Schwerner has in mind that famous moment in Pascal's *Pensées*: "The eternal silence of these infinite spaces fills me with dread" (95). The infinite spaces inside and outside the self that open for the archaic speakers in the poem, these spaces where Divinity is understood to have its domain, are at least as dreadful as Girard's notion of sacred violence, and, I think, equally capable of leading to sacred acts and, eventually, a culture of holiness.

This is where the real comes into play, especially as Schwerner understands Wallace Stevens's sense of the term. For instance, in Tablet X, which consists almost entirely of the Scholar/Translator's absurd diacritical symbols for "missing," "untranslatable," and "confusing," we encounter two words in brackets, located directly in center of the text: [the the]. According to the key to *The Tablets*, words in brackets have been "supplied by the scholar translator"; they are, in other words, speculations as to the meaning of unidentified ideograms, though the Scholar/Translator, as he admits himself, is drastically unsure of his linguistic reconstructions.[8] In this case, of course, "The the" are the last two words in Stevens's "The Man on the Dump," though there is no sign that the Scholar/Translator is aware of this. It is an expression of "the truth" (*Collected Poems* 203), the definite article, grammatical marker of the singular, which I would connect to "the wrapper on the can of pears, / The cat in the paper-bag, the corset, the box / From Esthonia" (201) and all the other detritus of material existence that is identified earlier in Stevens's poem. "The the" and "the truth" are two phrases that have been the source of much critical contention. A. Walton Litz identifies "The the" with "a poetry of the irreducible minimum" (262), which I presume is what Stevens means by "the janitor's poems / Of every day" (*Collected Poems* 201). If such is the case, then "the the" signifies a poetic of the quotidian and the immediate: in other words, an Objectivist poetic of the sort represented by Stevens's friend and rival William Carlos Williams, and a precursor to the kind of poetic that Schwerner also ponders in the work of George Oppen. In Stevens's poem, the post-romantic poet, wondering if he should "hear the blatter of grackles and say / *Invisible priest*" (203), is highly ambivalent toward such a poetry: "One feels the purifying change. One rejects / The trash" (202) he declares, yet the dump remains his ineluctable reality. "[I]t is indeed there that one first heard the truth," argues Harold Bloom, "when with a heightened sense of self one emulated Whitman by returning to the object, any object" (*Wallace Stevens* 148). For Bloom, "'The the' is any object whatsoever, outside the self, which is in the process of being taken up again into language" (147). It is because this Whitmanian process takes place that the man on the dump, even when fixated on trash, is still "the American High Romantic, perpetually at work reconstructing itself" (148).

Following these readings, we can say that "The the" produces a critical crux: is it a mark of Stevens's uneasy acknowledgment of (and probable resistance to) an objectivist aesthetic that he understood to be a rival of his own? Or is it the final gesture in another triumphant struggle for poetic transcendence, a sublime moment of linguistic transformation, the work of an *"invisible priest"* in the midst of the modern junk heap? "One beats and beats for that which one believes" (*Collected Poems* 202), declares the poet. But what does he believe—about the dump, which is our modern reality, and more importantly, about the sort of poem that is to be written on the dump? Should the modern poem continue to be a search for "the truth," whether found in the object world or in linguistic transcendence? As Schwerner understands him, Stevens vacillates between an older, romantic mode of perception and expression, in which the poem is the poet's *act of power*, and of a more recent modernist, or even postmodernist mode, in which the poet, as Schwerner notes, "becomes part of the process which itself is change." As Stevens himself knows, what is at issue is the nature of the transaction between subjective imagination and objective reality, and the kind of language-act that will result from it.

Let us return to "[the the]" in Tablet X. The appearance of this most vexed of modern signifiers in what is supposedly a text from about 5000 B.C.E. leads one to believe that "the truth" that the modern world finds so hard to comprehend was known at the beginning of civilization. Or was it? Since the Scholar/Translator supplies the phrase, we cannot know if our modern epistemological dilemma, what Stevens ironically calls "a philosopher's honeymoon" (203), is being projected back into our archaic origins. Schwerner's Tablet thus becomes the site of a philosophical dialogue that the present must hold with itself, in the mute presence of an inscrutable but weirdly familiar past. Perhaps Schwerner's Akkadians feel the same alienation from the object world that Stevens expresses in "The Man On the Dump," and likewise yearn doubtfully for transcendence. On the other hand, they may be more at home with quotidian reality, experiencing a kind of immanence in the presence of things that one associates with Williams and his fellow Objectivists. "The the" in Tablet X poses this problem, but cannot in itself provide an answer, for just as there is no consensus as to the phrase's meaning in Stevens's poem, there can be no definite understanding of the archaic sensibility from its dubious insertion in Schwerner's text. But if we read a little further, we find more clues.

:::

Throughout *The Tablets*, the object world of both nature and human artifact impinges upon, and thus shapes, the archaic consciousness. The voices in these texts betray a deep concern—one could even say a cathexis—for specific *things*. Tablet XIII, for instance, begins with an almost ecstatic litany of objects:

> this chair this yellow table these pots this tablet-clay this lettuce this lettuce
> this stone jar these blue flowers this silver lioness this electrum ass on her
>   rein-ring
> here's my eye and here's the great emptiness surrounding the object hating
>   me
> this tablet-clay hating me separated from its name
> this stone jar hating me separated from its name outlining
> a piece of the air to sliver me through this piece of blue flower hating me (45)

Moments such as these bear a strong resemblance to the Objectivist notion of sincerity, as explicated by Charles Altieri: "Insistence on the surface of the poem concerned primarily with direct acts of naming as signs of the poet's immediate engagement in the areas of experience made present by conceiving the act of writing as a mode of attention" (33). Yet such attention through perception and writing proves inadequate: thus we also read that "here's my eye and here's the great emptiness surrounding the object hating me." How to account for that "great emptiness," the threatening void in the seeming plenitude of the material world? Because consciousness is also shaped by a desire for metaphysical experience, the speakers in the poem often move between attempted union with the object world and a movement away from it, toward a level of being that may be defined as spiritual or possessed of the divine.

In effect, the opening lines of Tablet XIII record a psychic, even a spiritual crisis, brought on by the loss of immanence and the recognition of the space, the "great emptiness," between the perceiving subject and the perceived object. The writer experiences the objects as hating him; they are named, but the act of naming has lost its magical, unifying power, for the objects are now "separated" from their names. Language, or at least written language, may be the source of this problem, which is why the tablet-clay, the writing medium itself, is the first object mentioned as hating the speaker. Derrida's distinction between speech and writing is appropriate here: "In every case, the voice is closest to the signified, whether it is determined strictly as sense (thought or lived) or more loosely as thing. All signifiers, and first and foremost the written signifier, are derivative with regard to what would wed the voice indissolubly to the mind or to the thought of the signified sense, indeed to the thing itself. . . . The written signifier is always technical and representative. It has no constitutive meaning" (*Of Grammatology* 11).

No longer able to experience the thing as lived, the writing subject in Tablet XIII suffers a loss of constitutive meaning. The Scholar/Translator's comment on these lines are particularly revealing, for he calls them a "psychotic rant; what surprises however involves the degree of non-analogical type of reasoning, atypical personally and culturally, of the thought-modes of archaic literatures, Sumerian, Hebrew, Ugarit etc. But the author of XIII was very likely a 'cured' schizophrenic looking back, intensely directed to assess her past" (*Tablets* 45). As absurdly pedantic—and anachronistic—as this may be, the Scholar/Translator may be on to something here, which is typical of Schwerner's use of him. Terms like "psychotic" and "schizophrenic" may not be the best ones to apply to such an ancient text, but we are at a moment of psychic rupture or at least the recollection of such a moment. Perhaps one can say that the moment of unity with the object world, as far back in history as we can imagine verbal expression, is always already lost. The last "translated" lines of Tablet XIII consist of an exhortation addressed to the self, urging a renewed experience of the body and of the objects around it, and calling for the lost immediacy of the naming process:

> begin to begin
> give the eye to the socket
> surround the nostrils with the nose
> encircle the cave of the mouth with lips
> and the asshole with fat cheeks
> the mantis eats her lover after all is done
> neck first let it come down but begin
> begin to begin
> jar name table name lettuce object tablet-clay name
> name name

> eye mouth eye nostril lip cave ass tablet-clay mouth name
> take light wash away light together eye nose face name name (46)

What makes these lines so poignant is the recognition of loss that necessitates their very utterance. Because the process of naming has lost its magical potency, Schwerner's poem grows increasingly elegiac, and the language magic that was once a part of everyday life shifts toward the realm of divinity, or of the divinely inspired poet. Only here might an unmediated relation to the object world be found.

As we shall see, this tension between the magic of this mundane object world and the magic of the divine is related in turn to the equally important tension between orality and literacy, for *The Tablets* unfolds at that moment when what was an oral culture is giving way to one in which reading and writing have only recently come into being. Here, for instance, is the first half of Tablet XIV, a relatively brief Tablet and one that does not have any of the Scholar/Translator's commentary:

> from nothing, from nothing, the stone beginning, tell me my name,
> when I write letters and do accounts I am that other man
> and keep from trembling, o at the heart's root is not cauldron but . . . .
> come come in come in come in says my pain
> run from the sun, wander around in me and profit, the stars tell North
> but little else.
>   From nothing from nothing find me my name, say
> in some clear way if the end is sadness, how the days of fishing are numbered, say
> whether my name begins to rage or music rooting about for its pleasure
> o draw me from my Alabaster Self
> my millstone quartz marl me take me from my smooth whiteness my absence
> o Oualpaga Dammara Damalo Karhenmou Amagaa Arigaa Adambpaga
> as a night lightens in dream rivers
> +
> where does the hunger grow? never never ever
> in the lines of force stowed motionless in my thighs and afloat in the mineral roe
> Of ground o let my secret name Dammara Damalo Karhenmou implode and boil
> in my balls frozen in my body's boat (48)

One of the more noticeable aspects of this passage is the speaker's concern with his "secret name." As Walter Ong observes in *Orality and Literacy*, a work that Schwerner studied carefully,[9] "the fact that oral peoples commonly and in all likelihood universally considered words to have magical potency is clearly tied in, at least unconsciously, with their sense of the word as necessarily spoken, sounded, and hence power-driven. . . . Oral peoples commonly think of names (one kind of word) as conveying power over things" (32–33). The name invoked in Tablet XIV comes "from nothing, the stone beginning," the world of things, of inanimate objects that existed prior to sentient being. Nevertheless, the name has the power to guarantee the speaker a kind of life apart from his "Alabaster Self" and the sadness of ending or mortality, in a world where "the days of fishing are numbered." To find this name, then, is to be freed from what the speaker variously calls the "pain" or "hunger" of mortality; the name will "implode and boil / in my balls frozen in my body's boat," renewing his sexual potency and granting him the blessing of more life.[10] Through the name, the power of the spirit in the self is directed back upon the body; indeed, in the context of the speaker's religious belief, the binarism of spirit and flesh simply does not obtain.

One binarism that does obtain, however, involves the act of writing. The speaker declares that "when I write letters and do accounts I am that other man / and keep from trembling." Throughout The Tablets, writing is a highly charged activity that has about it the double nature of the sacred, its beneficence and its threat. Even writing letters and accounts (as opposed to, say, prophecy or prayer) provides the speaker with a sense of otherness that is experienced as relief, freedom from an existential fear of being caught in the limitations of the self, and hence, of mortality.[11] Is the "other man" created by writing the bearer of the secret name? As is said in Tablet VIII, "the right words wait in the stone / they'll discover themselves as you chip away" (29). Writing as an engagement with a form of being that is both of and beyond the self—that participates, in other words, in a process of transcendence— is fundamental to Schwerner's poesis in The Tablets.

But this primal experience of writing, premised on the fiction that we are reading translations of some of the oldest known texts, is always juxtaposed against the observations of the modern Scholar/Translator, who takes a rather different view of literacy. In the "Laboratory Teachings Memoirs of the Scholar/Translator" of Tablet XXVI, he asks, "Did the Old Ones, like me in my dawn, live in the revivifying newness of discovery? The history of my mind besieged by 5,000 years of written documents is the history by turns of a weary and oppressed animal and that of repeated and sometimes galling insistence on confronting and mastering the unabsorbable" (70). The Scholar/Translator associates his own youthful enthusiasm for books with the "Old Ones," who, at the dawn of literacy, are discovering the power of writing for the first time, a power to create Otherness that they invest with religious awe. In his old age, however, he feels oppressed and harassed by that which once offered him freedom. He suffers from what Santner would call "Egyptomania," a psychically rigidifying defense mechanism resulting from "coming too close to a surplus of validity over meaning, necessity over truth, that is at some level operative in all institutions that regulate symbolic identities" (53). Egyptomania forces upon one "a surplus, *fantasmatic labor* at the core of the sovereign relation"; particularly in figures invested with social (and textual) authority, it "most powerfully captures life, undeadens it, makes it rigid with energy" (64). Appropriately, Egyptomania is that which "constrains our capacities to respond to the Other" (122)—"not simply to the thoughts, values, hopes, and memories of the Other, but also to the Other's touch of madness, to the way in which the Other is disoriented in the world, destitute, divested of an identity that firmly locates him or her in a delimited whole of some sort" (82). Just this sort of encounter with the Other, human or divine, occurs again and again in the "ancient" sections of *The Tablets*, but the Scholar/Translator, unable to grasp these relations as they are inscribed through the new technology of writing, rigidly rejects them. As we observed, in one instance (Tablet XIII) he goes so far as to describe the text as a "psychotic rant" and the writer "very likely a 'cured' schizophrenic" (45).

The exhaustion that the Scholar/Translator feels when confronted with "5,000 years of written documents" is comic and pathetic, linking him to the Kafkan bureaucrats and Borgesian librarians who are his literary precursors.[12] Yet his sense of weary oppression in the face of the text's impossible demands also indicates the importance of *The Tablets* as a fictive investigation into the origin and end of writing itself: an "adventure," as Derrida names it in the *Grammatology*, "that merges with the history that has associated technics and logocentric metaphysics for nearly three [Schwerner would say five] millennia. And now it seems to be approaching what is really its own *exhaustion*; under the circumstances—and this is no more than one example among others—of this death of the civilization of the book, of which so much is said and which manifests itself particularly through a convulsive proliferation of libraries" (8). If this description truly applies to the situation of the Scholar/Translator, then his "Egyptomania," the impasse in his research to which he so painfully returns throughout *The Tablets*, is the inevitable outcome of a labor that coincides with the end of an epoch, the very origin of which the Scholar/Translator seeks to uncover. Like the Old Ones themselves, the Scholar/Translator attempts "to recoup the powers of the past without the sacrifice of the present—instinct with the knowledge of the doom attendant upon any creative thrust which thumbed its nose at its own time" (*Tablets* 98). This may be one of the many instances in *The Tablets* when the Scholar/Translator projects his own existential and textual situation back upon the ancient scribes he so desperately wishes to understand. His ensuing spiritual crisis is precisely the doom he describes, for what he fails to realize is that the present moment in which he works marks the end of an epoch that no scholarship, no translation, can ever fully recoup.

    :::

"The sign and divinity," Derrida writes, "have the same place and time of birth. The age of the sign is essentially theological. Perhaps it will never *end*. Its historical *closure* is, however, outlined" (*Of Grammatology* 14). The connection of writing to the spirit that we observe coming into being at the start of literate civilization in *The Tablets* is often cast in an elegiac register, which one would think is more appropriate to its end. In Tablet XX (from a group of "clearly epistolary Tablets," according to the Scholar/Translator), the writer addresses a friend (or perhaps a god), declaring that "I'm left with words and no flesh / of your moving spirit to dawn the world" (60). Forced to choose between the spirit in the flesh and the spirit in the word, the archaic consciousness of *The Tablets* would choose immanence every time. But Schwerner does not permit this: instead, his masterpiece boldly proposes that the separation of the human and the divine coincides with the advent of literacy and together constitute a *fall*. It could be, at least allegorically speaking, that what is "missing" or "untranslatable" in *The Tablets* is the story of that fall, and that literacy itself is a belated response to that primal crisis in the religious sensibility.[13] The ruptures in being represented by the imposition of the sacred into human life, and by the entrance of the written sign into consciousness, are experienced together as loss; the beginnings of what Grossman calls a "culture of holiness" and what Derrida calls "the civilization of the book" are together met with elegy. Earlier I called *The Tablets* a sort of divine comedy, and taking the work in its totality, I believe that to be true. But Schwerner's archaeology of the sacred and the real has about it something of a divine tragedy as well. As Ong observes, "there is hardly an oral culture or a predominantly oral culture left in the world today that is not somehow aware of the vast complex of powers forever inaccessible without literacy. This awareness is agony for persons rooted in primary orality, who want literacy passionately but who also know very well that moving into the exciting world of literacy means leaving behind much that is exciting and deeply loved in the earlier oral world. We have to die to continue living" (15). If such is the case for oral cultures in the world today, one can only imagine what Ong calls the "agony"—but at the same time the excitement—for human beings facing the cultural prospects of literacy for the first time in history. In *The Tablets*, Schwerner gives us that moment, investing it with a religious awe that is in no way eclipsed by the manifold ironies of the poem's comic premises and methods.[14]

The loss and the gain, the agony and the excitement of the passage into literacy, can be glimpsed—but only glimpsed—throughout the poem, partly aided and partly impeded by the Scholar/Translator. In Tablet XXI, another epistolary text, we are given the following plangent lines:

> and in the remembered travail
> of our tearing desire for clarity
> I write these forms to you whom I have lost
> having learned again with you
> the masked lure of truth
> the double impersonal faces of love (62)

Here, Schwerner's concern for the new technology of writing intersects with the changes taking place in the human capacity for belief and in the nature of the affective life. Writing is related to "our tearing desire for clarity" and "the masked lure of truth"; that is, writing becomes a means of fulfilling the desire for a greater knowledge of reality.[15] Yet in the travail of this quest, the friend to whom the text is addressed has been lost, though again, as in the case of Tablet XX quoted above, there is the distinct possibility that this friend is a god or at least some sort of spiritual Other. Thus writing—a technology that allows communication at a distance—is also related to "the double impersonal faces of love." The relative *impersonality* of writing, lack-ing the intimacy of face-to-face speech, means a previously unimaginable form of love at a distance and a "double" experience of affective communi-cation that entails both absence and presence. Literacy opens a promising but also threatening emotional space between one person and another, and likewise unsettles the human relationship to the divine.

What happens to religious experience when divinity no longer *speaks*? The writer in Tablet XXI calls his "scribe-companions dismissible, all risible / clowns of adulthood met by your irony or the silence / of your discomfort and I / could do nothing we have begun / to say goodbye" (62). Confronted by the ironic silence of divinity, the writer's "scribe-companions" are dis-missible, risible, and immature, presumably because the figure of the scribe cannot compare in religious authority to the priest or prophet in an oral culture. The writer in this Tablet wonders how "to bear the propulsive / sea-change of your spirit in the presence of my scribe-life" (62). Whose spirit has undergone this change? In effect, it does not matter whether it is that of humanity or divinity, for the fundamental conditions of what the writer calls his "scribe-life" have irrevocably altered his relations to both. Despite his supposed distance from us in time, he has undergone a painfully modern experience. As Santner describes it, we are

> always haunted, surrounded by the remainders of lost forms of life, by concepts and signs that had meaning within a form of life that is now gone and so persist, to use Lacan's telling formulation, as "hieroglyphs in the desert." We are thus al-ways, in a certain sense, within the dimension of loss and abandonment. But what is more, we are in the midst of loss we cannot even really name, for when you lose a concept you also lose the capacity to name what has been lost. When, for ex-ample, one has lost the capacity to pray, "God," in essence, assumes the status of a designified signifier, a stand-in for an otherwise *nameless loss*; the word signifies, *but not for us* even though we continue, in some sense, to be addressed by it. (44)

I would not go so far as to say that "God" has been totally transformed into a "designified signifier" for the melancholy scribe in Tablet XXI. Neverthe-less, he begins his lament with the lines "we have begun to say goodbye to each other / and cannot say it finally" (61), and for once, the pedantic Schol-ar/Translator gets it right: "The tone of XXI manifests remarkably contem-poraneous psychological harmonics" (61).

:::

In the passage from *The Coming Community* that serves as the epigraph to this chapter, Giorgio Agamben declares that "God is in every thing as the place in which every thing is, or rather as the determination and the 'topia' of every entity. The transcendent, therefore, is not a supreme entity above all things; rather, *the pure transcendent is the taking-place of every thing.*" The transcendent as the taking-place of every thing makes sense before and after the "age of the sign" or the "civilization of the book" (which, according to Derrida, may or may not ever really end), but during that long and perhaps interminable period, the transcendent remains a matter of separation, difference, and sacrificial distance. We may ultimately judge Agamben's formulation to be utopian, but it still sheds light on the current relationship in our culture between poetry and religion, whether the civilization of the book is on the wane or not. In any case, the postmodern (re)turn to a theology of immanence seen in Agamben's extraordinary manifesto bears an uncanny resemblance to the pre-literate forms of belief to which the voices in *The Tablets* desperately cling. One of the last passages in XXVI, the penultimate Tablet, begins:

> *He is someone else, perhaps an animal.* He lives inside plant names.
> He races inside his messages of fleet means. He is the calling voice
> Of the names inside the wheat and barley. He can't say them
> Forever. He tells them ++++++++++++++++++++++++++++++++++
> Through the inside of his eyes, he sees
> The inside of his eyes and describes the animal names of plants.
> He looks and tells. (93)

It is impossible to ascertain if these lines refer to a god or to a deified poet, but in either case, it is clear that the power he possesses is now out of reach of the ordinary mortal. This is the power to "receive the good names," to find "the sound, the proper / Voice for the saying, the murmuring, the uttering, the chant / Of wheat and barley changed by murmur into animal liveliness" (93). The magic of naming enters the domain of the transcendent, becoming a practice exclusive to that domain.

Likewise, in Tablet XXVII, the last tablet, which includes excerpts from the "Laboratory-Teachings-Memoirs of the Scholar/Translator," we find his translation of what he calls a "Derived Sympathy-Meditation Song," in which metaphysical speculation is intimately bound to and yet resignedly separated from bodily functions and the cycles of nature. Here is the beginning of the Song:

> shine attempted birth of closed regions
> and fall in slave incantations plenitude—
> cut honey, separate silence and anus, web grains
> for pregnancy conduct of a great mouth a
> lost harvest, palsy, & sweet
> stress of muscle fear to burn
> gather exudae in a quiet
> & swear tomorrow
> for talk better talk sadder
> mouths of loud grains
> unassailable & sad, teeth. (109)

Despite the difficulties posed by the parataxis of these lines, it would appear that what the Scholar/Translator calls the "Path of Sympathy-Meditation" (104) involves the recognition that "the attempted birth of closed regions" is always just that: an attempt. "Plenitude," or Agamben's notion of the transcendent as the taking-place of every thing, shines forth in this attempt, but also risks falling into "slave incantations." Human limits, both spiritual and physical, compel those who would practice "Sympathy-Meditation" to "separate silence and anus" and undergo a "lost harvest" of being. In the course of the meditation (and the poem), the initiate can only "swear tomorrow / for talk better talk sadder." Indeed, as Schwerner nears the end of *The Tablets*, to "talk better" is to "talk sadder," for language marks the separation of body and spirit, and physical birth inevitably leads to spiritual closure. Language—and in the world of the Old Ones, language is practically synonymous with poetry—both preserves and unmakes our link with the divine.

In the beginning—that is, in the archaic imaginary of *The Tablets*—the space between poetry and religion was hardly there at all, for poetry voiced the taking place of every thing. Today, I am tempted to say that this both can and cannot be. One of Schwerner's last notes in the Tablets Journals reveals "the pain I felt when I interrupted a lyric song by any of my unknown archaic speakers by intercalating—or rather by finding necessary the presence of—the S/T's discursive, apparently irrelevant comments. . . . I remember part of me would almost agree with a hearer's wish that I omit the S/T's commentary as unnecessarily clotting; I'd almost want to accede. But precisely such ambiguities, left somewhat to integrally radiate, is useful work done. The thing is, I wanted not to separate the song from the entropic world. This *and* that" (157). It is in this inseparability, the "this *and* that," that we find Schwerner's—and poetry's—continued importance.

"The maxim of poetic thinking is this: DO NOT BE CONTENT WITH AN IMAGINARY GOD. Poetry is the most realistic of arts" (xi). So Allen Grossman tells us at the start of his remarkable book of poems, *How to Do Things with Tears*. For Grossman, "Poetic knowledge is useful KNOWL-EDGE (knowledge that helps out with tears), but only when it encounters, and forces, into visibility (puts where you can see), whatever it is that resists your will to know and to love" (xi). An imaginary God, therefore, would mitigate poetry's "realism" and the useful knowledge that it provides. With the exception of Jack Spicer, who would probably agree with Grossman on this point, whether the poets whose work I have examined in this book are content with an imaginary God must remain an open question. But it seems clear that the struggle with the sacred that we have observed over and over in their work does indeed force into visibility whatever resists their (and our) will to know and to love. Divinity enters this poetry not merely as a significant cultural construct, not merely as a question of personal belief, but as an Other that challenges the basic function of poetry in the modern world. It calls upon poets to open themselves to powers of being and of language that they would otherwise overlook or even deny. The traditional, often archaic patterns of myth, ritual, and religious practice with which we have seen these poets engage, still represent, to use a basic theological term, a kind of revelation, which as Eric L. Santner observes, "is an opening of space of human possibilities organized by the claims made upon me by the Other" (105). Often deploying the most radically defamiliarizing forms and procedures, the contemporary poets under discussion here have variously responded to these claims with extraordinary generosity. A measure of their importance lies in their formal originality, through which they revise and renew the oldest of our psychic and spiritual necessities. The fact that they frequently draw upon some of the more dubious and volatile religious traditions, such as gnosticism, antinomianism, shamanism, spiritualism, and theosophy, the fact that they often present their work as a kind of heresy, reminds us of the fundamental uneasiness (Duncan's "primary trouble") of poetry's relation to the sacred. And yet the endurance of this relationship—and its formative power over poetry as a living art—is undeniable.

But the resistance to this idea is worth noting. As is often the case in academic criticism, while writing this book I had occasion to submit individual chapters in essay form to various scholarly journals. The work was generally well received, my approach to the poetry was welcomed, and the essays were published. The reader reports I would be sent, however, sometimes struck me as rather curious. My research was regarded as solid and my writing as lucid and effective. But some readers expressed frustration, bafflement, and exasperation over what they perceived to be mystical religious commentary disguised as literary criticism. As one reader put it, "there are times at which the author confuses reading poetry with spiritual exercise and presumes a reader who is too much a worshiper at the temple." In a certain respect, I confess I was pleased with such responses. This is not to say that I seek to mystify this poetry. On the contrary, I would argue that my critical practice, if not a demystification of this poetry, is at least an *unveiling* of a partly hidden, partly repressed, partly neglected dimension of the work. It is not, therefore, that the *author* (that is, the critic or commentator) confuses reading poetry with spiritual exercise. Rather, it is the *poet* who understands that his or her work must be involved in just this sort of "confusion."

And of course, it is not confusion at all. Like Scholem, Corbin, and Eliade, the Historians of Religion in Steven M. Wasserstrom's study, the poets considered here participate in "transgression as norm," which is "not so much a release from the modern condition so much as it [is] a heightened characterization of it" (81). This does not only mean poetry's transgressions in relation to normative religious traditions; it means writing the sacred itself as transgression, when such discourse seems to have lost relevance to the modern world. When historicism becomes the critical norm, reading the poets as I have done may appear to take their work out of history, but in fact, there is every reason to believe that the esoteric meanings, arcane intertextuality, and hermeneutical mysteries we find here are not only fundamental to the poetry, but very much a part of the work's historical significance. As Schwerner's mad Scholar/Translator writes of the "Utterance/Texture/Indicators" he finds in the Tablets, "We might with a greater chance of accuracy understand such linguistic inventions as *sacred forgery*, or rather forgery prompted by a dazzled and mournful reconsideration, retrospective as well as perhaps economically profitable, of the sacred" (98). *The Tablets* is indeed a sacred forgery, and the same may be said for a great many of the other poems we have considered. This would mean that the critic of such work, himself "dazzled and mournful" in his reconsideration of the sacred, may be every bit as crazy as the figure whom Schwerner fondly calls the "S/T." But we know that in the end, the S/T always gets it right despite himself. With the tenth anniversary of his creator's death just months away, I give him the last word:

> The function of this U/T/I concerns performance and relationship, not the reification of an isolation threatening to enshroud a solitary reader faced with a "text." Although we generally conceive of that reader as separated from the dance and music ordinarily associated with archaic and tribal modes of "poetry," it's a common and insistent mistake to envision the post-archaic world as the site of increasing numbers of civilized sad troglodytes existing in a hell of separation and loss. The rites and poetry/music/dance didn't end. They entered the mind. (98–99)

Notes

Introduction

1. I employ the term "experimental" to refer primarily to matters of technique and procedure, as opposed to "avant-garde," which I understand to signify a socio-logical formation, or to "postmodern," which is usually used as a matter of historical periodization (for my discussion of the term "avant-garde," see *Lyrical Interference* 67–85; for a discussion of the term "postmodern" in regard to recent long poems, see McHale, *Obligation* ix–xi and 1–3). Since form, as we have been told repeatedly, is always an extension of content, no experiment in technique or procedure can be that alone. Perhaps this is why Wallace Stevens writes in his "Adagia" that "all poetry is experimental poetry" (*Opus Posthumous* 187). Then again, it is clear from some of Stevens's other statements in the "Adagia" that poetry means a great deal more to him than words, however "experimentally" composed. Most important for our purposes is his remark that "after one has abandoned a belief in god, poetry is that essence which takes its place as life's redemption" (185), about which I will have more to say below. For the time being, we can note that if all poetry is experimental poetry, it is because the poem is an attempt to find new understanding or meaning in life, which always requires a renewed sense of form. As George Oppen puts it in a somewhat different context, poetry becomes "a test of truth" (Dembo and Pon-drom 174).

2. I have addressed the issue of sacred versus secular literature, both in regard to Bloom's thought and more generally, in *The Ritual of New Creation*. That book fo-cuses on works by Jewish authors, but many of my formulations apply to the poems under discussion here as well.

3. Grossman's concept of poetic vocation is also worth noting: "Vocation is the sense, of which a persona may become aware, of having been assigned a cosmic task he did not choose, may not be able to perform, but to which he nonetheless is obligated" ("On Communicative Difficulty" 144).

4. For a detailed analysis of this poem, see chapter 5.

5. I refer to my three-volume serial poem *Track: Track* (1999), *Columns* (2002), and *Powers* (2005).

6. My use of the term "power," particularly in relation to "knowledge," is best defined by Poirier in Emersonian terms: "The recognition that 'knowledge' is to be the 'effect,' and is not therefore the source of 'power,' is crucial. It is a way of admit-

ting that we do not act out of subservience to something we already know; we act so as to discover something presumably worth knowing. 'Power' is not obedient to established meanings but opposed to them; it wants to decreate them within the process of some larger creative urge. 'Urge and urge and urge, / Always the procreant urge of the world,' as Whitman puts it near the beginning of *Leaves of Grass* in 1855. 'Power' in large defines itself by challenges to the already authorized use of words, including those the poet or philosopher will himself make use of" (43).

7. Not only does Whitman influence Duncan directly, but he also mediates the latter's relationship to modernism, as Duncan makes clear: "Once I returned to Whitman, in the course of writing *The Opening of the Field* when *Leaves of Grass* was kept as a bedside book, Williams's language of objects and Pound's ideogrammatic method were transformed in the light of Whitman's hieroglyphic of the ensemble" (*Fictive Certainties* 190–91). As for Dickinson's influence on Spicer, the probing and scrupulous review that Spicer wrote for the Boston Public Library's newsletter of Johnson's three-volume edition of Dickinson's poems and letters indicates how deeply he considered the complex issues of composition, inspiration, and identity made manifest in Dickinson's writing (Spicer, *House That Jack Built* 231–37). Peter Gizzi, who edited Spicer's lectures in *The House That Jack Built*, discusses the relationship between Dickinson's and Spicer's uses of letters as poems; he also analyzes the connection between Spicer's poetry of dictation and Dickinson's remark that "Nature is a Haunted House" (184, 206–7).

8. Consider, for example, the case of Lionel Trilling, whose Arnoldianism, however tempered by his Freudianism, shapes his critical stance throughout his career. Comparing Trilling to the Emersonians, as Richard Poirier defines them, Mark Krupnick observes that "Conservative by disposition, Trilling distrusted the Emersonian invention of private, counterhistorical worlds. Rather, he had Matthew Arnold's Oxonian love of great institutions and old traditions and seems always to have been intellectually most comfortable within the ready-made academic humanistic culture of Columbia College" (33). The preservation of "great institutions and old traditions" is a hallmark of Arnoldian thought, and is a powerful determinant in Arnold's own working out of the relation between poetry and religion.

9. In the essay that originally served as the preface to an edition of Wordsworth's poetry that Arnold chose and edited (1879), Arnold represents Wordsworth as the preeminent poet of moral ideas, arguing that "A poetry of revolt against moral ideas is a poetry of revolt against *life*; a poetry of indifference towards moral ideas is a poetry of indifference towards *life*" ("Wordsworth" 46). Furthermore, Arnold insists that "Nature herself seems, I say, to take the pen out of his hand, and to write for him with her own bare, sheer, penetrating power" (53). Moral probity and intelligence, natural sincerity and strength: Wordsworth embodies the poetic virtues that are for Arnold equally religious virtues. Arnold ends the piece with a quote

from Wordsworth himself on his poems: "They will co-operate with the benign tendencies in human nature and society, and will, in their degree, be efficacious in making men wiser, better, and happier" (55). This view of Wordsworth combining morality and nature to produce what amounts to the religious dimension of his work is passed on to Lionel Trilling, Arnold's greatest American follower, as may be seen in Trilling's remarkable exercise in devotional criticism, "Wordsworth and the Rabbis" (1950). For a discussion of this essay, see Finkelstein, *Ritual of New Creation* 21–22.

10. See Bloom, *Wallace Stevens* 151–53 and 226–28 and Poirier 138 for further discussions by Bloom and Poirier of "The Creations of Sound" and Stevens's Emersonian debate with Eliot. See also Stevens's sly "Tribute to T. S. Eliot," in which he concludes that "Reading Eliot out of the pew, so to speak, goes on keeping one young. He remains an upright ascetic in a world that has grown exceedingly floppy and is growing floppier" (*Opus Posthumous* 240). Taking Eliot's poetry "out of the pew," the church in both the religious and literary canonical senses that Eliot engineered, vitalizes Stevens because it reminds him that religious asceticism is precisely the path that his own poetry never takes in order to achieve its youthful vitality, however "floppy" the modern world has become.

11. For a full consideration of H.D. and Duncan, especially in regard to psychoanalysis and the occult, see O'Leary, *Gnostic Contagion* 28–70. Two points in O'Leary's chapter are especially important: "The convergence of Freud and the occult can be reckoned in terms of the theory of correspondence that prevails in the work and thought of both H.D. and Duncan, most especially in the notion that what you see is not the real meaning of what you see: something more is hidden from the eyes, even from the eyes of the mind" (35); and "The religious connections H.D. and Duncan make in their writings, at times facilitated by Freudian insight, are realized through poetry. There are no rituals, no services, no prayers to this 'religion' that do not involve poetry. Religion, then, acts as a metaphorical vehicle to describe the inchoate 'beyonds' with which poetry interacts" (53).

Robert Duncan

1. One of the most severe but also insightful critiques of Duncan's career, culminating in a very harsh assessment of its "last mingy decades" (72), is found in "Some Thoughts about Objectivism" by the late poet, novelist and critic Ross Feld, who was originally what could be termed a second-generation New Americanist (see his volume *Plum Poems*, and for a recent reconsideration of that book, Henry Weinfield's "The Rigor of His Refusals"). Originally presented at a conference called "Intersections of the Lyrical and the Philosophical," where it provoked great controversy (see Fredman), "Some Thoughts about Objectivism" is mainly an even

more unsympathetic interrogation of George Oppen, who became friends with Duncan when he moved to San Francisco in 1967. Generally approving of Duncan's early work, Feld sees him engaging in an unsuccessful attempt at "poetic empire-building" with his two "largely unreadable" serial poems, The Structure of Rime and Passages. As Feld puts it, "Duncan allows the long poetic sequence to evict him from his magic cottage and install him instead into a palace. Where before Duncan 'with placated subjectivity' was Poet Pretender, now he was God: 'In poetry God is resurrected; He seeks in His Creation intensifications of Its orders'. But in the heavenly palace he never seemed comfortable and its echoes drowned out the re-markable poet of earlier years" (72)—the one exception being "My Mother Would Be a Falconress." Although I am fundamentally at odds with this interpretation, I believe that Feld's wit and intelligence makes a reconsideration of late Duncan all the more necessary.

2. As will be seen throughout this chapter, I owe a great debt of thanks to O'Leary, first through his book on Duncan and then through his generous reading of the present work.

3. An essay remains to be written on Duncan as love poet, or more precisely, as the embodiment of Eros within the Form of Forms. In such an essay, the central text would undoubtedly be "A Poem Beginning with a Line by Pindar." It would ex-tend backward to the darkly sexual Medieval Scenes and forward to "The Torso, Pas-sages 18" and to the astonishing "Circulations of the Song," in which Eros, in effect, bids farewell to Psyche and returns to Thanatos. Arguably, Eros as the principle of Form first appears in Duncan's poetry with the very early "Among My Friends Love Is a Great Sorrow." The graceful syntactic turns and repetitions in that lyric consti-tute the response or answer to love as the "painful question" or "old debt" (Years As Catches 74) among the poet's friends.

4. See O'Leary, Gnostic Contagion 92–98 and 167–70.

5. In "The Truth and Life of Myth," Duncan already indicates the degree to which his thinking is saturated with gnostic myth in conjunction with other spiritual tra-ditions. "In the imperative of Poetry," he declares, "three forces move to incarnate themselves in the poem: the words, come alive in their resonances of sound, pulse and meaning—this is the reservoir of our humanity; the life experience and imagi-nation of the poet—this is the reservoir of his craft and recognitions, the range of his creation of person; and the actual body of the poet—the reservoir of his life-style. But name two First Movers of the Poem. Name Seven. Name the Seventy-Two. In every configuration the Myth of the Poem will write itself anew" (Fictive Certainties 18). Note also how important this passage is for Duncan's understanding of the poem's relation to tradition as it is continually revised and reconstructed by the individual poet.

6. In addition to O'Leary and Mackey, another perceptive critic, Michael André

Bernstein, raises a set of related issues in what remains one of the single best essays on Duncan, "Robert Duncan: Talent and the Individual Tradition." According to Bernstein, "the critical terms with which we might account for success or failure in a poetics in which there is no *telos* to identify, and in which we cannot measure the individual poem's trajectory in terms of an already known project are still vexingly imprecise. . . . It is often difficult to give clear expression to the reasons why certain of Duncan's poems move us more deeply than others which are composed according to similar principles and with similar thematic concerns" (189, 190). For Bernstein, most readers are more attracted to Duncan's post-Romantic lyrics, such as "My Mother Would Be a Falconress," but "it is the longer, more exploratory sequences like 'Passages' and 'The Structure of Rime' that contain much of Duncan's finest work, and will inevitably provide a store-house of new possibilities for the future of the art" (189). As evidence, Bernstein mentions "Circulations of the Song," which is actually one of the more self-contained works in the *Ground Work*. In a certain respect, the present chapter is a further attempt to develop the critical terms needed to understand Duncan's nonteleological poetics.

7. Cf. "Man's Fulfillment in Order and Strife," in which Duncan writes of "that wholeness, that is made up of a multitude of individualities, [that] has become for me the central theme—a Man of all men, multiphasic, beyond what we can know but central, as are immediate realities of Man, to what we are. This was the Adam in whom all the species have their identity. In the traditions of the Jewish Kabbala this Adam falls apart into the lives of all men—his identity hidden in our identities" (*Fictive Certainties* 115).

8. Also see Beach 136–61. As for H.D., the modernist with whom Duncan has the closest literary and personal connections, it would appear that, given the recent research of O'Leary and Johnston, the relationship of Duncan to H.D. and the writing that results from it is deeply Romantic in every sense of the term.

9. Lyn Hejinian discusses Stein's version of realism as it evolves from nineteenth-century realistic fiction in "Language and Realism" (86–93), the first of her "Two Stein Talks." Given Duncan's romanticism, it is worth noting that, according to Hejinian, "the spirit of artistic commitment to the world, and the designation of that as realism, had in the nineteenth century followed on a rejection of religious (transcendent, inspirational) and secular (escapist) fantasies as the principal function of writing" (90).

10. He did, however, also continue to write in the romantic vein during this period, with the first draft of "Often I Am Permitted to Return to a Meadow" completed in 1953.

11. For Hejinian, apropos of Stein, "the opposite of realism is not imagination (which exists within style) but idealism (which is imposed on subject matter)" (95). Whether or not her second parenthetical remark is accurate (I do not believe it ap-

plies to Duncan among other poets in the Romantic tradition), this is still a further indication of the distance between Duncan's and Stein's sensibilities, and the degree to which he puts himself to school under her philosophically antithetical tutelage.

12. Written between May 1953 and December 1955 and published by the Jargon Society in 1958.

13. In contrast with my reading, Feld connects these lines to Duncan as "Objectivist . . . in that he reveals no personality behind his poem save one—that of the Poet Pretender" ("Some Thoughts" 71). But Duncan is hardly an Objectivist because he seeks an Eliotic "escape from personality." I think Feld is closer to the truth about Duncan and Objectivism when he observes that "Duncan knew where lay the artesian entry of the beautiful into his world, and he loved the world for it, for giving him permission to tap it" ("Some Thoughts" 71). But this too is only half the story, since the gnostic in Duncan, who grows stronger the further Duncan goes, has little love for or patience with the world and forcefully dissociates his sense of beauty from it to a greater and greater extent.

14. Consider Stein's remarks in *The Autobiography of Alice B. Toklas* apropos the poems in *Tender Buttons*: "They were the beginning, as Gertrude Stein would say, of mixing the outside with the inside. Hitherto she had been concerned with seriousness and the inside of things, in these studies she began to describe the inside as seen from the outside" (*Selected Writings* 147).

15. It is important to note that in his consideration of *The Book of Questions*, Duncan invokes a third figure in addition to Saussure and de León: Sigmund Freud. A devoted Freudian, Duncan relates the work of Jabès not only to structural linguistics and kabbalah, but to Freud's understanding of the dream-work as a language, "hieroglyphic and yet presenting letters and phones—a rebus that he [Freud] thinks to be identical with the poem-work" (*Selected Prose* 212–13). Thus, it may be said that Duncan's understanding of poetry derives equally from linguistic, psychoanalytic, and religious/theosophical sources.

16. Arguably, Duncan's poetic alliances undergo a change at this point as well, as he distances himself from Jack Spicer and Robin Blaser, his old comrades in the "Berkeley Renaissance," and moves closer to Charles Olson, Denise Levertov, and Robert Creeley, the Black Mountain poets with whom he will be associated in the late fifties and sixties (and with whom he will be grouped by Donald Allen in *The New American Poetry*).

17. For Duncan's relationship to Olson, and the importance of Whitehead to their poetic, see Byrd, and Johnston 72–76. Conte (47–54) demonstrates how Duncan's reading of Schrödinger amplifies the influences of Olson and Whitehead.

18. See also Handelman 79–82 for an application of Barthes and Derrida to specifically rabbinic ideas of scripture, ideas with which Duncan would have been fa-

miliar given his study of both Barthes and kabbalah. For a witty and insightful view of Duncan as "Jewish" poet, see Selinger, "Shekhinah in America" 255–57.

19. For a reading of "The Fire," see O'Leary, *Gnostic Contagion* 80–85.

20. In addition to Mackey's essay, see Reid 168–73. Both Mackey and Reid respond to Mersmann's reading of Duncan in *Out of the Vietnam Vortex* 159–204.

21. In O'Leary's comparison of Duncan and Mackey, "Mackey's cross-culturality is in conflict, whereas Duncan's theosophical background yields a holistic theory of correspondences he both relies on and refutes. Mackey, like Duncan, is gnostic, but he is not an emanational gnostic who believes divine knowledge is pulsating down through the cosmos from the hyperrealm above. Rather, his descriptive adjective of choice is "discrepant," which he uses to suggest a "creaking" of things, especially words, whose gruffness he willingly abides in. As a discrepantist, he keeps his distance from Duncan's holism with the poetic equivalent of a negative theology" (*Gnostic Contagion* 197). Or as Mackey himself puts it, "No doubt the easiest to make and most often made criticism of Duncan is that he is intoxicated with the idea of poetry, pushing a romance of the poem at the expense of everything else a poem could be about. . . . His friendly relations with What Is, alongside his sense of poetry's privileged access to It, appear too complacent at times, especially in the context of political and social problems like the war. He sometimes appears to be saying that whatever is is right, especially if—or exactly because—it contributes to the writing of poems. The delight he takes in poetry, his own 'riding high', runs its particular risks of narcosis" (*Paracritical Hinge* 175–76).

22. The last of the numbered Passages is "Passages 36" (it does not have any other name), which interrupts the progress of "A Seventeenth Century Suite." The rest of the series is unnumbered; each poem bears a title followed by the bracketed "[Passages]." The one exception, as indicated in the table of contents, comes late in *Ground Work II*: it is "You, Muses, Passages 22," which, as it were, fills the space in *Bending the Bow*, where between 21 and 23 there is a poem called "In Place of a Passage 22."

23. For a thorough examination of Duncan's method of composition, see Johnston 83–96. Johnston also notes the "professionalism" (ix) of Duncan's habit of wearing a three-piece suit when he sat down to write, as illustrated in the R. B. Kitaj drawing on the cover of *Ground Work II*.

24. For more on the Atlantis dream, see Davidson, *The San Francisco Renaissance* 59–62, and O'Leary, *Gnostic Contagion* 85–92.

25. See Grossman, *The Sighted Singer* 356–63. Grossman's elaboration of "mother tongue" and "father tongue" sheds a good deal of light on Duncan's situation as I interpret it here. According to Grossman, "the natural is female, maternal, earth-born, tragically compelled, not meaningful in itself but the ground on which meaning is inscribed . . . poetry in the mother tongue is a return of the child to the mother, the

choosing of necessity and therefore the defeat of choice" (356–57). Furthermore, "the past as mother is the earth as tradition, the body as cosmic-participant which is the dark companion of every meaning-intending soul. . . . The past as mother is the death-bound past which threatens the immortality of the son by redeeming the male figure in the female ground of oblivion" (361).

26. Cf. the rhapsodic "(Close)" to "Apprehensions" (*Roots and Branches* 42–43), a magnificent litany of the orders that constitute the poet's lyric domain.

27. Arguably, a gnostic sense of impending catastrophe has always been a fundamental part of Duncan's personal *mythos* of the poet, as indicated in the disastrous flood that ends his Atlantis dream, after the poet has been chosen as King or "It." In this respect, as Peter O'Leary suggested to me, Duncan "composed himself" into the last phase of his work, having predicted and received "permission" for it much earlier in his career (e-mail).

28. John Norris (1657–1712), regarded as the last of the Cambridge Platonists, is remembered today more as a philosopher (he was the first English respondent to Locke's *Essay Concerning Human Understanding*) than as a poet.

29. It is worth noting that "Jamais" is written as an *"Homage to the youthful Zukofsky, his looking forward in the 1920s to prove his Art in A-23"* (*Ground Work I* 147). The first line of the poem contains the letter (or word) "a" in quotations, and the last word of the poem is "the": the former referring to *"A,"* Zukofsky's huge masterpiece; the latter referring to *Poem Beginning "The"* (1927), Zukofsky's first published work. "A"-23 (1972–1973), the penultimate section of the poem, is an extraordinarily dense thousand-line movement written in the five-word line that Zukofsky employs in much of his later work, certainly a "proof" of Zukofsky's brilliant, obdurate artistry. Duncan also may be thinking of Zukofsky's remark that "a case could be made out for the poet giving some of his life to the use of the words *the* and *a*: both of which are weighted with as much epos and historical density as one man can perhaps resolve" (10). But the weight that Duncan places on these articles in his poem—that is, their transcendental implications—are rather different from Zukofsky's use of them. The specifics of Duncan's relation to Zukofsky remains to be explored; my sense is that he honors Zukofsky as a great craftsman, but is actually quite unlike him philosophically, given the linguistic skepticism that Zukofsky espouses. It could be, therefore, that Duncan's appropriation of Zukofsky's work is similar to his earlier appropriation of Stein's.

30. For my earlier reading of "Circulation," see *The Utopian Moment* 77–79.

31. According to Lewis, "Duncan probably encountered Rumi through the San Francisco Sufi movement of Rabia Martin, reinvigorated in the 1960s by Samuel Lewis and Pir Vilayat Khan, and the publicity surrounding the 700th anniversary of Rumi's death in 1973" (584).

32. Davidson (*Ghostlier Demarcations* 192) associates Duncan's horror of these

diseases with the AIDS epidemic, and though AIDS is not mentioned in the text, I think he is correct.

33. See Schwartz 17–18, who reports that Duncan showed the poem to Michael Palmer after "he had felt the writing had to have come to an end." Schwartz rightly observes that in the poem, "there is an extraordinary contiguity between the personal self and its impersonal ground, an oscillating border between the self and the limits of the self." But he misinterprets the phrase "I didn't have a prayer" as a rejection of religion, when the poem, though certainly not "religious" in any conventional sense, goes beyond religion because of its movement beyond Creation.

34. See also Jonas 320–40 for his remarkable epilogue, in which he compares the gnostic notion of thrownness to Heidegger's *Geworfenheit*, drawing important parallels between gnosticism and existentialism. For more on this formula, see Pagels, *Gnostic Gospels* xviii–xix. Harold Bloom has recourse to it as well in many of his gnostic readings of poets both canonical and contemporary, and draws extensively from Jonas. It is ironic, therefore, that Bloom has never addressed Duncan's work, since of all twentieth-century American poets (at least), Duncan was the most serious student of gnosticism.

35. See Schuchard 175–97. As we have seen, Duncan's reworking of Herbert and other seventeenth-century poets differs significantly from Eliot's.

Ronald Johnson

1. Eric Selinger observes that Beam 10 "makes quite explicit the links between one's genius or inspiring self ("*daimon*"), the Deity as First Cause and figure of universal Unity ("monad"), the self ("I"), and the Original or Primordial Adam of the Kabbalah ("Adam Kadmon") ("*ARK* as a Garden of Revelation" 163). What follows here may be regarded as a further unpacking of Selinger's brief interpretation.

2. When Duncan writes self-reflexively about architecture in his poetry and about his poetry as architecture, the effect is quite different from that of Johnson in *ARK*. Conte's reading of "Passages 9: The Architecture," based on Gustave Stickley's *Craftsman Homes*, confirms this: Stickley's "home with many recesses, corridors, and adjacent rooms provides Duncan with an analogue for serial composition" (62). Stickley's sinuous, romantic notion of home design, in which a feeling of mystery is achieved through the placement of recesses and corridors, aptly applies to the movement of the Passages sequence, but not to Johnson's building of what he calls in "*ARK* 70" (probably thinking of "Kubla Khan") his "Walled Demesne."

3. Tree and human body together yield, of course, the mythic figure of the Green Man, the nature deity who rules Johnson's earlier book-length poem.

4. Somewhat closer to home, from Johnson's own reading, comes Elizabeth Sewell's analysis of Sir Francis Bacon's orphic project in her *Orphic Voice*. Accord-

ing to Sewell, Bacon at his most acute develops "a vision of a method of thinking, in which enfoldment and enlightenment are one and the same thing, *in which there is no division between figure and meaning*. This is hieroglyphic, myth, and poetry, the Orphic darkness to which Bacon, whether he would or not, was dedicated. It is a darkness which is its own light, or, to change the Baconian figure for a moment, a labyrinth which is its own clue" (98; my emphasis). The resemblance here to Wasserstrom's "tautegorical sublime" and hence to Johnson's method is striking.

5. In his essay comparing Johnson and Zukofsky, Mark Scroggins reminds us that Zukofsky's intentions in *"A"* apparently shift from the writing of "a Marxist version of *The Cantos*" to "a loosely articulated series of formal experiments, all disposed upon the 'foreseen curve' of a twenty-four-section structure and the unfolding events of Zukofsky's own life. The problem of form in the long poem, Zukofsky came to realize midway through his labors, need not be a problem of ideology" (147). Such being the case, it might well be said that *ARK* begins where *"A"* ends, that it is late Zukofsky whom Johnson emulates, just as it is early Zukofsky (and Pound) whom he criticizes. Further proof of this may be found in Johnson's last work, *The Shrubberies*, with its strong family resemblance to Zukofsky's *80 Flowers*.

6. Unlike Duncan, Johnson does not have a gnostic sensibility, but what he does share with gnosticism is its rejection of Original Sin as the cause of human unhappiness. Various gnostic sects worshiped the serpent, celebrating its role as the bringer of knowledge in the story of Adam and Eve. See Lacarrière 81–86 and Pagels, *Adam, Eve, and the Serpent*, 69.

7. In the early 1990s, Johnson privately circulated an autobiographical text called "Legend," in which he describes moving to San Francisco "at the threshold of a new generation of change and question." There, he tells us, he "conceived and built a lofty Temple of words, images, music, called ARK." He then notes that "For camaraderie, he formed and led, as Road Captain, a band of lusty, roistering men called the Rainbow Motorcycle Club, often partying until dawn. Of numerous underground groups in that city this was one of the most enduring and abandoned." As Mark Scroggins writes of the Rainbow Motorcycle Club in his review of Johnson's *The Shrubberies* (a more explicitly homoerotic text compared to *ARK*), "picnics and campouts were frequently held; much leather was worn, cigars were smoked, beer was drunk; nobody in the club actually owned a motorcycle."

8. In *The Heads of the Town up to the Aether*, Spicer's most sustained critique of the orphic position, Orpheus is usually portrayed as a narcissistic "asshole" who cannot recognize that poetry comes not from the self, but from possession by "ghosts" or "spooks." See, for instance, the poem "Elegy" and Spicer's mordant "Explanatory Note" below it (*My Vocabulary* 259). I also refer the reader to my brief essay "Hail Nothing: A Reading of Jack Spicer's 'Orfeo.'"

9. I owe my awareness of this phrase to Henry Weinfield, who discusses its signif-

icance to Mallarmé's oeuvre in the introduction to his translation of the *Collected Poems*.

10. Rachel Blau DuPlessis argues that Johnson never truly succeeds in working through the myth, since he loses "the conflict and contradictions of what female dangerous agency [the Maenads] and stunned passivity [Eurydice] mean to the myth of the male singer" ("Echological Scales" 111). DuPlessis's feminist analysis of what she appropriately calls Johnson's "Orpheus Complex" has broad implications for our understanding of the relationship of myth to gender in contemporary poetry. Although she is critical of some of the effects of the "Orpheus Complex," she also acknowledges the "odic limitlessness," the "[s]pilling sound of bliss" of this poetic lineage, which includes, of course, both Whitman and Duncan. "[W]ould it be possible," DuPlessis speculates, "briefly to note the intense 'feminine' 'masculinity' of these often homosexual writers? . . . By which 'feminine' I mean a certain boundarylessness, a willingness to dissolve into otherness, the 'loss' of the ego that is a gain of the larger itness, almost an idness, of your specific language" (104). This describes Johnson's vision, if not his architectural procedure, and it certainly applies to much of Duncan's work.

11. Cf. a similar conflation of the two myths in the opening lines of the first of Rilke's *Sonnets to Orpheus*, a work familiar to both Duncan and Johnson: "Da stieg ein Baum. O reine Übersteigung! / O Orpheus singt! O hoher Baum in Ohr!" [There rose a tree. O pure transcendency! / O Orpheus singing! O tall tree in the ear] (16–17).

12. For a discussion of "the dance" and related figures in *The Opening of the Field*, see Davidson, "A Book of First Things."

13. I do not want to overlook one other brief homage to Duncan, Johnson's contribution to the special Duncan issue of *Sagetrieb*. This poem runs as follows: "Rodin did every day / betray the flesh to clay / so Duncan flay a soul / to ray our rafters whole" ("For R.D." 15). The comparison of Duncan to a great sculptor and the reference to "rafters" both indicate Johnson's pervasive thinking of poetry as a "constructed" art. At the same time, however, he also acknowledges Duncan's darker vision: it is difficult to imagine Johnson's poetry "flaying" a soul, though this is precisely what Duncan's late work enacts.

14. Cf. 1 Thessalonians 4:15–17: "[15] According to the Lord's own word, we tell you that we who are still alive, who are left till the coming of the Lord, will certainly not precede those who have fallen asleep. [16] For the Lord himself will come down from heaven, with a loud command, with the voice of the archangel and with the trumpet call of God, and the dead in Christ will rise first. [17] After that, we who are still alive and are left will be caught up together with them in the clouds to meet the Lord in the air. And so we will be with the Lord forever." The rapture is now well known in popular culture due to the sensationalistic Left Behind series by Tim La-

Haye and Jerry B. Jenkins, though *ARK* was completed before the 1995 publication of the first Left Behind novel.

15. An altogether more pious reference to Lothlorien and the mallorn trees may be found in *The Book of the Green Man* 45. In the notes to this poem, Johnson refers to "J. R. R. Tolkien's *Book of the Rings* [*sic*], the most magical imaginative work of the twentieth century" (85).

16. If my interpretation is at all accurate, there is something strangely portentous in these lines, since at the end of his life, when Johnson was ill with a brain tumor, he had to leave San Francisco and move back to his home in Kansas to be helped by his father and sister.

Jack Spicer

1. For a further discussion of this idea, and the related notion of the poem's "pressing for the end," see my *Lyrical Interference* 20–23.

2. In the beginning his short but very useful book on Spicer, Edward Halsey Foster proposes that "Jack Spicer's poetry is an argument against the American voice that Walt Whitman projects—optimistic, expansive, political. . . . The sublime self of *Leaves of Grass* was entirely foreign to him. It was as if from the beginning Spicer had determined to see and do everything the opposite of Whitman" (5).

3. The shamanic notion that poetry is both a disease *and* a remedy, and that the poet is a "cured sick man," who has been initiated into his vocation through a process of self-healing, is discussed at length by O'Leary. See particularly *Gnostic Contagion* 19–27, 71–72, and 144–49.

4. Feld's "Lowghost to Lowghost" and "The Apostle's Grudge at the Persistence of Poetry" remain, to my mind, two of the very best essays on Spicer's work. Feld's extraordinary sympathy for the peculiarities of Spicer's poetic and religious agon may also be felt in his remarkable volume of poetry, *Plum Poems*.

5. In "The Practice of Outside" (318), Blaser notes that the poem is a response to both Duncan and George Stanley, while Ellingham and Killian report that, according to Stanley, the images of god, star, and totem refer specifically to volumes of poetry by Duncan (*Bending the Bow*), Harold Dull (*The Star Year*), and Stanley himself (*Beyond Love*). This sounds quite plausible, considering Spicer's modus operandi of encrypting specific personal references in his poems. Be that as it may, given Duncan's overall poetic significance and his status in the Bay Area literary community of the period, I think it is safe to say that Duncan is the most important target of the poem, and, hermeneutically speaking, the figure against which Spicer's position must be juxtaposed.

6. Thanks to John Vincent for this particular interpretation.

7. In *Fifteen False Propositions against God*, Spicer adopts as a refrain Pound's

lines (slightly misquoted) from "Villanelle: The Psychological Hour, "*Beauty is so rare a thing. / So few drink of my fountain*" (158). These lines, already deeply ironic in Pound's poem, are appropriated by Spicer in order to demonstrate the inadequacy of beauty as an ideal in the spiritually haunted world of his dictated poetry—despite its persistence in his work, and what we might call its ontological indispensability. For a further discussion of *Fifteen False Propositions*, see below.

8. In "Jack Spicer's Ghosts and the Gnosis of History," I argue that gnosticism, which permeates Spicer's work but is most overt in *Heads of the Town*, may be related in turn to an ironic but still ultimately empowering vision of poetic tradition and to a strong inclination toward critique of the cultural if not political status quo of the late fifties and early sixties. More than twenty years later, I would still acknowledge this dimension of Spicer's writing, but I must also emphasize the often despairing pessimism derived from his gnostic and Calvinist worldview, a pessimism for which poetry hardly compensates.

9. Cf. *The Holy Grail*, where we learn that "The grail is the opposite of poetry / Fills us up instead of using us as a cup the dead drink from" (*My Vocabulary* 332).

10. Vincent's close reading of these concluding lines are worth quoting at length, for they shed light on the remarkable connections between Spicer's verbal play and his struggle for belief. According to Vincent, "the commands 'Be / like God' and 'Believe the birds' that close sections III and IV have combined to become 'Be – / Leave in it / Like God.' The poet's final command has changed from a more-or-less straightforward piece of advice to a double simile doubled by a pun. The two similes are that the reader ought 'believe' in this door that leads to the outside of the poem like one believes in God and that the reader ought to concurrently 'be' and 'leave' in one's situation like God is in His situation. The similes are each doubled by the pun on 'believe.' Neither sonic 'Believe' nor graphic 'Be-leave' take the fore; they are equally active and indicate ambivalence at the center of both belief and being" (164).

11. According to Ellingham and Killian (138–39), *Fifteen False Propositions* was written while Spicer was breaking up with Russell Fitzgerald, with whom he had lived for some months and to whom the book is addressed. Thus the "Dear Sir" and other personal remarks in the book probably refer to Fitzgerald. The breakup apparently had a religious component; Nick Diaman notes that "Jack would attack Russell on religious grounds, Russell being Roman Catholic and Jack identifying himself as a Calvinist Protestant" (139). Hence the lines "There is born a child / Like we Protestants say in our Christmas carols" (*My Vocabulary* 200) and the references throughout to the "Joyful mysteries," related, at least to some extent, to a series of Fitzgerald paintings called The Mysteries of the Most Holy Rosary.

12. In *God's Caress*, Charles Lloyd Cohen observes that "although both agreements are pacts of salvation, the Covenant of Works perpetuates the ingrained at-

titudes that, as much as sin, inhibit the successful completion of God's business. Only the Covenant of Grace promotes that way of thinking contributive to someone's implementing the Law while tainted by Original Sin" (48). According to Cohen, "those without faith live permanently under the Covenant of Works; only the Elect enter the Covenant of Grace, publicized to all but established with few." Thus, "people do not earn salvation by deeds; they receive it, and the means to it, as a gift" (68, 69).

13. Regarding the question of prose and verse, which strikes me as fundamental to Spicer's project, we may also consider the following, from his review of the variorum edition of *The Poems of Emily Dickinson*: "The reason for the difficulty of drawing a line between the poetry and prose in Emily Dickinson's letters may be that she did not wish such a line to be drawn. If large portions of her correspondence are considered not as mere letters—and indeed, they seldom communicate information, or have much to do with the person to whom they were written—but as experiments in a heightened prose combined with poetry, a new approach to both her letters and her poetry opens up" (*House That Jack Built* 234).

14. In the first Vancouver Lecture, Spicer tells his audience before reading from the *Textbook* that "this, I think, is as near to dictation, without interference from me, as I've written" (*House That Jack Built* 19).

15. The text of original, gnostic *Heads of the Town* of the Peratae has never been found: scholars know of its existence and something of its content only through an encyclopedic religious work of the second century c.e. commonly known as the *Philosophumena* (Doresse 6). My discussion of the original *Heads of the Town* (as described by Doresse) in relation to Spicer's *Heads of the Town*, is drawn in part from "Jack Spicer's Ghosts and the Gnosis of History" 89–90. It is also worth noting that the original gnostic work, the title of which may also be translated as *The Rulers of the Cities up to the Ether*, may have been one of a number of "manuals of initiation, inspired by magic, designed to show the disciple how, after his death, he can traverse the different circles by pronouncing the name of each Aeon or guardian in turn" (Lacarrière 133).

16. See Pagels, *The Gnostic Gospels* 84–122, for a discussion of the dispute between gnostic and orthodox Christians over the Passion of Christ.

17. In Vincent's polysemic reading of this text, he notes that "the final lines might parse: 'Mocking the light that sometimes makes it through the canopy of dark, time leaves us, words leave us, and love leaves us'" (161).

18. The notion of the ideal poem having an infinitely small vocabulary first appears in the second letter in *After Lorca*, the same letter in which Spicer declares that "Words are what stick to the real. . . . They are as valuable in themselves as rope with nothing to be tied to" (*My Vocabulary* 123). In this regard, Spicer's thinking remains consistent until the end of his career.

19. In addition to Howe's own work, see the discussions of Howe and antinomianism in Back 44–49 and 121–24.

Susan Howe

1. Drawing extensively on Jacques Derrida's *Archive Fever*, Stephen Collis demonstrates the importance of the archive (along with such related terms as "archon" and "anarchy") to Howe's project. See Collis 18–22. Howe herself observes that "if you are a woman, archives hold perpetual ironies. Because the gaps and silences are where you find yourself" (*Birth-mark* 158).

2. She does, however, apparently believe in telepathy, if not literally, then metaphorically: "Poetry is thought transference," she writes in *Melville's Marginalia*. "Free association isn't free" (*Nonconformist's Memorial* 105). This is followed by a description of her realization that Melville's Bartleby is based on the figure of James Clarence Mangan: "I saw the pencilled trace of Herman Melville's passage through John Mitchel's introduction [to Mangan's *Poems*] and knew by shock of poetry telepathy the real James Clarence Mangan is the progenitor of fictional Bartleby" (106). For a consideration of Howe and "poetry telepathy," see Montgomery 36.

In his section on Howe in *Precipitations: Contemporary American Poetry as Occult Practice*, Devin Johnston observes that Howe's poetry "would seem concerned with the failure of telepathy, the impossibility of leaping across the hegemonic structures for transmission that determine history. The pathos of her work (and its ethical emphasis), one might argue, lies in its foregrounding of erasure, or the fragmentary marks of a passing presence. While such an emphasis is reasonable, I would also argue that Howe's poetry valorizes a moment of cultural exchange, an encounter with otherness that is almost violent in her work. What is channeled through Howe's poetry is not so much the fragmentary record of an other, but rather the frictional moment of encounter, conversion, or repression" (148). Given Johnston's suggestive use of such terms as "passing presence," "channeled," and "frictional moment of encounter," I find it curious that he does not connect his analysis with the idea of a séance, especially given the overarching theme of his book. Nevertheless, the idea of spiritual communication is implicit in this view of how the poetry opens itself to otherness.

3. Cf. Walter Benjamin, from *Theses on the Philosophy of History*: "Only the historian will have the gift of fanning the spark of hope in the past who is firmly convinced that *even the dead* will not be safe from the enemy if he wins. And this enemy has not ceased to be victorious" (255). In the introduction to *The Birth-mark*, Howe declares that "I know records are compiled by winners, and scholarship is in collusion with Civil Government" (4), a remark that strongly echoes another passage from Benjamin's *Theses*, in which he considers historicism's "empathy with the vic-

tor" (256). This is the same passage in which Benjamin observes that "there is no document of civilization which is not at the same time a document of barbarism" (256), concluding that it is the task of the historical materialist to "brush history against the grain" (257). Howe obviously sees her historical writing as accomplishing much the same task, telling Lynn Keller "I love his interest in very short essays, his interest in the fragment, the material object, and the entrance of the messianic into the material object" (Howe, "Interview" 29). For more on Howe and Benjamin, see Back 59–60.

4. "An antinomian is a religious enthusiast" writes Howe in *The Birth-Mark* (11), and then proceeds to unpack the term historically and etymologically. For an analysis of this concept in Howe's work, see Nicholls 591–92.

5. In the Introduction to *The Birth-mark*, Howe suggests that marginalia "may be called speed reading or ghost writing" (15). Her insistence on the importance of handwriting culminates, of course, in her essay on Emily Dickinson's handwritten manuscripts, "The Flames and Generosities of the Heart," in which she remarks—shedding as much light on her own practice as on Dickinson's—that "in the precinct of Poetry, a word, the space around a word, each letter, every mark, silence, or sound volatizes an inner law of form—moves on a rigorous line" (*Birth-mark* 145).

6. Howe's understanding of the religious—that is, sacrificial—aspect of the hunt in American literature and culture is based partly on Richard Slotkin's *Regeneration through Violence: The Mythology of the American Frontier 1600–1860*, which she calls "a crucial book for anyone interested in American literature" (*Birth-mark* 167). Of particular relevance are Slotkin's sections on captivity narratives (94–145), on hunting and initiation (146–79), and on *Moby-Dick* (538–50). Poetic dictation, spiritual possession, and hunting all come together, of course, in Emily Dickinson's "My Life had stood – a Loaded Gun –," to which Howe devotes some of her most inspired criticism in *My Emily Dickinson*. As Howe declares, "power is pitiless once you have put it on. The poet is an intermediary hunting form beyond form, truth beyond theme through woods of words tangled and tremendous. Who owns the woods? Freedom to roam poetically means freedom to hunt" (*My Emily Dickinson* 79–80).

7. Howe draws on Burke's "Dialectic of the Scapegoat" and Girard's *The Scapegoat*, quoting from their analyses of the psychology of persecution but adding, apropos of Hutchinson's fate, that the "mechanism is peculiarly open to violence if the attacker is male; his bloodbrother, female" (*Birth-mark* 53).

8. According to Back, "the charting of her own childhood and ancestral geographies, the uncovering of the points of convergence between biography and history, and the frank foregrounding of the intensely personal are foundational to Howe's poetry and poetics. The uncovering of each historical tale is propelled *also* by the wholly individual and idiosyncratic historical details of the poet's own life" (12).

9. Howe herself uses the term "indeterminacy," most notably in the introduc-

tion to *Thorow*, which concerns the changing names of Lake George: "In paternal colonial systems a positivist efficiency appropriates primal indeterminacy" (*Singularities* 41). But what does "primal indeterminacy" mean? If primal refers to nature, then it seems that Howe is resorting to a Romantic, indeed, even colonial view of the unbounded, edenic world before the advent of human language and culture. If primal refers to tribal, as in the case of Native American tribes prior to their encounters with Europeans, then she is again assuming an essentializing, Romantic perspective on tribal culture, which she herself criticizes later in the poem when she invokes "The literature of savagism / under a spell of savagism" (49)—savagism referring to either the myth of the noble savage or its polar opposite, the colonial notion of the savage who cannot be civilized. Consider, by contrast, Girard's remark in regard to ancient or tribal societies: "'Conservative' is a word too weak to describe the rigidity of spirit and terror of change that characterizes those societies in which the sacred holds sway. The imposition of a socio-religious order appears as an enormous boon, an unhoped for act of grace that could at any moment be withdrawn" (*Violence* 282). Thus there is nothing "primal" about indeterminacy. *Language* may be indeterminate and meaning may be a function of difference, as structuralism demonstrates, which means that to a greater or lesser extent, linguistic indeterminacy is a feature of all literature. But the indeterminacy of writing such as Howe's, despite its many identifiable antecedents, is not a return to the primal, but a modern (or postmodern) refunctioning of sacred, ritualistic structures. For more on the contradictory qualities of *Thorow*, see later in this chapter.

10. In his obscure, incoherent, but truly inspired *Swallowing the Scroll: Late in a Prophetic Tradition with the Poetry of Susan Howe and John Taggart*, Lew Daly writes that, apropos of sacrifice, language, and poetic experimentalism, "contrary to the reigning oppositional ideology in contemporary poetry, the altar on which we lay our writings down is not of language, but language is itself the sacrifice: we must indeed lay it on the altar of the other person. Not the altar of language—but, of the other, the altar on which it is sacrificed is the milestone poetry seeks" (86). This statement is part of Daly's argument against the oppositional claims of language poetry, an argument that is also at the heart of the journal *apex of the M*, which he coedited with Pam Rehm, Alan Gilbert, and Kristin Prevallet while they were students in the Poetics Program of the University of Buffalo. This group, which criticized the language poets' emphasis on the materiality of the signifier, spoke instead for an innovative poetics open to spiritual concerns. As Daly claims, poetic language is to be seen not "as a mirror held up to division and absence, compounding the forces which keep us apart, but rather, and indeed more precisely, in a final resistance to these forces, to all that, including critique, keeps the people from taking the stage as a chorus of the gloriously redeemed" (87). Despite the extravagance of this presentation, I find Daly's basic idea of language as sacrifice fundamentally

in accord with my understanding of alternative or avant-garde writing, at least in regard to Howe and the other poets under consideration in this book. For another view of the *apex of the M* controversy, see Lazer 213–17.

11. One of the most important precursor texts for Howe's poem, as she explains in her interview with Edward Foster, is Marx's *The 18th Brumaire of Louis Bonaparte*, in which Marx famously declares that "the tradition of all dead generations weighs like a nightmare on the brains of the living." Here is the pertinent passage from Marx; note the way Howe has appropriated the last phrase: "But unheroic though bourgeois society is, it nevertheless needed heroism, sacrifice, terror, civil war, and national wars to bring it into being. And in the austere classical traditions of the Roman Republic the bourgeois gladiators found the ideals and the art forms, the self-deceptions, that they needed to conceal from themselves the bourgeois-limited content of their struggles and to keep their passion on the high plane of great historic tragedy. Similarly, at another stage of development a century earlier, Cromwell and the English people had borrowed from the Old Testament the speech, emotions, and illusions for their bourgeois revolution. When the real goal had been achieved and the bourgeois transformation of English society had been accomplished, Locke supplanted Habakkuk. Thus the awakening of the dead in those revolutions served the purpose of glorifying the new struggles, not of parodying the old; of magnifying the given task in the imagination, not recoiling from its solution in reality; of finding once more the spirit of revolution, not making its ghost walk again." Howe comments: "Marx saw the revolutionary situation as theatrical spectacle. And the idea of the dead generations weighing like a nightmare on the brain of the living—the idea of the ghost of the old revolution walking is so right. The spectacle of killing the king accomplished the bourgeois transformation of English society, Marx wrote. It was real, and it was a theatrical event. The ghost is still walking around" (*Birth-mark* 176).

12. Drawing on research by historian Lois Potter, Back reminds us that King Charles, who had a speech impediment, favored the use of images rather than words, and had a "particular affection for, patronage of, and participation in the dramatic form of the court masque wherein dialogue was minimal, plot and action slight, while costumes, scenery, and other elements of pageantry were all lavish, meant to enrapture through visual appeal" (147). This emphasis on the spectacular extends to Charles's self-dramatization at his execution, which Howe herself notes. Thus, the iconic poem recapitulates the iconic historical events, with the highly contested sacrificial death of the king at their "absent center." For a full consideration of theater in Howe's *Bibliography*, see Back 147–50.

13. One figure whom Back does not mention, but I believe is invoked through the image of the "blank page," is the goddess who appears in section 38 of *Tribute to the Angels*, the one of the most crucial moments in the second volume of H.D.'s

Trilogy: "she is the Vestal / from the days of Numa, // she carries over the cult / of the *Bona Dea*, // she carries a book but it is not / the tome of the ancient wisdom, // the pages, I imagine, are the blank pages / of the unwritten volume of the new ..." (570). Howe turns the goddess herself into a blank page and associates her with ghost writing, thereby revising H.D.'s triumphant feminist scripture, making the blankness more threatening, more uncanny, and perhaps more pessimistic. Howe also has recourse to a related passage from section 35 ("under her drift of veils, / and she carried a book" [568]), which serves as an equally ambivalent epigraph to *Singularities*.

14. In her essay on *Thorow*, Jenny L. White demonstrates the poem's debt to the novels of James Fenimore Cooper, including the use of "Mount Vision," which proves to be, in *The Pioneers*, "a place-name coined by Judge Marmaduke Templeton in connection with his first encounter with what was at the time a trackless wilderness. . . . Mount Vision is therefore the location from which Cooper's novel effects the rhetorical emptying of the landscape that marks the American pastoral" (252). Part of White's point is that Mount Vision is a literary referent that Cooper employs in his historical revisionism; it is part of what Cooper failed to realize was "an already-peopled landscape"; thus, in the "word Forest," a "metaphoric or linguistic construct does not have to be abstracted from the 'real' world" (254).

Michael Palmer

1. O'Leary cites Palmer's account of Duncan's teaching in the Poetics Program of the New College in San Francisco, when both poets were on the faculty in the early eighties. Duncan's immense erudition, his demanding presence, and his emotional volatility, especially after he became ill, produced a tense, stressful environment, especially for the students. According to Palmer, "I don't pretend that I was unaffected by these events, but I was certainly not made ill. They seemed to me part of the atmosphere of the place, though . . . I made a very distinct effort to monitor the emotional state of the program's students in the aftermath, as I think most of us did. It was perhaps too late for Robert to change in any dramatic way" (*Gnostic Contagion* 4). But as O'Leary tells us, gnostic contagion is primarily a form of psychic transmission, to which Palmer proved most receptive. It is on this level that he certainly was "made ill," and became the poet he is today.

2. These three books, *Notes for Echo Lake*, *First Figure*, and *Sun*, were originally published by North Point Press, which ceased operation in 1991, leaving Palmer temporarily without a publisher. This probably contributed to the time lag, but Palmer's work definitely undergoes some significant changes in the interim as well. The three North Point volumes have since been republished by New Directions under the title *Codes Appearing* (2001).

3. This is due partly to Palmer's longstanding critique of self-expression in lyric poetry, which is one of the theoretical pillars on which the style of his poetry rests. As he puts it in an interview in 1984, "I'm not interested in *myself*—that's just this guy who sits here drinking coffee and making a fool of himself. If only a *self* got posited in a poem we might as well be having lunch somewhere and not bothering with poems. A self that is transformed through language, however, interests me, though that already includes the reader as we are all part of a shared language. . . . It seems to me to become reductive exactly at that point where you focus on the self alone and thus end up with a poetry of personality, and that exhausts itself as soon as the personality exhausts itself" ("A Conversation" 77). The logical outcome of this position is the title series in Palmer's *The Promises of Glass* (2000). In this series of eighteen lyrics, each poem ironically bears either the title or subtitle "Autobiography," and each in its own way contributes to the deconstruction of the autobiographical impulse, life writing's narcissistic "promises of glass." That these are also some of Palmer's funniest and most poignant poems turns the critique against itself; the possibility that one can draw on one's life for the matter of a lyric poem remains *sur rature*.

4. For Benjamin's discussion of aura in regard to Baudelaire, see *Charles Baudelaire* 145–52. Baudelaire's awareness of the increasing loss of the auratic relationship between human subjectivity and the object world (particularly art objects) leads Benjamin to observe that "the greater Baudelaire's insight into this phenomenon, the more unmistakably did the disintegration of the aura make itself felt in his lyrical poetry" (149).

5. The opposite of this dilemma of self-sacrifice, which nevertheless yields the same results, is *self-parody*, which Baudelaire presents in the prose piece "A Lost Halo," from *Paris Spleen*. In this piece, which Benjamin analyzes in "Some Motifs in Baudelaire," an erstwhile poet loses his halo in the street and is freed to "indulge in vulgar behaviour like ordinary mortals" (*Charles Baudelaire* 153). Following Benjamin's initial insights, Marshall Berman brilliantly analyzes "A Lost Halo," noting that for both Baudelaire and Marx in *The Communist Manifesto*, "one of the crucial experiences endemic to modern life, and one of the central themes for modern art and thought, is *desanctification*" (*All That Is Solid Melts into Air* 157). Berman further observes that "one of the paradoxes of modernity, as Baudelaire sees it here, is that its poets will become more deeply and authentically poetic by becoming more like ordinary men" (160).

6. To put this in more positive terms, consider Ronald Schuchard's remark that T. S. Eliot saw Baudelaire "as the first desert father of the reaction against romanticism" (131). Eliot did not count Baudelaire among the heretics at all, since he reserved that term for romantics, romanticism itself being the greatest heresy. To him, Baudelaire's poetry is a prime instance of *blasphemy*. For a thorough analysis

of Eliot's understanding of blasphemy in relation to poetry and belief, especially in Baudelaire, see Schuchard 131–47.

7. The deconstruction of modern heroism is fundamental to the postmodern project; it accompanies what Jean-François Lyotard calls the postmodern's "incredulity toward metanarratives" (xxiv) including "the Enlightenment narrative, in which a hero of knowledge works toward a good ethico-political end—universal peace" (xxiii–xxiv). Another name Lyotard gives this figure, in the political register, is the "hero of liberty" (31), whose function as an enlightening educator may be seen in the modern poet's self-denial, his giving himself up to his poems, which will then provide a new level of truth to his readers. Palmer's work calls this function radically into question.

8. Although Palmer puts the phrase "blooming field of weeds" in quotation marks, I have been unable to locate it in any of Celan's poems, though it is certainly reminiscent of phrases from his early work. For more on Palmer's relationship to Celan, especially in regard to "The White Notebook" (*Promises of Glass* 3–55), see Zawacki.

9. Palmer's treatment of Rilke in the Baudelaire Series poems is discussed briefly but with great insight by Eric Murphy Selinger in his groundbreaking essay "Important Pleasures and Others: Michael Palmer, Ronald Johnson."

10. Cf. Palmer's understanding of this situation: "I think there's a relationship that's almost impossible to examine between thought and poetry. The Romantic ideal, of course, was that poetry aspire to a condition of thought, which was a kind of prelapsarian dream—that it aspire to a condition prior to utterance. But in fact it aspires to something as imperfect as utterance too" ("Interview" 164).

11. Cf. Spicer, in one of his desperate poems near the end of his career: "The poem begins to mirror itself. / The identity of the poet gets more obvious" (*My Vocabulary* 423).

12. See his remarks quoted above in note 3.

13. The most remarkable and fully sustained experiment of this sort, yielding a number of the most important instances of the philosophical lyric, is William Bronk's volume *To Praise the Music* (*Life Supports* 123–49), a sequence of fourteen-line poems that constitutes, in effect, a modern rethinking of the sonnet form.

14. For a complete reading of Celan's poem, including its origins and early publication history, see Felstiner 26–41.

15. For Celan's understanding of this situation and his response, see Felstiner 118–19, 165, 232.

16. Somewhere behind the *Letters to Zanzotto* is probably *After Lorca* (1957), Jack Spicer's breakthrough work, the first of his "books" or serial poems and one of his most important statements of poetic principles. Spicer exploits the multiple meanings of the word *correspond* to develop a number of his crucial concepts. For Spicer,

"The poem is a collage of the real. . . . Things do not connect; they correspond. That is what makes it possible for a poet to translate real objects, to bring them across language as easily as he can bring them across time" (*My Vocabulary* 133). Thus the things in two poets' poems may correspond, even when they are separated by time and language. And as Spicer concludes, "That is how we dead men write to each other" (134). In other words, that is how a community of like-minded poets comes into being, or, across time, a poetic tradition. Palmer and Zanzotto are not "dead," but they do "die" into language and "correspond" with and to each other. Hence Palmer's "Zanzotto," and not Zanzotto.

17. Following Duncan, it is no accident that Palmer's most explicit investigation of the sacred—or perhaps, the sudden eruption of the sacred in the poem as a category to be defined, condition to be analyzed, illness to be cured—occurs within the context of a seemingly heterogeneous series of poems that defy categorization and definition, even to the point of being called, paradoxically, Untitled. This is the longest sequence of *At Passages*, a book bearing a title that is, of course, an homage to Passages, the open, serial poem that winds its way through the last twenty-five years of Duncan's career. And like the open work of Duncan's last books, where serial texts are woven among other, seemingly discrete poems, Untitled poems appear in other sections of *At Passages*, within the section called "Untitled" (though some of the poems in the series *do* have titles) and beyond the section, even into Palmer's most recent book, *Company of Moths* (2005).

18. In his interview with Peter Gizzi, Palmer explains that in addition to echoing Duncan's Passages, the poems in the sequence, including this one, are connected to an evening-long dance piece he did with his long-time collaborator, Margaret Jenkins, called *The Gates Far Away Near* (the title of another poem in the sequence is "Untitled (Far Away Near)" [*At Passages* 65–66]). Palmer notes of the dance piece that "we wanted a grid on which to place it—of a prologue, plus seven gates to a city. And these gates were named, in a deliberately arbitrary fashion, the Gate of Desire, the Gate of Public Words, et al., to mirror the wildly disparate reality of the city depending on which gate you entered" ("Interview" 165).

Nathaniel Mackey

1. See Mackey's discussion of *The Gnostics* in his interview with Paul Naylor, *Paracritical Hinge* 340.

2. There is nothing serendipitous in the connection between psychoanalysis, shamanism, and poetry, as O'Leary's work amply demonstrates. According to Eliade, "the shaman is not only a sick man; he is, above all, a sick man who has been cured, who has succeeded in curing himself" (27). Like analysts who have undergone their own courses of treatment, if shamans "have cured themselves and are

able to cure others, it is, among other things, because they know the mechanism, or rather, the *theory* of illness" (31). Psychoanalysis is preeminently a theory of illness, in which analysts ideally lead their patients to the point at which their patients can cure themselves. As for poetry, especially such fevered, obsessively repetitious poetry as Mackey's, "poetry is the sickness of the poet; writing poetry is the cure" (O'Leary, *Gnostic Contagion* 15).

3. See chapter 1, n. 21, for O'Leary's comparison of Duncan and Mackey in regard to the issue of cross-culturality and "oneness" in the serial poem. Mackey speaks of his resistance to Duncan's notion of the "world-poem" in an interview with Brent Cunningham: "The term suggests all-inclusiveness and I balk at that. It's a misnomer. The thing about the world-poem that needs to be stressed is that it is not an all-inclusive poem" (*Paracritical Hinge* 320).

4. Mackey's crucial essay "Cante Moro" (*Paracritical Hinge* 181–98) thoroughly examines the interrelations among flamenco, Arabic music, African American jazz and blues, Lorca's poetry and essays on *duende*, and the poetics of the New American poetry, including Duncan and Spicer.

5. Mackey elaborates on whatsaying in his interview with Paul Naylor: "'Whatsaidness' ups the ante on witness, not wanting to abide by simple oppositions between narrativity and reflexivity, expressivism and constructivism. The what-sayer is the recipient of the narrative and a co-producer of the narrative, a weave or tangle of roles the Kalapalo, I think, usefully acknowledge" (*Paracritical Hinge* 339).

6. In her thorough essay "Trickster Poetics: Multiculturalism and Collectivity in Nathaniel Mackey's *Song of the Andoumboulou*," Simpson reads Mackey's serial poem "as a kind of trickster discourse which can enable a deeper understanding of how the poem's disjunctive formal characteristics function in relation to one of the work's central concerns: the possibility of a collective subjectivity that might allow the poem's explorers to partake of the 'discrepant engagement' necessary for the realization of a cross-cultural identity, neither essentialist nor assimilationist, but improvisational" (39).

7. Mackey's fascination with dissonance, raspy sounds, etc. is worth considering in the light of Northrop Frye's discussion of the musical qualities of poetry. Attacking the sentimental idea that highly musical poetry is mellifluous and smoothly flowing, Frye notes that "it is more likely to be the harsh, rugged dissonant poem (assuming some technical competence in the poet) that will show in poetry the tension and the driving accented impetus of music" (256).

8. Mackey's program on KUSP radio, *Tanganyika Strut* (named after the Wilbur Harden/John Coltrane piece), has for many years served as a showcase for this vast knowledge of jazz and world music. He has also recorded what may be the definitive synthesis of spoken poetry and jazz, the album *Strick: Song of the Andoumboulou 16–25* (Spoken Engine) with percussionist Royal Hartigan and woodwind player

Hafez Modirzadeh. For a discussion of this album, see Mackey's essay "Sight-Specific, Sound-Specific . . ." (*Paracritical Hinge* 228–36).

9. For the links between shamanism and the Orpheus myth, see Eliade 391. Mackey's engagement with the figure of Orpheus may not be as extensive as that of his precursors Duncan and Spicer, but it does serve as the basis for at least one important poem, "Song of the Andoumboulou: 55," subtitled "—*orphic fragment*—." The poem is based on *Black Orpheus* (1959), the immensely popular award-winning film by Marcel Camus, which introduced samba and bossa nova to an international audience. Retelling the myth of Orpheus and Eurydice in the Afro-Brazilian context of Carnival, the film is as much a "lyric" as a "narrative," and is a perfect expression of the cross-cultural sensibility that Mackey seeks throughout his work. The erotic, occult, and musical intensities of the film are also congruent with Mackey's project: it features an extraordinary scene in which Orpheus, seeking the lost Eurydice, attends an Umbanda ceremony conducted by a shamanic, cigar-smoking priest, a scene that features spiritual possession and the ventriloquizing of Eurydice's voice.

10. For the power of the *saeta* and its relation to *duende*, see *Paracritical Hinge* 192.

Armand Schwerner

1. For further discussion of this aspect of *The Tablets*, as well as an introduction to Schwerner's major themes, see Finkelstein, *Not One of Them* 110–20.

2. Appropriately, one of Schwerner's last projects was an experimental translation of the *Inferno*, of which Cantos I–X, XV, and XXI were completed before his death. In his preface to this work, Michael Heller discusses the unique prosodic structure of Schwerner's translation, which abandons any approximation of terza rima for "a prosodically tighter form, assigning narrative on the left side of the page, juxtaposing it with speech and oration on the right. This lineation, unlike other versions, and with perhaps a Bakhtinian dialogics in mind, focuses on the opposition between interior voicing of narration and rumination and the externality of speech, between psychic state and self-presentation" (vi). The opposition that Heller posits is particularly suggestive in the light of the dialogic nature of *The Tablets*, which likewise vacillates "between psychic state and self-presentation" (vi).

3. I address the vexed issue of *The Tablets*'s modernist lineage in terms of epistemology, genre, and poetic methodology in "Wallace Stevens, Armand Schwerner, and 'The The.'"

4. For the best in recent scholarship on the Objectivists, see DuPlessis and Quatermain, including the comprehensive essays by Charles Altieri and Burton Hatlen.

5. Curiously, this important statement is not reprinted in Oppen's *New Collected Poems*.

6. Of the many Objectivist formulae, three in particular are worth considering in regard to Schwerner's work: (1) from Williams's *Spring and All* (1923), "that 'beauty' is related not to 'loveliness' but to a state in which reality plays a part (204); (2) from Zukofsky's "An Objective" (1930), "writing occurs which is the detail, not mirage, of seeing, of thinking with the things as they exist" (12); and (3) from Oppen's interview with L. S. Dembo (1968), "the attempt to construct meaning, to construct a method of thought from the imagist technique of poetry—from the imagist intensity of vision. If no one were going to challenge me, I would say, 'a test of truth'. If I had to back it up I'd say anyway, 'a test of sincerity'—that there is a moment, an actual time, when you believe something to be true, and you construct a meaning from these moments of conviction" (Dembo and Pondrom 174). Since Schwerner was influenced by both Stevens's and the Objectivists' understanding of a "poetry of reality," readers may wish to consult Gelpi's "Stevens and Williams: The Epistemology of Modernism" for a useful comparison.

7. Always scrupulous in his personal and literary relations, Oppen mentions that he is quoted by Schwerner in his review of *Seaweed*, observing that "some community of interest will be assumed, I hope, without suggesting the prior existence of cliques" (72).

8. Cf. the Scholar/Translator's hilariously self-reflexive anxiety in a crucial note following Tablet VIII: "There is a growing ambiguity in this work of mine, but I'm not sure where it lies. Some days I do not doubt that the ambiguity is inherent in the language of the Tablets themselves; at other times I worry myself sick over the possibility that *I* am the variable giving rise to ambiguities. Do I take advantage of the present unsure state of scholarly expertise? On occasion it almost seems to me as if I am inventing this sequence, and such a fantasy sucks me into an abyss of almost irretrievable depression, from which only forced and unpleasurable exercises in linguistic analysis rescue me" (*Tablets* 32).

9. Schwerner refers to *Orality and Literacy* a number of times in a long interview with Willard Gingerich. See Gingerich, "Interview" 35–36, and "Armand Schwerner" 32.

10. The blessing of more life is a concept that originates with Harold Bloom and is found throughout his work, including *The Book of J* (210–11, 307–15). Citing Bloom's "Freud and Beyond," Santner makes extensive use of the notion as he discusses "the difference between, on the one hand, an *identity* mediated by institutional resources of recognition and authorization—an identity that locates us and determines our part within a socially intelligible whole—and, on the other hand, the *singularity* we assume thanks to what the biblical traditions understand as the blessings of divine love" (27–28 and passim). Though the writer in Tablet XIV supposedly predates the

monotheism of the Hebrew Scriptures by some thousands of years, he still seeks this singular relationship with divinity. And while it is unlikely that Bloom would include Schwerner in his pantheon of "strong poets," I suspect that despite their differing methods and aesthetics, the two share an understanding of how an ancient religious sensibility may be translated into a modern poetic one.

11. According to Ong, "it has been suggested that the cuneiform script of the Sumerians, the first of all known scripts (*c.* 3500 BC) grew at least in part out of a system of recording economic transactions" (86). But he also notes that "writing is often regarded at first as an instrument of secret and magic power" (93).

12. Gingerich calls *The Tablets* "probably the only North American texts which honestly merit the label Borgesian, despite several decades of Borges wannabees in English" ("Sacred Forgeries" 23). McHale ("Archaeologies of Knowledge" 250–53) offers a full account of *The Tablets'* family history in relation to literary hoaxes, forgeries, fragments, ruins, and archaeologies.

13. I am indebted to my colleague Tyrone Williams for this insight, which he offered after reading an earlier draft of this chapter.

14. Apparently, the question of *The Tablets* as comedy or tragedy was very much on Oppen's mind as he read the poem and watched it grow over the years. In a 1968 letter to Jerome Rothenberg, he observes that "Armand's Tablets of course dis-embowel [*sic*] the nouns but is therefore the account of tragedy" (*Selected Letters* 180). Then in a 1977 letter to Schwerner himself, in which Oppen praises Schwerner's *the work, the joy and the triumph of the will*, he writes that "I remember (you may not) that you were angry years ago when I objected to your manner of reading The Tablets - - - reading as comedy, tho the poem was tragedy . . . for the poet-translator was a lost man, the words were disappearing. . ." (342). From these remarks, I would speculate that Oppen reads *The Tablets* as tragedy because he recognizes the loss, often accompanied by disruptive violence, that is manifested in the poem about the issue of naming. For Oppen, Schwerner's excursions into the archaic origins of speech and writing ritualistically "disembowel" the nouns, leading to the "poet-translator's" sense that words are disappearing. Oppen's parapraxis—"poet-translator" for Schwerner's "Scholar/Translator"—makes perfect sense: Oppen identifies the figure in the poem with the poet himself, for whom, given Schwerner's methods, words are painfully stripped of their Heideggerian *presence*. Oppen's remark about nouns in *The Tablets* may be compared to the reverence in his paradigmatic lyric "Psalm." There, the deer in the forest ("That they are there!") are bound, in an almost prelapsarian fashion, to their signifying nouns: "The small nouns / Crying faith / In this is in which the wild deer / Startle, and stare out" (*New Collected Poems* 99). Moments such as these, so frequent in Oppen's work, almost never occur in *The Tablets*.

15. Cf. Oppen, for whom the term *clarity* is one of the most important in his per-

sonal poetic lexicon, connoting both the immediate reality of the object-world and the poet's task, even though it may be virtually impossible, to find the language through which he or she may address the social and philosophical complexities that lie behind this world. Thus, "Of Being Numerous," section 22, reads in its entirety: "Clarity // In the sense of *transparence,* / I don't mean that much can be explained. // Clarity in the sense of silence" (*New Collected Poems* 175). Even more directly, in "Route" Oppen declares that "Clarity, clarity, surely clarity is the most beautiful thing in the world, / A limited, limiting clarity // I have not and never did have any motive of poetry / But to achieve clarity" (193).

Works Cited

Adorno, Theodor. "Lyric Poetry and Society." Trans. Bruce Mayo. In *The Adorno Reader*. Ed. Brian O'Connor. Oxford: Blackwell, 2000. 212–29.

———. *Prisms*. Trans. Samuel and Shierry Weber. Cambridge, MA: MIT P, 1981.

Agamben, Giorgio. *The Coming Community*. Trans. Michael Hardt. Minneapolis: U of Minnesota P, 1993.

Altieri, Charles. "The Objectivist Tradition." In DuPlessis and Quartermain, *The Objectivist Nexus*. 25–36.

Arnold, Matthew. *Culture and Anarchy*. Ed. R. H. Super. The Complete Prose Works of Matthew Arnold. Vol. 5. Ann Arbor: U of Michigan P, 1965.

———. "The Study of Poetry." In *English Literature and Irish Politics*. Ed. R. H. Super. The Complete Prose Works of Matthew Arnold. Vol. 9. Ann Arbor: U of Michigan P, 1973. 161–88.

———. "Wordsworth." In *English Literature and Irish Politics*. Ed. R.H. Super. 36–55.

Back, Rachel Tzvia. *Led by Language: The Poetry and Poetics of Susan Howe*. Tuscaloosa: U of Alabama P, 2002.

Barron, Jonathan N., and Eric Murphy Selinger, eds. *Jewish American Poetry: Poems, Commentary, and Reflections*. Hanover, NH: Brandeis UP/UP of New England, 2000.

Barthes, Roland. *Image Music Text*. Trans. Stephen Heath. New York: Farrar, Straus and Giroux, 1977.

Basso, Ellen B. *A Musical View of the Universe*. Philadelphia: U of Pennsylvania P, 1985.

Beach, Christopher. *ABC of Influence: Ezra Pound and the Remaking of American Poetic Tradition*. Berkeley: U of California P, 1992.

Benjamin, Walter. *The Arcades Project*. Trans. Howard Eiland and Kevin McLaughlin. Ed. Roy Tiedemann. Cambridge, MA: Harvard UP, 1999.

———. *Charles Baudelaire: A Lyric Poet in the Era of High Capitalism*. Trans. Harry Zohn. London: Verso, 1973.

———. "Theses on the Philosophy of History." In *Illuminations*. Trans. Harry Zohn. New York: Schocken, 1969. 253–64.

Berman, Marshall. *All That Is Solid Melts into Air: The Experience of Modernity*. New York: Penguin, 1988.

Bernstein, Michael André. "Robert Duncan: Talent and the Individual Tradition." *Sagetreib* 4.2/3 (Fall/Winter 1985): 177–90.

Bertholf, Robert J., and Ian W. Reid, eds. *Robert Duncan: Scales of the Marvelous.* New York: New Directions, 1979.

Blake, William. *The Poetry and Prose of William Blake.* Ed. David V. Erdman. Garden City, NY: Doubleday, 1965.

Blaser, Robin, ed. *The Collected Books of Jack Spicer.* Los Angeles: Black Sparrow, 1975.

Bloom, Harold. *Agon: Towards a Theory of Revisionism.* New York: Oxford UP, 1982.

———. *The Anxiety of Influence: A Theory of Poetry.* New York: Oxford UP, 1973.

———. "Introduction." In Hart Crane, *The Complete Poems of Hart Crane.* xi–xxxii.

———. *Kabbalah and Criticism.* New York: Continuum, 1984.

———. *Ruin the Sacred Truths: Poetry and Belief from the Bible to the Present.* Cambridge, MA: Harvard UP, 1987.

———. *Wallace Stevens: The Poems of Our Climate.* Ithaca, NY: Cornell UP, 1977.

———. *The Book of J.* Trans. David Rosenberg. New York: Grove Weidenfeld, 1990.

Botman, Darius. "A Glossary of Jazz." *A Passion for Jazz.* http://www.apassion4jazz.net/ (accessed 5 January 2007).

Bronk, William. *Life Supports: New and Collected Poems.* Jersey City, NJ: Talisman House, 1997.

Bruns, Gerald L. *Modern Poetry and the Idea of Language: A Critical and Historical Study.* New Haven, CT: Yale UP, 1974.

Byrd, Don. "The Question of Wisdom as Such." In Bertholf and Reid, *Robert Duncan.* 38–55.

Caldwell, Patricia. "The Antinomian Language Controversy." *Harvard Theological Review* 69.3/4 (1976): 345–67.

Cambon, Glauco. "Foreword." In Zanzotto, *Selected Poetry.* xiii–xxii.

Cohen, Charles Lloyd. *God's Caress: The Psychology of Puritan Religious Experience.* New York: Oxford UP, 1986.

Collis, Stephen. *Through Words of Others: Susan Howe and Anarcho-Scholasticism.* Victoria, BC: ELS Editions, 2006.

Conte, Joseph M. *Unending Design: The Forms of Postmodern Poetry.* Ithaca, NY: Cornell UP, 1991.

Corbin, Henry. *Avicenna and the Visionary Recital.* Trans. Willard R. Trask. Bollingen Series 66. New York: Pantheon, 1960.

———. *Creative Imagination in the Sūfism of Ibn 'Arabī*. Trans. Ralph Manheim. Bollingen Series 91. Princeton, NJ: Princeton UP, 1969.

Crane, Hart. *The Complete Poems and Selected Letters and Prose of Hart Crane*. Ed. Brom Weber. Garden City, NY: Anchor Books, 1966.

———. *The Complete Poems of Hart Crane*. Ed. Marc Simon. New York: Liveright, 1986.

Daly, Lew. *Swallowing the Scroll: Late in a Prophetic Tradition with the Poetry of Susan Howe and John Taggart*. Published as supplement #1 of the journal *apex of the M*. Buffalo, NY: M Press, 1994.

Dante Alighieri. *Cantos from Dante's Inferno*. Trans. Armand Schwerner. Jersey City, NJ: Talisman House, 2000.

Davidson, Michael. "A Book of First Things: *The Opening of the Field*." In Bertholf and Reid, *Robert Duncan*. 56–84.

———. *Ghostlier Demarcations: Modern Poetry and the Material Word*. Berkeley: U of California P, 1997.

———. *The San Francisco Renaissance: Poetics and Community at Mid-Century*. New York: Cambridge UP, 1989.

Dembo, L. S., and Cyrena N. Pondrom, ed. *The Contemporary Writer: Interviews with Sixteen Novelists and Poets*. Madison: U of Wisconsin P, 1972.

Derrida, Jacques. *Of Grammatology*. Trans. Gayatri Chakravorty Spivak. Baltimore: Johns Hopkins UP, 1976.

———. *Writing and Difference*. Trans. Alan Bass. Chicago: U of Chicago P, 1978.

Dickens, Charles. *David Copperfield*. Ed. Nina Burgis. New York: Oxford UP, 1980.

Dickinson, Emily. *The Complete Poems of Emily Dickinson*. Ed. Thomas H. Johnson. Boston: Little, Brown, 1960.

Doresse, Jean. *The Secret Books of the Egyptian Gnostics*. New York: MJF Books, 1968.

Duncan, Robert. *Bending the Bow*. New York: New Directions, 1968.

———. *Derivations: Selected Poems 1950–1956*. London: Fulcrum Press, 1968.

———. *Fictive Certainties*. New York: New Directions, 1985.

———. *Ground Work: Before the War*. New York: New Directions, 1984.

———. *Ground Work II: In the Dark*. New York: New Directions, 1987.

———. *The H.D. Book*. 1984. Frontier Press. http://www.ccca.ca/history/ozz/english/books/hd_book/HD_Book_by_Robert_Duncan.pdf (accessed 24 May 2000).

———. *Letters: Poems 1953–1956*. Chicago: Flood Editions, 2003.

———. *The Opening of the Field*. New York: New Directions, 1973.

———. "Preface." In Jack Spicer, *One Night Stand*. ix–xxvii.

———. *Roots and Branches*. New York: New Directions, 1969.

———. *A Selected Prose*. New York: New Directions, 1995.

———. *The Years as Catches: First Poems (1939–1946)*. Berkeley, CA: Oyez, 1966.

DuPlessis, Rachel Blau. "Echological Scales: On *ARK* of Ronald Johnson." *Facture* 1 (2000): 99–119.

———. "Introduction." In Oppen, *Selected Letters*. vii–xx.

———, and Peter Quartermain, eds. *The Objectivist Nexus: Essays in Cultural Poetics*. Tuscaloosa: U of Alabama P, 1999.

Eliade, Mircea. *Shamanism: Archaic Techniques of Ecstasy*. Trans. Willard R. Trask. Bollingen Series 76. Princeton, NJ: Princeton UP, 1992.

Ellingham, Lewis, and Kevin Killian. *Poet Be Like God: Jack Spicer and the San Francisco Renaissance*. Middletown, CT: Wesleyan UP, 1998.

Eliot, T. S. *The Complete Poems and Plays 1909–1950*. New York: Harcourt, Brace and World, 1971.

———. *Selected Prose of T. S. Eliot*. Ed. Frank Kermode. New York: Harcourt Brace Jovanovich, 1975.

———. *The Use of Poetry and the Use of Criticism*. London: Faber and Faber, 1964.

Emerson, Ralph Waldo. *Essays and Poems*. New York: Library of America, 1996.

Feld, Ross. "The Apostle's Grudge at the Persistence of Poetry." *Ironwood* 14.2 (1986): 188–94.

———. "Lowghost to Lowghost." In Henderson, *The Pushcart Prize*. 430–55.

———. *Plum Poems*. New York: Jargon Society, 1972.

———. "Some Thoughts about Objectivism." *Sagetrieb* 12.3 (Winter 1993): 65–77.

Felstiner, John. *Paul Celan: Poet, Survivor, Jew*. New Haven, CT: Yale UP, 1995.

Finkelstein, Norman. "The Case of Michael Palmer." *Contemporary Literature* 29.4 (Winter 1988): 518–37.

———. *Columns: Track, Volume II*. NY: Spuyten Duyvil, 2002.

———. "Hail Nothing: A Reading of Jack Spicer's 'Orfeo.'" *Colorado Review* 25.2 (Fall–Winter 1998): 168–72.

———. "Jack Spicer's Ghosts and the Gnosis of History." *Boundary 2* 9.2 (1981): 81–100.

———. *Lyrical Interference: Essays on Poetics*. New York: Spuyten Duyvil, 2003.

———. *Not One of Them in Place: Modern Poetry and Jewish American Identity*. Albany: State U of New York P, 2001.

———. *Powers: Track, Volume III*. New York: Spuyten Duyvil, 2005.

———. *The Ritual of New Creation: Jewish Tradition and Contemporary Literature*. Albany: State U of New York P, 1992.

———. *Track*. New York: Spuyten Duyvil, 1999.

———. *The Utopian Moment in Contemporary American Poetry*. Lewisburg, PA: Bucknell UP, 1993.

———. "Wallace Stevens, Armand Schwerner, and 'The The.'" *Wallace Stevens Journal* 24 (2000): 151–60.

Foster, Edward Halsey. *Jack Spicer*. Boise: Boise State U, 1991.

Fredman, Stephen. "Intersections of the Lyrical and the Philosophical: Introduction." *Sagetrieb* 12.3 (Winter 1993): 7–11.

Freud, Sigmund. "The Uncanny." Trans. Alix Strachey. In *The Standard Edition of the Complete Psychological Works of Sigmund Freud*. Ed. James Strachey. Vol. 17. London: Hogarth Press, 1955. 217–56.

Frye, Northrop. *Anatomy of Criticism: Four Essays*. Princeton, NJ: Princeton UP, 1957.

Gelpi, Albert. "Stevens and Williams: The Epistemology of Modernism." In *Wallace Stevens: The Poetics of Modernism*. Ed. Albert Gelpi. Cambridge: Cambridge UP, 1985. 3–23.

Gingerich, Willard. "Armand Schwerner: An Interview with Willard Gingerich." *American Poetry Review* 24.5 (September/October 1995): 27–32.

———. "An Interview with Armand Schwerner." *Hambone* 11 (Spring 1994): 28–51.

———. "Sacred Forgeries and Translations of Nothing in the *Tablets* of Armand Schwerner." *Talisman* 21/22 (Winter/Spring 2001): 18–26.

Girard, René. *The Scapegoat*. Trans. Yvonne Freccero. Baltimore: Johns Hopkins UP, 1986.

———. *Violence and the Sacred*. Trans. Patrick Gregory. Baltimore: Johns Hopkins UP, 1977.

Grossman, Allen. *How to Do Things with Tears*. New York: New Directions, 2001.

———. *The Long Schoolroom: Lessons in the Bitter Logic of the Poetic Principle*. Ann Arbor: U of Michigan P, 1997. 179–88.

———. "On Communicative Difficulty in General and 'Difficult' Poetry in Particular: The Example of Hart Crane's 'The Broken Tower.'" *Chicago Review* 53.2/3 (Autumn 2007): 140–61.

———. *The Sighted Singer: Two Works on Poetry for Readers and Writers*. Baltimore: Johns Hopkins UP, 1992.

Handelman, Susan A. *The Slayers of Moses: The Emergence of Rabbinic Interpretation in Modern Literary Theory*. Albany: State U of New York P, 1982.

Hartman, Geoffrey H. *Criticism in the Wilderness: The Study of Literature Today*. New Haven, CT: Yale UP, 1980.

———. "Text and Spirit." In Hartman and O'Hara. *The Geoffrey Hartman Reader*. 191–204.

———, and Daniel T. O'Hara. *The Geoffrey Hartman Reader.* Edinburgh: Edinburgh UP, 2004.

Hatlen, Burton. "Robert Duncan's Marriage of Heaven and Hell: Kabbalah and Rime in *Roots and Branches.*" In Trawick, *World, Self, Poem.* 207–26.

H.D. [Hilda Doolittle]. *Collected Poems 1912–1944.* Ed. Louis L. Martz. New York: New Directions, 1983.

Heller, Michael. "Preface." In Dante Alighieri, *Cantos.* vi–vii.

Hejinian, Lyn. *The Language of Inquiry.* Berkeley: U of California P, 2000.

Henderson, Bill, ed. *The Pushcart Prize, II: Best of the Small Presses.* Yonkers, NY: Pushcart P, 1977.

Hesiod. *Theogony and Works and Days.* Trans. Catherine M. Schlegel and Henry Weinfield. Ann Arbor: U of Michigan P, 2006.

Howe, Susan. *The Birth-mark: Unsettling the Wilderness in American Literary History.* Hanover, NH: Wesleyan UP / UP of New England, 1993.

———. *The Europe of Trusts.* Los Angeles: Sun and Moon P, 1990.

———. "An Interview with Susan Howe." By Lynn Keller. *Contemporary Literature* 36.1 (1995): 1–34.

———. *My Emily Dickinson.* Berkeley, CA: North Atlantic Books, 1985.

———. *The Nonconformist's Memorial: Poems.* New York: New Directions, 1993.

———. *Singularities.* Hanover, NH: Wesleyan UP / UP of New England, 1990.

Hulme, T. E. *The Collected Writings of T. E. Hulme.* Ed. Karen Csengeri. Oxford: Clarendon, 1994.

Isaacs, Ernest. "The Fox Sisters and American Spiritualism." In Kerr and Crow, *The Occult in America: New Historical Perspectives.* 79–110.

Johnson, Ronald. *ARK.* Albuquerque: Living Batch P, 1996.

———. *ARK 50: Spires 34–50.* New York: Dutton, 1984.

———. *The Book of the Green Man.* New York: Norton, 1967.

———. "For R.D." Sagetrieb 4.2&3 (Fall & Winter 1985): 15.

———. "From *Hurrah for Euphony.*" *Chicago Review* 42.1 (1996): 25–31.

———. "An Interview with Ronald Johnson." By Peter O'Leary. *Chicago Review* 42.1 (1996): 32–53.

———. Letter to the author. 24 December 1990.

———. *To Do as Adam Did: Selected Poems of Ronald Johnson.* Jersey City, NJ: Talisman House, 2000.

Johnston, Devin. *Precipitations: Contemporary American Poetry as Occult Practice.* Middletown, CT: Wesleyan UP, 2002.

Jonas, Hans. *The Gnostic Religion: The Message of the Alien God and the Beginnings of Christianity.* 3rd ed. Boston: Beacon Press, 2001.

Kahn, Charles H. *Anaximander and the Origins of Greek Cosmology.* Indianapolis: Hackett, 1960.

Kaufman, Robert. "Lyric's Expression: Musicality, Conceptuality, Critical Agency." *Cultural Critique* 60 (Spring 2005): 197–216.

Keats, John. *The Poems of John Keats*. Ed. Jack Stillinger. Cambridge, MA: Belknap P, 1978.

Kermode, Frank. "Introduction." In Eliot, *Selected Prose*. 11–27.

Kerr, Howard, and Charles L. Crow, eds. *The Occult in America: New Historical Perspectives*. Urbana: U of Illinois P, 1983.

Krupnick, Mark. *Lionel Trilling and the Fate of Cultural Criticism*. Evanston, IL: Northwestern UP, 1986.

Lacarrière, Jacques. *The Gnostics*. Trans. Nina Rootes. San Francisco: City Lights Books, 1989.

Lazer, Hank. *Lyric and Spirit: Selected Essays, 1996–2008*. Richmond, CA: Omnidawn Publishing, 2008.

Lewis, Franklin D. *Rumi: Past and Present, East and West: The Life Teaching and Poetry of Jalâl*. Oxford: Oneworld Publications, 2000.

Litz, A. Walton. *Introspective Voyager: The Poetic Development of Wallace Stevens*. New York: Oxford UP, 1972.

Lyotard, Jean-François. *The Postmodern Condition: A Report on Knowledge*. Trans. Geoff Bennington and Brian Massumi. Minneapolis: U of Minnesota P, 1984.

Mackey, Nathaniel. *Discrepant Engagement: Dissonance, Cross-Culturality, and Experimental Writing*. Tuscaloosa: U of Alabama P, 2000.

———. *Eroding Witness*. Urbana: U of Illinois P, 1985.

———. *Paracritical Hinge: Essays, Talks, Notes, Interviews*. Madison: U of Wisconsin P, 2005.

———. *School of Udhra*. San Francisco: City Lights Books, 1993.

———. *Splay Anthem*. New York: New Directions, 2006.

———. *Whatsaid Serif*. San Francisco: City Lights Books, 1998.

Mallarmé, Stéphane. *Collected Poems*. Trans. Henry Weinfield. Berkeley: U of California P, 1994.

———. *Selected Prose Poems, Essays, and Letters*. Trans. Bradford Cook. Baltimore: Johns Hopkins UP, 1956.

Mann, Paul. *The Theory-Death of the Avant-Garde*. Bloomington: Indiana UP, 1991.

Marx, Karl. *The 18th Brumaire of Louis Bonaparte*. Trans. Saul K. Padover. http://www.marxists.org/archive/marx/works/1852/18th-brumaire/ch01.htm (accessed 31 July 2008).

Matt, Daniel C. *The Essential Kabbalah: The Heart of Jewish Mysticism*. San Francisco: Harper San Francisco, 1995.

McHale, Brian. "Archaeologies of Knowledge: Hill's Middens, Heaney's Bogs,

Schwerner's Tablets." *New Literary History* 30.1 (Winter 1999): 239–62.

———. *The Obligation toward the Difficult Whole: Postmodernist Long Poems.* Tuscaloosa: U of Alabama P, 2004.

Mersmann, James F. *Out of the Vietnam Vortex: A Study of Poets and Poetry against the War.* Lawrence: U of Kansas P, 1974.

Montgomery, Will. "Appropriating Primal Indeterminacy: Language, Landscape and Postmodern Poetics in Susan Howe's *Thorow.*" *Textual Practice* 20.4 (2006): 739–57.

Naylor, Paul. *Poetic Investigations: Singing the Holes in History.* Evanston, IL: Northwestern UP, 1999.

Nicholls, Peter. "Unsettling the Wilderness: Susan Howe and American History." *Contemporary Literature* 37.4 (1996): 586–601.

O'Leary, Peter. E-mail to the author. 7 May 2000.

———. *Gnostic Contagion: Robert Duncan and the Poetry of Illness.* Middletown, CT: Wesleyan UP, 2002.

Olson, Charles. *Collected Prose.* Ed. Donald Allen and Benjamin Friedlander. Berkeley: U of California P, 1997.

Ong, Walter J. *Orality and Literacy: The Technologizing of the Word.* London: Methuen, 1982.

Oppen, George. *The Collected Poems of George Oppen.* New York: New Directions, 1975.

———. *New Collected Poems.* Ed. Michael Davidson. New York: New Directions, 2002.

———. "On Armand Schwerner" [review of *Seaweed*]. *Stony Brook* 3/4 (1969): 72.

———. *The Selected Letters of George Oppen.* Ed. Rachel Blau DuPlessis. Durham, NC: Duke UP, 1990.

Otto, Rudolf. *The Idea of the Holy: An Inquiry into the Non-Rational Factor in the Idea of the Divine and Its Relation to the Rational.* Trans. John W. Harvey. 2nd ed. London: Oxford UP, 1950.

Owen, Alex. *The Place of Enchantment: British Occultism and the Culture of the Modern.* Chicago: U of Chicago P, 2004.

Pagels, Elaine. *Adam, Eve, and the Serpent.* New York: Vintage Books, 1989.

———. *The Gnostic Gospels.* New York: Vintage, 1981.

Palmer, Michael. *At Passages.* New York: New Directions, 1995.

———. *Codes Appearing: Poems 1979–1988.* New York: New Directions, 2001.

———. *Company of Moths.* New York: New Directions, 2005.

———. "A Conversation." *American Poetry* 3.1 (1986): 72–88.

———. "'Dear Lexicon': An Interview by Benjamin Hollander and David Levi Strauss." *Acts* 2.1 (1986): 8–36.

———. E-mail to the author. 17 January 2002.

———. "Interview with Michael Palmer." By Peter Gizzi. *Exact Change Yearbook* 1 (1995): 161–79.

———. *The Promises of Glass*. New York: New Directions, 2000.

———. "Robert Duncan and Romantic Synthesis." *Poets.org*. http://www. poets.org/viewmedia.php/prmMID/15949 (accessed 9 September 2008).

Pascal, Blaise. *Pensées*. Trans. A. J. Krailsheimer. London: Penguin, 1966.

Perloff, Marjorie. *Poetic License: Essays on Modernist and Postmodernist Lyric*. Evanston, IL: Northwestern UP, 1990.

———. *The Poetics of Indeterminacy: Rimbaud to Cage*. Princeton, NJ: Princeton UP, 1981.

Poirier, Richard. *The Renewal of Literature: Emersonian Reflections*. New York: Random House, 1987.

Pound, Ezra. *Personae: The Collected Shorter Poems of Ezra Pound*. New York: New Directions, 1971.

Reid, Ian W. "The Plural Text: 'Passages.'" In Bertholf and Reid, *Robert Duncan*. 161–80.

Riley, Peter. "The Narratives of *The Holy Grail*." *Boundary 2* 6.1 (1977): 163–90.

Rilke, Rainer Maria. *New Poems: A Revised Bilingual Edition*. Trans. Edward Snow. New York: North Point, 2001.

———. *Sonnets to Orpheus*. Trans. M. D. Herter Norton. New York: Norton, 1970.

Rizzo, Gino. "Afterword: Zanzotto, 'fabbro del parlar materno.'" In Zanzotto, *Selected Poetry*. 307–23.

Rothenberg, Jerome, ed. *Technicians of the Sacred: A Range of Poetries from Africa, America, Asia and Oceania*. Garden City, NY: Anchor Books, 1969.

Santner, Eric L. *On the Psychotheology of Everyday Life*. Chicago: U of Chicago P, 2001.

Scholem, Gershom G. *Major Trends in Jewish Mysticism*. New York: Schocken, 1954.

Schuchard, Ronald. *Eliot's Dark Angel: Intersections of Life and Art*. New York: Oxford UP, 1999.

Schwartz, Leonard. *A Flicker at the Edge of Things: Essays towards a Poetics: 1987–1997*. New York: Spuyten Duyvil, 1998.

Schwerner, Armand. *Seaweed*. Los Angeles: Black Sparrow, 1969.

———. *The Tablets*. Orono, ME: National Poetry Foundation, 1999.

———. "Wallace Stevens: The Movements within the Rock" [part I]. *Kulchur* 18 (Summer 1965): 59–81.

———. "Wallace Stevens: The Movements within the Rock" [part II]. *Kulchur* 19 (Autumn 1965): 43–69.

Scroggins, Mark. "'*A*' to *ARK*: Zukofsky, Johnson, and an Alphabet of the Long Poem." *Facture* 1 (2000): 143–52.

———. Review of *The Shrubberies* by Ronald Johnson. *Jacket* 16. http://jacketmagazine.com/16/senog-r-john.html (accessed 18 January 2005).

Selinger, Eric Murphy. "*ARK* as a Garden of Revelation." *Facture* 1 (2000): 153–71.

———. "Important Pleasures and Others: Michael Palmer, Ronald Johnson." *Postmodern Culture* 4.3 (May 1994). http://muse.jhu.edu/journals/postmodern_culture/V004/4.3selinger.html (accessed 9 September 2008).

———. "Shekhinah in America." In Barron and Selinger, *Jewish American Poetry Reflections*. 250–71.

Sewell, Elizabeth. *The Orphic Voice: Poetry and Natural History*. New Haven: Yale UP, 1960.

Simpson, Megan. "Trickster Poetics: Multiculturalism and Collectivity in Nathaniel Mackey's *Song of the Andoumboulou*." *MELUS* 28.4 (Winter 2003): 35–54.

Slotkin, Richard. *Regeneration through Violence: The Mythology of the American Frontier 1600–1860*. Norman: U of Oklahoma P, 1973.

Spicer, Jack. *The House That Jack Built: The Collected Lectures of Jack Spicer*. Ed. Peter Gizzi. Hanover, NH: Wesleyan UP, 1998.

———. *My Vocabulary Did This to Me: The Collected Poetry of Jack Spicer*. Ed. Peter Gizzi and Kevin Killian. Hanover, NH: Wesleyan UP / University Press of New England, 2008.

———. *One Night Stand & Other Poems*. Ed. Donald Allen. San Francisco: Grey Fox, 1980.

Stein, Gertrude. *Lectures in America*. In *Writings, 1932–1946*. Ed. Catherine R. Stimpson and Harriet Chessman. New York: Library of America, 1998. 191–336.

———. *Selected Writings of Gertrude Stein*. New York: Vintage, 1990.

Stevens, Wallace. *The Collected Poems*. New York: Vintage, 1990.

———. *Opus Posthumous*. Ed. Milton J. Bates. New York: Vintage, 1990.

———. *The Palm at the End of the Mind: Selected Poems and a Play*. Ed. Holly Stevens. New York: Vintage, 1990.

Trawick, Leonard W., ed. *World, Self, Poem: Essays on Contemporary Poetry from "Jubilation of Poets."* Kent, OH: Kent State UP, 1990.

Valéry, Paul. *Oeuvres*. Ed. Jean Hytier. Vol. 1. Paris: Gallimard, 1957.

Van Spankeren, Kathryn. "Moonrise in Ancient Sumer: Armand Schwerner's *The Tablets*." *American Poetry Review* 22 (July/August 1993): 15–18.

Vincent, John. *Queer Lyrics: Difficulty and Closure in American Poetry*. New York: Palgrave Macmillan, 2002.

Walker, Jayne L. "Exercises in Disorder: Duncan's Imitations of Gertrude Stein." In Bertholf and Reid, *Robert Duncan*. 22–35.

Wasserstrom, Steven M. *Religion after Religion: Gershom Scholem, Mircea Eliade, and Henry Corbin at Eranos.* Princeton, NJ: Princeton UP, 1999.

Weinfield, Henry. "Commentary." In Mallarmé, *Collected Poems.* 149–275.

———. "Introduction." In Mallarmé, *Collected Poems.* xi–xix.

———. "The Rigor of His Refusals: The Poetry of Ross Feld." *Notre Dame Review* 16 (Summer 2003): 195–204.

White, Jenny L. "The Landscapes of Susan Howe's 'Thorow.'" *Contemporary Literature* 47.2 (2006): 236–60.

Whitman, Walt. *Complete Poetry and Collected Prose.* New York: Library of America, 1982.

Williams, William Carlos. *The Collected Poems of William Carlos Williams, Volume I: 1909–1939.* Ed. A. Walton Litz and Christopher J. MacGowan. New York: New Directions, 1986.

Yeats, W. B. *The Collected Poems.* New York: Macmillan, 1956.

———. *Per Amica Silentia Lunæ.* In *Mythologies.* New York: Collier, 1959. 317–69.

Zanzotto, Andrea. *Selected Poetry of Andrea Zanzotto.* Trans. Ruth Feldman and Brian Swann. Princeton, NJ: Princeton UP, 1975.

Zawacki, Andrew. "'Relation without Relation': Palmer, Celan, Blanchot." *New German Critique* 91 (Winter 2004): 117–28.

Zukofsky, Louis. *Prepositions +: The Collected Critical Essays.* Hanover, NH: Wesleyan UP/UP of New England, 2000.

Index

Adam Kadmon (primal man), 31, 34, 70–72, 84–86
Adorno, T. W., 155–57
Agamben, Giorgio, 229–30
Altieri, Charles, 221
antinomianism, 111, 114–15, 118
Arnold, Matthew, 2, 14–17

Back, Rachel Tzvia, 118, 122
Barthes, Roland, 37
Basso, Ellen B., 184, 193
Baudelaire, Charles, 56–57, 145–48
Benjamin, Walter, 144–46
Blake, William, 18, 127
Blaser, Robin, 100–02
Bloom, Harold, 2, 7, 20, 24, 219
book: idea of the, 58, 143, 180, 190. *See also* Derrida
Bruns, Gerald, 196

Caldwell, Patricia, 109–10
Calvinism, 100–04
Celan, Paul, 148, 155, 158–59
Charles I, 122–30
Cioran, E. M., 182
Conte, Joseph M., 37, 73, 144
Corbin, Henry, 185–86
Crane, Hart, 22–24

Davidson, Michael, 51, 54
Derrida, Jacques, 38, 58, 143, 180, 222, 225–27
Dickens, Charles: *David Copperfield*, 129–30
Dickinson, Emily, 11–14, 121, 134

Doresse, Jean: *The Secret Books of the Egyptian Gnostics*, 107–08
Duncan, Robert, 4–6, 10, 18, 24, 27–64, 120–21, 178; and gnosticism, 29–30, 38–39, 49–51, 63–64; and Eliot, 61–63; and Johnson, 66–67, 77–83; and Palmer, 139–41; and Spicer, 98–100; and Stein, 31–37
DuPlessis, Rachel Blau, 84, 86, 215

Egyptomania, 154–55, 158, 225
Eliade, Mircea, 183, 194, 200, 202–03, 205–06
Eliot, T. S., 16–20, 61–63
Emerson, Ralph Waldo, 7–9, 15
ethnopoetics, 208–09

Feld, Ross, 99–100, 104
Freud, Sigmund, 3, 154, 188
Frye, Northrop, 198

García Lorca, Federico, 189, 195
Gingerich, Willard, 216
Girard, René, 118–21, 126, 185, 186–87, 191, 206, 217–18
gnosticism, 29–30, 49–50, 59–60, 63–64, 107–08, 185–90
Grossman, Allen, 2–3, 23, 47, 151–52, 217, 226, 232

H. D., 24–26
Hartman, Geoffrey, 1–2, 104–05
Hatlen, Burton, 70–71
Hejinian, Lyn, 32
Herbert, George, 47–48

Hesiod: *Works and Days*, 44–45
Howe, Susan, 11, 109, 114–37; and anti-
    nomianism, 111, 114–15; *Bibliography
    of the King's Book, or Eikon Basilike*,
    121–30; *The Nonconformist's Memo-
    rial*, 135–37; and spiritualism, 115–17;
    Thorow, 130–35
Hulme, T. E., 80
Hutchinson, Anne, 109–10

Jabès, Edmond, 36, 38, 163–64
Johnson, Ronald, 65–94; and Adam
    Kadmon, 70–72; *ARK*, 67–94; as
    orphic poet, 81–86
Jonas, Hans, 29–30, 39, 49

kabbalah, 70–71, 142
Kaufman, Robert, 155–56
Keats, John, 201
Kermode, Frank, 17
kosmos: in Duncan, 49, 64; in Johnson,
    65–72. *See also* Adam Kadmon

Lacarrière, Jacques: *The Gnostics*, 185
Lewis, Franklin D., 53–54

Mackey, Nathaniel, 30, 42, 183–207;
    and gnosticism, 185–90; music and
    poetry, 189, 195–97; and shamanism,
    184, 200–06
Mallarmé, Stéphane, 51–53, 57–58, 99,
    144
Mann, Paul, 162–63
Matt, Daniel C., 71–72
McHale, Brian, 209–10
Milton, John, 123
Montgomery, Will, 131–33

Naylor, Paul, 131
Nicholls, Peter, 128
Norris, John, 49
Numen, 35, 39

O'Leary, Peter, 18, 27–28, 29, 30, 57, 60,
    66, 96, 178, 188–89, 191
Olson, Charles, 15, 97–98, 195
Ong, Walter J., 223–24, 227
Oppen, George, 214–16
Orpheus myth, 81–87, 150–53, 196
Otto, Rudolf: *The Idea of the Holy*, 35

Pagels, Elaine, 63
Palmer, Michael, 138–82; and Baudelaire
    Series, 144–57; and heresy, 138–40;
    Letters to Zanzotto, 163–74; and the
    sacred, 3–4, 174–82; *Sun*, 158–63;
    "Untitled," 175–82
Perloff, Marjorie, 31–33
Poirier, Richard, 7–8, 20
Pound, Ezra, 31
psychotheology, 26, 155, 211

Rilke, Rainer Maria, 148–53
Rothenberg, Jerome, 208
Rumi, 53–54

sacrificial crisis, 118–21, 206, 217–18. *See
    also* Girard
Santner, Eric L., 26, 154–55, 158, 211–12,
    217, 225, 228, 232
Scholem, Gershom, 70
Schuchard, Ronald, 16
Schwerner, Armand, 208–31, 233–34;
    and ethnopoetics, 208–09; and Op-
    pen, 214–16; on Stevens and the real,
    212–13, 219–20; *The Tablets*, 210–12,
    216–31
séance, 115–18, 130
Selinger, Eric Murphy, 79, 90
serial form: in Duncan, 37–38; in
    Mackey, 191–97; in Palmer, 143–45,
    174–75
Sewell, Elizabeth, 82–83
shamanism, 187, 191, 194, 200–06
Spicer, Jack, 14, 17, 95–113, 143–44, 232;

and antinomianism, 110–12; and Cal-
vinism, 100–04, 113; and gnosticism,
107–08
spiritualism, 116–17
Stein, Gertrude, 31–37
Stevens, Wallace, 19–22, 212–13, 219–20

Tolkien, J. R. R., 92

Valéry, Paul, 99, 177
Vincent, John, 103, 106

Walker, Jayne L., 31–32
Wasserstrom, Steven M., 6, 75–76, 233
Weinfield, Henry, 51–52, 99
White, Jenny L., 131
Whitman, Walt, 9–11, 41, 47, 69–70, 72
Williams, William Carlos, 109, 196–97

Yeats, W. B., 18, 55–56, 69

Zanzotto, Andrea, 163, 166–70
Zukofsky, Louis, 76–77

Contemporary North American Poetry Series

Industrial Poetics: Demo Tracks for a Mobile Culture
By Joe Amato

On Mount Vision: Forms of the Sacred in Contemporary American Poetry
By Norman Finkelstein

Form, Power, and Person in Robert Creeley's Life and Work
Edited by Stephen Fredman and Steve McCaffery

Jorie Graham: Essays on the Poetry
Edited by Thomas Gardner
University of Wisconsin Press, 2005

Gary Snyder and the Pacific Rim: Creating Countercultural Community
By Timothy Gray

We Saw the Light: Conversations between the New American Cinema and Poetry
By Daniel Kane

History, Memory, and the Literary Left: Modern American Poetry, 1935–1968
By John Lowney

Paracritical Hinge: Essays, Talks, Notes, Interviews
By Nathaniel Mackey
University of Wisconsin Press, 2004

Frank O'Hara: The Poetics of Coterie
By Lytle Shaw

Radical Vernacular: Lorine Niedecker and the Poetics of Place
Edited by Elizabeth Willis